The Life of Selina Campbell

RELIGION AND AMERICAN CULTURE

Series Editors
David Edwin Harrell Jr.
Wayne Flynt
Edith L. Blumhofer

THE LIFE OF
SELINA CAMPBELL

*A Fellow Soldier
in the Cause
of Restoration*

LORETTA M. LONG

THE UNIVERSITY OF ALABAMA PRESS
Tuscaloosa and London

1 3 5 7 9 8 6 4 2
02 04 06 08 09 07 05 03 01

Typeface: Sabon

∞

The paper on which this book is printed meets the minimum requirements of
American National Standard for Information Science–Permanence of Paper
for Printed Library Materials, ANSI Z39.48-1984.

Long, Loretta M. (Loretta Marie), 1971–
The life of Selina Campbell : a fellow soldier in the cause of restoration /
Loretta M. Long.
p. cm. — (Religion and American culture)
Includes bibliographical references and index.
ISBN 0-8173-1059-2 (cloth. : alk. paper)
1. Campbell, Selina Huntington, 1803?-1897. 2. Disciples of Christ—West
Virginia—Biography. 3. Women in Christianity—United States—History—
19th century. I. Title. II. Religion and American culture (Tuscaloosa, Ala.)
BX7343.C2 .L6   2001
286.6′092—dc21
00-011120

British Library Cataloguing-in-Publication Data available

Credit for frontispiece, p. ii: Selina and Alexander Campbell, while attending
the annual convention of the American Christian/Missionary Society in
Cincinnati, OH, c. 1861. (Courtesy of Archives and Special Collections,
Bethany College)

Contents

Acknowledgments

I have been blessed throughout this project by the generosity of many different people without whom this project would never have been possible. Perhaps the most crucial individual was Jeanne Cobb, archivist and coordinator of special collections at Bethany College. Mrs. Cobb opened not only her archives but also her house and her dinner table to a starving graduate student. Without her guidance and suggestions, I would never have had such access to the wonderful material on which this book is based. My debt of gratitude to her is immense.

The entire staff of the Disciples of Christ Historical Society played a special role as well in this project. I want to recognize especially David McWhirter, who was particularly patient in guiding me through his many sources on the Campbell family.

A special thank-you goes to John Robinson and Fred Arthur Bailey of Abilene Christian University, who went above and beyond the call of collegiality to edit this document and bring it into its current form.

The Life of Selina Campbell

Introduction

In the *Millennial Harbinger* of July 1845, Alexander Campbell, leader of the burgeoning Disciples of Christ movement, printed a biography of "The Right Honorable Selina, Countess of Huntingdon," a woman who for him epitomized Christian womanhood. His attention to her life attested to both his "deep interest" in the "moral worth and spiritual excellence . . . [of] our young sisters" and his belief "that in modern times, as well as in more ancient times, the gospel . . . works effectually and results in the formation and production of female excellence."[1]

Lady Selina (1707–1791), though a member of the English nobility, nevertheless represented the feminine ideal for American women. Particularly exemplary, Campbell believed, was her desire to remain committed to her "family engagement" and to "lay herself out to do good" including "devis[ing] plans for the diffusion of the gospel."[2] For Campbell, a church leader, Lady Selina not only modeled the appropriate role for women in religion but also exemplified the spiritual qualities of his wife, Selina Huntington Bakewell, whose parents had named her for the great activist. Like her namesake, Mrs. Campbell was known for her efforts in promoting missions and serving the physical and spiritual needs of those around her, activities that often defined the private sphere for many women in antebellum America. The life of Selina Campbell illustrates the importance of this role.

Selina Campbell's life exhibits two fundamental themes in the history of American women. First, it highlights the significance of the role of Christian faith and values in the development of the "separate spheres" ideology. Since Barbara Welter's article "The Cult of True Womanhood" introduced the concept in 1966, the idea of separate spheres for nineteenth-century men and women has received a great deal of attention, but few writers have probed its religious dimensions.[3] Selina Campbell's life suggests that faith played a central part in the lives of many women in nineteenth-century America.

Selina was brought to western Virginia at the age of two in 1804 and was raised in Wellsburg on the Ohio River. Apart from extended visits to her children after the death of her husband, she lived in what would become West Virginia for another ninety-three years. After marrying Alexander Campbell, she moved to his home on Buffalo Creek, which soon became known as Bethany Mansion. As the wife of a prominent evangelist, Selina Campbell came into contact with many women. Moreover, her own writings and the private correspondence she maintained with a host of friends and acquaintances suggest that she belonged to a sizable group of women in American society who shared a particular view of women's proper function in the family, the world, and the church.

These women were not intent on political and social equality with their husbands and brothers. Rather, they focused their attention on faith in God and how they might each serve Him. This concern manifested itself in an emphasis on spiritual parity that gave each gender equal standing before God but provided different gender-specific assignments in society. In the separate spheres that the two genders occupied, spiritual meaning outweighed temporal considerations. A role might be private (and outwardly submissive), but for Selina Campbell and many other women it was not necessarily inferior (although it certainly connoted inferiority for many women). Service and dedication to others were perceived as duties that God had assigned to women for His own purposes. These duties did not undermine the essential balance between husbands and wives. In fact, for many they endowed this balance with a divine significance.

Although the ideas that came to be regarded as the foundation of the separate spheres system are described as "Victorian," they antedated the British queen. They originated not exclusively in a puritanical conception of social relations but rather also in the dynamic interaction between the forces of industrial capitalism and the Christian understanding of the world advanced by specific interpretations of the Bible. An exploration of Selina Campbell's conception of women as a member of the Restoration Movement (a larger term for the reforms promoted by the Disciples of Christ) sheds light on the ways in which evangelistic religion shaped perceptions of women. By probing Selina's views of her proper role in her family and in her church, we are better able to grasp the true meaning of domesticity in the lives of nineteenth-century American women.

Ann Braude in her essay "Woman's History *Is* American Religious History" has suggested several reasons why American women's history cannot be separated from the history of American religion. As she indicates, the connection between the two cannot be ignored. Braude points out that the majority of the members of nearly all religious groups in North America have been women, a fact generally overlooked by historians. Braude expresses no wonder at "the willingness of women to participate in the institution that enforces their subordination and provides the cosmological justification for it." Instead, she attributes their participation in American religion to the "special meaning" they found there "for their lives as women." Indeed, religious instruction harmonized well with women's ideas about family life and social relations and frequently shaped their consciousness as a separate gender. Moreover, domestic ideology (dealing with the role of the home in American society) was flexible enough to accommodate many different theological orientations, but at the same time these orientations were in some way informed by the religious thought of the men and women involved.[4]

A second theme emerging from the life of Selina Campbell is the importance of the private sphere for many nineteenth-century women. Lori Ginzberg (*Women and the Work of Benevolence*) saw the identification of gender difference as hindering the women's movement for equality. It might be argued, however, that the separate spheres ideology reflected, at least in part, a recognition of an important role that women must perform in the family and the church, a role that superseded equality. The Disciples of Christ invite examination because they were perhaps the fastest growing Protestant faith of the nineteenth century, and their leaders wrote prolifically about the proper role for women in the church and the church in the world.[5] Furthermore, Selina Campbell's many surviving letters, essays, and articles permit deep analysis of the view of her role taken by one particular Disciple woman.

At its core, the Campbell marriage involved a division of labor that relied on separate spheres of activity; at the same time, it emphasized the complementary nature of the spheres. Such an arrangement contrasts in a few important ways with the picture painted by others who have written on the subject. Many scholars have described the separate spheres arrangement of gender roles in the nineteenth century as creating a superior/inferior relationship between men and women such that women were always the junior partner—always excluded, always demeaned, always abused. Linda Kerber points out that Barbara Welter's "choice of the word 'cult' was intentionally pejorative," having been chosen specifically to convey her negative evaluation of the concept. According to Kerber, other scholars described the sphere of women "as separate from, and subordinate to, that of men," an interpretation that "was congruent with Marxist argument." Many of the studies of women's roles stress the economic importance of the separate spheres ideology and neglect its spiritual importance.[6]

In contrast, Alexander Campbell remained adamant that his wife's activities contributed as much to his success as his own actions did. Indeed he credited Selina with much of the success of his ministry. Friends writing after his death reaffirmed the importance of Campbell's wife in his life and work. Certainly, Campbell's own personality in part led him to emphasize his wife's role. Still, when a nationally prominent figure published his views in this area, they undoubtedly influenced many thousands not only in the matter of theology but also with respect to family organization. Both Campbells were less concerned with power and the control of social forces than with promoting the faith to which they had dedicated their lives.

Barbara Welter's pathbreaking article "The Cult of True Womanhood" in 1966 first enlivened the discussion of the specific nature of the separate spheres. Subsequent scholarship has greatly expanded our understanding of gender roles in the nineteenth century. An examination of Selina Campbell's life affords a fresh perspective on this body of literature. Building on Welter's article, historians have probed deeply into the meaning of the separate spheres in which men and women lived and worked. Many works on the subject, including Welter's, focus on the inequality perceived as resulting from the woman's position in the home, or more pointedly, from her exclusion from the public realm.

The common ideology of power relations entails a public position from which each person defends his or her interests. A Marxist-influenced interpretation of the importance of property relations has often been employed to understand women in the nineteenth century. The exclusion of women from such activities as voting and public speaking means that, according to such a philosophy, women are excluded from the important sources of power.

It is now generally accepted that women occupied one sphere, while men operated in another. There have been many interpretations of the antecedents and effects of this arrangement. Reflecting the prevailing theories of feminism of the 1970s and 1980s, Welter and others have concluded that the cult of true womanhood was at its heart a cover for male domination. Indeed, Carroll Smith-Rosenberg has identified power relations between the sexes as lying at the center of women's history. In *Disorderly Conduct*, she described women as trapped and dependent on men, feeling powerless and resentful of male hegemony.[7] But such an approach artificially narrows the scope of women's history. Smith-Rosenberg calls for an analysis of women's own words about their lives, but she stops short of divorcing nineteenth-century feminism from the twentieth-century women's movement. Before we can fully understand the history of American women, we must free ourselves from the feminist movement and instead analyze the lives of actual historical subjects. The worldview of nineteenth-century women, the sum of their own knowledge and experiences, must not be filtered through the experience of twentieth-century women. The separate sphere meant more than tyranny in the eyes of nineteenth-century women; far from being purely negative, it frequently offered women a more active role in creating in their lives meaning that was shaped in large part by religious faith. Selina Campbell was to say much about this interpretation of her potential contribution.

The two major studies on women in the Disciples of Christ share several tendencies relevant to the issue of separate spheres. In particular they reflect the proclivity of many historians to attribute to women of the nineteenth century the struggle of twentieth-century women. In 1979, Fred Arthur Bailey's dissertation, "The Status of Women in the Disciples of Christ Movement, 1865–1900," introduced the first and only full-length scholarly treatment of women's role in the history of the movement. His analysis rested on the work done by Ann Douglas, Welter, and others who had concluded that the culture of America was infused with masculine and feminine values. The creative activity of the world of commerce and manufacturing reflected the masculine virtues of aggression and intellectual ability; the female world, marked by emotion, passivity, and cooperation, was clearly apparent in the home and increasingly in the churches.

For some historians, the rise of values associated with femininity in American society explained the withdrawal of so many American men from religious life and the exclusion of women from most forms of public life. Welter concluded: "Religion, along with the family and popular tastes, was not important, and so became the property of the ladies. Thus it entered a process of change whereby it became more domesticated, more emotional, more soft and accommodating—in a word, more 'feminine.'" Other writers, however, have suggested different interpretations of religion during the nineteenth century. Nathan Hatch discerned a dynamic world of religious change prompted by the democratizing aspects of the American Revolution. He describes American religion as growing in strength rather than becoming marginalized, as suggested by Welter.[8] The significance of this strength is that religion cannot easily be dismissed as a weak force in Jacksonian America or as a domain abandoned to women. Vitality rather than functional weakness characterized most American religion at the time. Certainly, women constitute the majority of church members for reasons that scholars have yet to explain fully. But in the case of Selina Campbell, the feminization of American religion is not the whole story. The preaching of the Gospel was the task to which Alexander Campbell devoted his life, and the steady growth of the churches he supported belies any charge that his work was insignificant. His wife's role in that work is thus imbued with greater significance.

Bailey discussed the greatly circumscribed role of women proposed by Welter and Davis in terms of "true women" and "new women." The true woman accepted her role in the home as passive, reflecting the leadership of her husband; the new woman sought a greater voice in public affairs and viewed her sphere as extending beyond her home. Though certainly both the new woman and the true woman were models readily available to Disciple women, Bailey's emphasis on the progress of feminism within American religion limits the value of his study. While Bailey drew his conclusions after reading hundreds of articles about women that appeared in various Disciple newspapers from 1865 to 1900, in many ways, the newspaper articles were but ideal conceptions of women's role advanced by both men and women.

In reality, many women, Selina Campbell among them, believed that feminism would harm the position of women. It threatened to undermine the American family and weaken the Christian Church. To them, gender roles were less important than other things. Edwin Groover maintains, for example, that the Disciples' formulation of gender roles was informed by their belief in the approaching millennium.[9] The wisdom and piety of the female-led home would directly affect the arrival of this long anticipated event, and the role of women in it seemed supported by Scripture. Groover's analysis agrees with Bailey's contention that the separate spheres served to exclude women from church life and prevent them from enjoying the same quality of life as men.

For most nineteenth-century women, marriage was a decision fraught with hidden pitfalls as well as with opportunities for fulfillment. When a woman chose a husband, with rare exceptions, she entered a permanent relationship that had significant social, legal, and emotional consequences. Prevailing attitudes about domesticity as well as statutory provisions shaped these consequences and were grounded on women's position in the home. Women exercised their authority and performed most of their duties in the home. In her study of American womanhood from 1780 to 1835, Nancy Cott outlined several qualities of nineteenth-century gender roles. "The central convention of domesticity," she suggested, "was the contrast between the home and the world." Specifically, "home was 'an oasis in the desert,' a 'sanctuary' where 'sympathy, honor, virtue are assembled,' where 'disinterested love is ready to sacrifice everything at the altar of affection.' "[10] The home was separate from the world and its qualities of competition and greed. A woman's role in the home was reinforced by societal expectations. Cultural values, like the view that women's domestic role was primary, had deep roots in American society and persisted through the socialization of children and the reinforcement of tradition. Such assumptions greatly shaped Selina's role in the Campbell home, but they do not tell the full story.

Domesticity was certainly a key factor in the life of Selina Campbell, but there was more to her life than passive devotion to her family. Selina's core responsibilities were clearly domestic in nature. She cared for her husband and family, anticipating their needs whenever she could. But Selina was more than just a simple housekeeper: she was also an active leader in local women's groups and an editor for her prolific husband, who valued her comments on his speeches and writing. He often called her his "fellow soldier" because of her equal participation in his work.[11] Campbell often used military language in his writings when he spoke of spreading the Gospel and advancing the "kingdom of God." His use of such language to describe his wife's role is significant.

Cott's analysis is in some ways a postfeminist analysis, because it goes beyond the superior/inferior axis of male/female relationships and seeks to account for the factors that made the Campbell marriage so dynamic. Cott notes that the affectionate bonds that women developed with their children and their husbands may have gratified wives as they went about caring for their households. The cult of domesticity was thus not merely a trial for women; many wives rejoiced in their role as servants and prospective participants in the millennium, finding deep satisfaction in their work.[12]

Selina Campbell was one such spouse. Belief in the coming millennium and other attitudes—which may distinguish nineteenth-century women from their twentieth-century counterparts—suggests that truly to comprehend the role of domesticity in women's lives requires a deeper understanding. We must reach beyond the twentieth century's casual disparagement of homemakers and seek to understand the meaning of domesticity for nineteenth-century women. In considering the life of Selina Campbell, too, we must focus on personal hopes, goals, and fears, which encompassed not only her domestic obligations but also issues of faith, love, and partnership in marriage.

Selina Campbell's general notions about the appropriate function of women in society bear out many of the conclusions reached by historians of women's roles. In particular, Selina's voracious reading attests to the important influence that popular literature exerted on women's thinking. Newspapers and journals like Sarah Hale's *Godey's Ladies Book* regularly published articles on the domestic concerns of women such as cooking, child rearing, and housecleaning. Barbara Welter used some of the publications that Selina read to analyze the issues that Selina's contemporaries faced.[13] Welter concluded that an ideal of "True Womanhood" reflected notions of piety, submissiveness, and other virtues with which women were commonly identified. Such values certainly permeate Selina Campbell's life, but the result did not always conform to Welter's conclusions. The voluminous amount of material Selina left behind regarding her views of women's proper role make it possible to probe deeply into her opinions for what they suggest about women of faith. While the public nature of women's popular literature can help us delineate the experience of many women, an analysis of Selina's life shows us how a specific woman digested and implemented the ideas to which she was exposed.

In contrast to Welter's portrayal, Selina's relationship with her husband indicates that men and women in the nineteenth century could sometimes be equal partners in marriage. The Campbells' union reflected in part the singular views of Alexander Campbell on the character and abilities of women in general. "No Christian man can ever set a higher estimate on woman than Mr. Campbell did, or place her in a higher niche or position of honor or esteem," Selina wrote. From such a basis of mutual respect Selina and her husband built a relationship founded on complementary contributions. She often shared with others the details of her husband's views of women and marriage, and she mentioned his support of women's activities as a means of spurring others on to greater involvement.[14]

Certainly Campbell supported conservative biblical interpretations, which limited the participation of women in public worship. When asked whether women should "deliver lectures, exhortations, and prayers in the public assembly of the church," the reformer replied, "Paul says, 'I suffer not a woman to teach nor to usurp authority over the man; but to learn in silence.' I Tim.ii.12. I submit to Paul, and teach the same lesson." But if he did not endorse public church activities for women, he greatly supported every other manner of feminine activity. He especially valued the role of women in marriage. "No *one* could ever value the relation of woman to Man more than did dear Mr. Campbell," Selina wrote to her friend Mrs. S. E. Smart, editor of the *Christian Monitor.* "She was indeed in his eyes a precious Gift from God to Man and as such he prized and valued woman!!"[15] Campbell often eloquently voiced his admiration for women. One of his most striking expressions appeared often in Selina's writing: "Man is the prose, and woman the poetry of humanity. The key note of the anthem of creation."[16]

It would be difficult to miss the obvious paternalism in Campbell's statements; certainly he felt men moved more naturally than women in the realm of public affairs. But when analyzed in their context, his statements become more positive. In a society struggling against the powerful forces of urbanization, industrialization, and the rise of popular culture, all of which threatened to undermine the simple message of the Gospel, piety—an imperative for women—translated into a private crusade to preserve traditional values. This perspective highlighted the importance of woman's moral influence in the church. Selina shared her husband's belief that women played a crucial role; she not only worked within its precepts but also sought to enlarge it for the betterment of all the churches. Bailey and others identify the process by which she did so as the shift from the true woman to the new woman, or the shift in women's role from the passive to the active.

The present study suggests, however, that the role of women in American society changed not because of the dichotomy between passive and active but rather because of the shift from a private role to a role with some public implications. As women entered the public sphere to defend the interests of the home, their activities became in their eyes an extension of their private role in response to new challenges of great interest: urbanization, immigration, and female preaching.[17] Women's basic role as defenders of home and family remained the same. But their activity expanded with shifts in the currents of their culture.

Another important role for women was motherhood. Most Disciples believed in a variation of the old saying "the hand that rocks the cradle rules the world": a mother's early instruction guided the hearts and minds of her children. Far from being taught to rule the world, however, the children needed to learn of salvation. In a church that greatly valued conversion to the Gospel, a woman's role in this process was critical. Both Alexander Campbell and Selina Campbell agreed that motherhood was a "sacred responsibility" not only as socialization but also as "spiritualization." Motherhood was part of domesticity. But Selina saw motherhood as more than just another domestic activity. In her eyes it was a commission from God to take responsibility for both the physical welfare *and* the spiritual welfare of her children. It is significant that Selina received her religious training through the influence of her mother. Indeed, the religious leadership in her family came not from her father but from her believing mother, whose Baptist faith prepared Selina for the teachings of her future husband. From her mother Selina learned the importance of female spiritual leadership.

Domesticity had a complex effect on nineteenth-century women. Women in general did not passively acquiesce to their own domination. They actively pursued their own goals and dreams, shaped in many instances by their faith and the values of nineteenth-century America. The role of women was private but far from negligible. The story of

Selina Campbell, then, is the story of the choices made by a woman who lived her life according to a certain set of ideas and beliefs, who lived within the world of domesticity but was neither dominated by it nor a rebel against it. Within this world she created a life of meaning for herself that incorporated the views of the culture around her and modified them to suit her own terms. Her life allows us to glimpse the experience of an individual and increases our understanding of domesticity by taking a new approach based on different assumptions.

Selina Campbell's own thoughts about her friends and family, as well as a number of other concerns, prompted her to write over a hundred letters and essays for publication in various journals and newspapers. The most prominent theme in her writings was always the centrality of her faith in God. In this respect Selina was representative of the great number of American women whose religious beliefs stood at the center of their conceptual framework, the women who constituted 60 percent to 70 percent of the church members in the pews every Sunday. These churchgoers responded to the values propounded from the pulpit and shared them with other women.

As a more than competent writer and thinker, Selina Campbell commented on a variety of issues that captured her attention—some cultural, others political or philosophical. The number of topics she addressed and the depth in which she discussed them establish her as a thinker and author worthy of close study. Her articulate analysis of many issues gives us an opportunity to examine the conclusions of a well-read woman of faith. Specifically, her chosen topics are subsumed under the umbrella of a worldview. They included political observations such as her view of the conflict that culminated in the Civil War, social issues such as the danger of public amusements, and spiritual questions such as the purpose of suffering. Her diverse responses to a variety of issues reflect the many different facets of her background and personality. In all, there seem to have been few issues on which Selina did not form an opinion and express herself frequently. The volume of letters, essays, and articles she left behind is sufficient for a detailed study of her life and thought, adding another dimension to the analysis of Selina's contributions as a woman and a Disciple. These materials also reveal her opinion on issues that went well beyond the role of women in the family and in society. Though many of her comments appeared in letters to her children, they touched on topics outside the domestic circle and illuminate the part that religious faith played in the lives of many nineteenth-century women.

The first (and probably last) principle immediately apparent when we analyze Selina's worldview is the importance of her faith in a personal, active, and righteous God. This faith provided the lens through which she interpreted most aspects of the society she observed. In the context of promoting service to God, Selina examined even issues that at first seemed to have no direct relationship to her faith, such as the importance of education in an individual's development. In the letters that detail her opinions on such issues, she wrote passionately about the depth of her faith. None of these letters was published apart from a few written to people outside her family. These documents probably reveal accurately most of her private thoughts and feelings. The opinions expressed in the letters reflect, in the main, the thoughts she deemed worthy of sharing with those close to her—primarily her children.

In her writings, several aspects of Selina's character become evident. First, she was a deeply moral person who distrusted the dizzying social scene she associated with town living. Dancing, parties, and fancy dress were distasteful to her and struck deep chords within her conscience. She laboriously wrote reasoned essays telling why such activities were counterproductive. She did not rush to condemn but rather strove to convert. Second, she was a widely read person capable of commenting intelligently on the topics that she addressed; her remarks in her personal correspondence and in the articles she wrote for publication attest to her extensive reading habits. She mentions having read nearly 150 books as well as dozens of newspapers, many of them published abroad. When Selina discussed issues, she discussed them as one who had read much of the available information, had considered it in light of scriptural precepts, and was concerned to present a balanced interpretation.

Naturally, the Bible figured prominently in Selina's writings. In common with many other Victorians, she quoted from it regularly and was extremely familiar with its contents. Studying Scriptures, she believed, prepared a person not only for the challenges of life in this world but also for the joys of the next. It is the best source of "wisdom to pass through this world with comfort and also prepare us for the next where no *sorrow* or temptations can ever assail us." Reading the Bible was part of her regular routine. She often shared insights from her readings in the letters she wrote to friends and family members. The Bible also assumed a particular significance in her thought and actions as a Disciple. The preaching of her husband, the most influential individual among the Disciples of Christ, often centered on the importance of Scripture as a "scientific manual or technical blueprint" containing all that a Christian needed to know about the nature of God and the theology of the ancient gospel.[18] Rejection of its teachings left one vulnerable to the wrath of God. A person could secure eternal welfare only through the grace of God as revealed in the Bible, which therefore required careful study.

Selina Campbell, like her husband, emphasized the Scriptures and also made her own observations about their importance. She believed that the Bible was "the only source of true knowledge concerning our life here and our eternal destiny." It was also a guidebook that "treats upon all the duties incumbent upon us while sojourners here below." Instruction in the Scriptures revealed promises of an inheritance from heaven for all of those who lived a "life of faith and holiness." There was an obvious dichotomy between the life lived on earth and the life awaiting the Christian in Heaven. For Selina, Scriptures provided all the necessary knowledge for both. The Bible was a Christian's only reliable source for advice on how to live in this world.[19]

At times, it is difficult to gauge the extent to which Selina Campbell's opinions were influenced by her husband rather than being solely her own. It is equally difficult to determine how much of what her husband wrote was influenced by his wife's input. Certainly, in some cases Alexander Campbell's imprint is quite evident in Selina's thinking. The emphasis on primitivist, nondenominational Protestantism and on the need for education in matters moral as well as intellectual are but two examples. But in other instances, one of which is the American Christian Missionary Society (ACMS), the two differed, and Selina's influence on her husband is more obvious.

I do not mean to suggest that the story of this one woman should be regarded as undercutting theories that seek to explain the lives of women in general. On the other hand, many such studies are based on evidence from the lives of women who have much in common with Selina Campbell. Cott's work examined educated New England women of some means whose husbands had above-average incomes. The life of Selina Campbell, who in both education and wealth resembled women studied by other writers, shows how large a role personality and religious beliefs could play. Also, Selina was a model for other women because of her marriage to Alexander Campbell. And though she did not often lead in her own right, she nonetheless demonstrated her own abilities in uniquely feminine ways.

While the Campbell marriage emphasized equality and partnership, in some respects it probably differed from other marriages and worked against an active role for Selina. For instance, the Campbells were united in their belief in primitive Christianity. Their common commitment to a particular theology probably made Campbell more supportive of his wife's role than he might otherwise have been and meant also that she agreed with his theological doctrines.

Although the role of women did not receive as much attention as the Lord's Supper, ecclesiastical authority, or infant baptism in the sharply denominational religious debates of the nineteenth century, it nonetheless often captured the attention of leaders of the Disciples of Christ. In his journal, *Millennial Harbinger,* Alexander Campbell frequently wrote on the issue of women's proper role. His conclusions and those published in other similar journals speak directly to many issues in nineteenth-century women's history and provide an important backdrop for his wife's activities. As early as 1824 words like "separate spheres" and the "modesty and delicacy" of women appear, reflecting a new worldview that was taking shape. Moreover, the middle decades of the nineteenth century witnessed the strongest growth in the Disciples since their beginning. By 1860, they were the fifth largest Protestant church, numbering about 200,000 members.[20] Thus the ideas of Alexander Campbell reflected the views of a significant segment of the population. Since many of his views of women were shaped by his relationship to his wife, her life and experience can help us understand the public writings of her husband.

Selina's religious practice reflected many of the aspects of Protestant evangelical religion that is often called the Stone-Campbell movement.[21] Indeed, the movement in which her husband was involved in its early stages resulted in the nineteenth-century church known as the Disciples of Christ, or the Campbellites; this group emphasized piety, a personal experience of the grace of God, and a conversion experience for each believer. The Disciples also supported the camp meetings and revivals of the era, although they later came to mistrust the hyperemotionalism of many such gatherings. Thus in many ways the Disciples were at the heart of the nation's theological and spiritual trends throughout the nineteenth century.

The Disciples of Christ were unique in several ways. Their emphasis on congregational autonomy set them apart from the common types of denominational hierarchy. With the exception of the American Christian Missionary Society, founded in 1849 to coordinate the missions efforts of the individual congregations, the Disciples understood the "Church" to be the body of believers in Jesus Christ throughout the world and not an individual institutional structure. In the absence of large denominational conventions or a hierarchical leadership to disseminate doctrine, the leaders of the movement often published their own newspapers to disseminate their ideas.

The earliest origins of the Disciples of Christ reach back to several key events. One of the most important documents, and one that illustrates many of the key aspects of the Disciples' theology, is the "Declaration and Address of the Christian Association of Washington," written in 1809. Thomas Campbell, the author of the document and Alexander Campbell's father, intended it as an exposition of a new effort to promote primitive Christianity, or the church established by Christ's Apostles in the first century, and a Christian faith free from all human additions. What it became was a manifesto for a growing group of Americans trying to free themselves from the strictures of denominationalism and return to the simplicity of first-century Christianity. Thomas Campbell had been a Presbyterian minister in western Pennsylvania, mainly the town of Washington, for several months when his relaxed requirements for administering the sacrament of the Lord's Supper drew criticism from the leaders of his synod. Increasingly frustrated with the rigidity of the synod, which had put him on trial for his practices, Thomas led several churches to join a "Christian Association" through which they could promote the centrality of the Scriptures over man-made creeds and the independence of each congregation over the interference of dogmatic hierarchies.[22]

Thomas was later joined by his talented son, who shared his desire to reform the Presbyterian church in the United States. Both had withdrawn from the Calvinist Seceder Presbyterians to found a new congregation, the Brush Creek Church. When they began their ministry, the Campbells intended not to create a new denomination but only to reform existing churches. In fact, for the entirety of his life Alexander Campbell referred to his efforts as the Reformation, not a new church. But Richard Hughes argues that by the middle of the nineteenth century, despite the Campbells' intentions, the Disciples' unique theology had set them apart.[23] Ironically, one of the stated goals of the "Declaration and Address" had been to unite all Christians, drawing on the centrality of the Scriptures, to form a loose "Christian Association," but the often complex process of interpreting the Bible had made plain to the Disciples the difficulty of attaining such a goal. After brief unions with the Baptists and Republican Methodists, the Disciples sought independence from all established denominations.

Both Campbells were profoundly influenced by Enlightenment ideas of order, reason, and the constancy of the laws of nature. Believing that these laws of nature could be identified and used to interpret the character of God in a rational manner, they especially identified with a philosophy often called "Scottish Common Sense Realism." Many Scottish philosophers in the eighteenth and nineteenth centuries specifically objected to the skepticism of David Hume and instead held to the belief that each person was capable of evaluating evidence and coming to rational conclusions based on several interacting but verifiable factors.

They built on John Locke's theories regarding human understanding. The Campbells, applying this philosophy to religious inquiry, emphasized the ability of individuals to understand Scripture through their own reasoning or "common sense" (the shared rational abilities of all humankind). Their scrupulous empiricism relied upon a deep trust of all the senses and the inherent reality of the world. At the same time, the Campbells were aware of the limits of the scientific method in documenting theological realities. They compensated for deficiencies in this area by encouraging slow and meticulous study of Scripture. To be a Disciple was thus to respect greatly the rationality of the human mind and the importance of devoting one's life to the study of the Bible.

The literacy rate of the Disciples was high enough to ensure that a large number of members could read the newspapers, magazines, and journals published by prominent leaders in the movement. Alexander Campbell's *Millennial Harbinger,* which succeeded his earlier journal, the *Christian Baptist,* informed thousands of readers on biblical interpretation, current events, and biographical examples of Christian devotion. Other journals such as the *Christian Standard,* published by Isaac Errett in Cincinnati, Ohio, and the *Christian Evangelist,* published by James H. Garrison and B. W. Johnson of St. Louis, Missouri, did likewise. In addition, such newspapers often published articles and letters written by a variety of men and women on the issues facing the Church. Articles by Selina Campbell appeared often on the pages of these periodicals and provide further information about her public ideas.

These newspapers represent a unique forum in American history that Selina used skillfully. Certainly the editors had the power to determine what would and would not be published. The varied and often contradictory nature of the opinions expressed in their newspapers, however, indicates at least some validity for the debates as expressions of public sentiment. Such newspapers were an effective means of communication for many Disciples' leaders.[24] By examining the viewpoints she advanced in the dozens of articles published in the journals of the Stone-Campbell movement, one can examine the nature of her ideas on a variety of subjects and the conclusions that she reached, especially regarding the nature of separate spheres for each gender.

Other primary sources on the life of Selina Campbell are equally useful, offering less edited versions of her thoughts. These sources come
from four major document collections. First, there are the Campbell
Family Papers, preserved at Bethany College in West Virginia. This collection includes letters mainly from Selina to her children that number
in the hundreds. There are also several dozen letters from Alexander
Campbell to his wife. Unfortunately, not a single letter from Selina to
her husband survives, but fortunately the abundance of other sources
mostly compensates for this lack.[25] The many surviving letters from her
husband frequently mention information contained in her earlier letters, and they hint at the nature of Selina's letters to Alexander. Second, there are the papers of Theron Hervey Bakewell, older brother of
Selina. Bakewell's papers have been preserved by the Virginia Historical
Society and number over 500 items. Several dozen of these are letters that Selina as a young woman wrote to her brother and her father.
The third major source of information on Selina Campbell is the correspondence of Julia Barclay, her close friend, preserved by the Disciples
of Christ Historical Society in Nashville, Tennessee. Fourth, in 1882
Selina wrote a memoir of her husband entitled *Home Life and Reminiscences of Alexander Campbell*. This 500-page book details their marriage, Selina's relationship with her children, and many other important
aspects of her life.

In 1985 historian Elizabeth Fox-Genovese suggested that current
models of women's history do not fit the relationship between women
and evangelical religion. Fox-Genovese underscored the need to understand theology and religion as a system of belief and not merely a function of economic or social values.[26] As a system of belief, religion had a
tremendous impact on the life and experience of Selina Campbell. Her
faith was not a mindless reflection or determinant of the society she
lived in. It was a powerful force in the formation of her worldview—
the way in which she analyzed the events of the world and responded
to them. In many cases, Christian values played a major role in shaping
the foundations of society, for example influencing laws, determining
class relationships, and outlining the role of the individual. Moreover,
though the Disciples of Christ (especially the more conservative south-

ern branch later called the Churches of Christ), espoused the Bible as
the foundation of their beliefs and practices, they also lived in a culture
whose dramatic changes did not leave them undisturbed. We must understand both Selina's theology and her culture if we are to grasp her
gender ideology.

The interaction between evangelical religion and the reform impulse also shaped the role of women in the nineteenth century. This interaction is most spectacularly evident in the sphere that women began
to occupy in nineteenth-century society. This sphere transcended the
public-private dichotomy commonly noted by historians. Women's benevolent activities, for instance, actually created a new definition of
public and private. Women succeeded in expanding the home to include large parts of society, thus establishing their authority in new
areas. Benevolent societies are probably the most important example of
this enlargement of women's sphere. No discussion of women's role in
American religion can be complete without an appreciation of the consequence of women's benevolent societies.

Selina Campbell, as a Disciple, was not particularly interested in
joining moral reform societies. The Disciples as a whole emphasized the
role of the church as a promoter of moral reform more than secular
societies.[27] Indeed, the early heritage of the Disciples' theology encompassed a distrust of large organizations, with their tendency to promote
the tyrannical control of a few religious leaders over the many. The importance of the individual contributed to the Disciples' emphasis on individual congregational efforts to promote reform. Selina therefore did
not join any temperance or other reform societies. But she did make one
important exception. The only accepted platform for national effort
among the Disciples was the missions effort. After her husband's death,
this effort received much of Selina's attention.

In 1866 Alexander Campbell died after a lingering illness. His widow,
then sixty-four, would live more than three decades longer. Though
Selina Campbell faced many challenges during the years of her widowhood, she also demonstrated the variety of her talents. Specifically she
revealed significant ability as a writer and analyst of public issues. Always a prolific letter writer, Selina redoubled her efforts. The volume of

Selina's writings escalated as her lessened domestic responsibilities allowed her more time to prepare articles for publication. Many of her articles were published in newspapers associated with the Disciples movement. The *Christian Standard,* for example, published several pieces attributed to her.[28] These included letters on various topics that Selina wrote to the editor of the paper but also some feature articles on subjects usually related to American culture, the role of women, and foreign or domestic missions efforts. In all, over thirty articles by Selina appeared in the pages of the *Christian Standard* alone. Other papers such as the *Christian-Evangelist,* the *Christian Record,* and the *American Christian Review* carried a similar number of items.[29] The articles Selina wrote bore such titles as "Dancing," "The English Language," "Titles," and "A Good Example." Though she did not deliberately seek a career as a writer, she considered writing one of her strongest skills and did not hesitate to share her ideas with others.

The domestic sphere remained important even after the Civil War, but new concerns began to capture the attention of women during the postbellum period when Selina's writing career blossomed. The desire to "lay herself out to do good" was one of Lady Huntingdon's most recognized qualities in Alexander Campbell's essay. And one of its most important components was to "devise plans for the diffusion of the gospel," a concern that received great attention from Selina Campbell in the years after the Civil War and the death of her husband.[30] The same ideology that encouraged her to assume a new role as head of the home also affirmed her part in spreading the Gospel. The postbellum atmosphere of religious change highlighted this role.

For a woman like Selina, according to her husband, "the poor around her were the natural objects of her bounty. These she relieved in their necessities [and] visited in sickness."[31] The rising need for amelioration of great social ills in the postbellum era spoke to the hearts of nineteenth-century Disciples and combined with other factors to introduce change into the expected function of women in the church. Thus for the postwar women Disciples, benevolent duties were greatly expanded. Selina's writings reflect this trend toward organizing women's efforts. Even before her husband's death in 1866 she had encouraged him to support the foundation of a Disciples missionary society in order to coordinate the efforts of all members. In 1874 when several Indianapolis Disciple women founded the Christian Women's Board of Missions, Selina was an enthusiastic supporter.

In general, the Disciples' call for women to meet the needs of the poor in American society resulted in action. The needs were seen as great and immediate, and the evangelical impulse encompassed an emphasis on the Holy Spirit's power to change one's life and turn one toward good deeds. Everyone was expected to answer the call in their everyday lives. Numerous articles exhorted women to "go forth, then, in the discharge of every duty, remembering that your country demands it, that society demands it, and that poor, suffering humanity will take no excuse for neglect."[32] Two different rationales were offered for the obligation of women to engage actively in benevolence work. For some, such activity was required in order to fulfill the missionary impulse. Others felt it was the appropriate response to the Christian religion that had offered women opportunities of a sort they had never before enjoyed.

Fewer Disciples women joined reform movements than did female members of other Protestant groups. The Disciples of Christ nevertheless valued the contributions of women. An editorial in the *Christian Standard* suggested that women had at least three areas of influence: the home, the neighborhood, and the press. Isaac Errett, the author, made it clear that they "intend no platitudes. . . . We know how fashionable it is just now, to sneer at the ignoble drudgeries of domestic life, and to protest against the slavery that bind women to a monotonous and dreary round of home duties. . . . Yet . . . what is the State or the Church worth unless supplied from truly Christian homes with the material strength and the elements of propriety?" He declared that women did have a place in influencing the families in their neighborhood through their example and the preaching of the Gospel. Furthermore, as editor of the *Christian Standard,* he encouraged women to produce articles to be published for the enlightenment of the entire Christian world and Sunday school literature for the instruction of young children. Indeed, most editors of Disciples' magazines encouraged women to write articles on a variety of topics and thereby to move beyond the stereotype of a woman useful only in the home. Mrs. H. W. Everest accepted Errett's offer and published articles urging women to realize that many opportunities "begin at home" but "they by no means end there."[33] She encouraged women to reach out to anyone they met and to help the youth in their neighborhood.

Many Disciples leaders accepted women's activism as a natural extension of their role in protecting the home. In a speech at the Women's Reform Club at Centerville, Ohio, on March 15, 1878, Jennie Kirkham outlined women's duty as follows: "We must work if we would save truth, purity, and liberty, home and native land from the falling chains of vice and intemperance. . . . Great changes are not only coming on the world, but are even now upon us."[34] To the mostly middle-class adherents of the Disciples of Christ, the rapid pace of the times and the concomitant changes in divorce laws, women's rights, and more had the potential to unravel society completely. Women's outreach offered a means by which society could be stabilized. More than just an extension of the home, the new activism of the postbellum era evinced an urgent cry for the preservation of cherished values in the face of the impersonal forces reshaping American society.

The issue of gender roles in religion is complex, involving such diverse factors as theology, sociology, and cultural studies. Lady Selina Huntingdon's commitment to her family and her community presaged the later involvement of Selina Campbell in the nineteenth century. But the nineteenth century proved formative in determining the position of women in the Disciples of Christ. The life of Selina Campbell helps flesh out these trends and give them meaning for all women in the nineteenth century. Most of all, the nineteenth century cannot be understood as a static era during which women were relegated to the narrow confines of the home. The life of Selina Campbell also indicates that women's issues shaped the church's goals and practices. Women were not imprisoned by their domestic responsibilities. Though Selina cared for her husband and children before she considered the needs of anyone else, she was not a passive participant in activities. She did not serve her community and church as a slave but instead worked to spread the faith to which she had dedicated her life. And her view of her role, seen through the lens of this faith, determined her response to each of the many challenges that life brought her.

I

The Bakewell Family

The story of the English brickmaker's daughter who became one of the most prominent women in America's fastest growing nineteenth-century churches begins in a small community in central England. The village of Lichfield, lying in the southern Staffordshire area, 118 miles northwest of London, numbered 4,842 inhabitants in 1801. Lichfield perhaps took its name from the "traditionary martyrdom of more than 1000 Christians, who are said to have been massacred here in the reign of the Emperor Diocletian."[1] An old town with a strong sense of history, in 1802 Lichfield also became the birthplace of a woman whose life is noteworthy for its demonstration of devotion to family, home, and faith. The history of Selina Bakewell's family in Lichfield and in the rest of England provides a fascinating backdrop for her life. Events in Selina's childhood shed great light on her character as an adult, tell us about the members of her family and illuminate their role in her development, and lay the foundation for consideration of her adult experience.

The original village of Bakewell from which the family took its name lies in Derbyshire. The name probably came from the invading Normans of the eleventh century.[2] Family records trace the Staffordshire Bakewells (Selina's branch) back as far as Levenettus Cancellarius, a thane of the king, who was appointed the "Rector de Bakewell" in 1158. Little is known about him except that he was believed to have been born in Renfrewshire, Scotland. Selina Campbell's branch of the

Bakewell family descends directly from John Bakewell (1638–1716) of Castle Donington, the eighteenth generation from Levenettus. His son John (1690–1761) was the first Bakewell of Selina's lineage to list his residence as Kingston, County Stafford, where Selina's father was probably born.[3]

In 1796 Samuel Bakewell married Selina's mother, Ann Maria Bean, at St. Chad's Cathedral, Shrewsbury, England. The couple soon settled in Lichfield.[4] There is no record of any other Bean children, but there is also no reason to believe that there were none. George Bean, Ann Maria's father, actively served the Shrewsbury Baptist Church as deacon for several years and through his diligent service to his church transmitted his faith to his daughter. The piety that would later so broadly characterize Selina's life thus had its roots deep in her family history. At the church itself two monuments inscribed with the Bean name illustrate the family's relationship with the congregation, as do the graves of many members of the Bean family in the cemetery of the church's courtyard.[5] Later, after Ann Maria Bean Bakewell and her children crossed the Atlantic to a new home, they joined a Baptist church in Wellsburg, Virginia—the ultimate testimony to the faith of George and Ann Bean.

The early years of the nineteenth century yielded momentous changes for the Bakewell family and for the young Selina. Probably responding both to a lack of opportunity in central England and to his own adventurous, entrepreneurial spirit, Samuel Bakewell left his family and sailed for the United States in 1803. This move obliged the family to build a new life in a new country. The special clay of the hills surrounding Samuel's home in Shrewsbury and Lichfield and the larger county of Staffordshire was especially suited to pottery, an industry that Samuel Bakewell apparently attempted to join. The market for pottery, however, had been declining around the turn of the century. The potters of Staffordshire, mostly journeymen and craftsmen, had formerly owned their own kilns and exercised great control over the production and sale of their products. Growing specialization and organization of the market increasingly drove production into mechanized factories, so that the journeymen and craftsmen now exerted less control over their employment.[6] As prices fell and opportunities evaporated, many potters tried to relocate. Samuel Bakewell was probably one such worker who wanted to establish a factory in America.

Bakewell sailed for the United States in 1803 and eventually reached York County, Pennsylvania. After residing in the area for a few months, he became a naturalized citizen at the Allegheny County courthouse in Pittsburgh in early 1804.[7] Ann Maria, Selina, and Selina's three brothers set sail from Liverpool on April 30, 1804, on the ship *Diana* to reunite all members of the family. Selina and her three older brothers had all been born before the family moved. Two more sons, Arthur and Edwin, would be born in Virginia. For fifty pounds sterling the family and their possessions, which included a bureau with brass handles, a 1790 cookbook, and an old tea canister, among other things, were brought to the United States.[8] After the arrival of the wife and children, the reunited family settled in Charlestown, Brooke County, (West) Virginia.[9] Samuel most likely chose the Wellsburg area because of the ready availability of a particular type of clay in the surrounding hills that was especially useful for firing pottery. The verdant gradients lining the Ohio River, where Wellsburg had been settled in the late eighteenth century, overlay a wonderful soil.

By 1816, after nearly thirteen years in the United States, Samuel Bakewell had abandoned his family to escape debtor's prison. None of his efforts to produce new types of stoneware and brick in Virginia had been successful, and his debts kept mounting. He held a patent on a new type of brick kiln and struggled vainly for several years to get the funding to promote it. As Samuel's debts accumulated, his family grew to eight members.

The first Bakewell child, George Bean, had been born May 18, 1797, seven years before the family moved to Virginia. We have little information about this eldest son of Samuel and Ann Maria Bakewell. Family records do not even mention him until he passed in 1822. His death, though the circumstances remain unknown, was an accident for which his father, it seems, blamed himself. The family apparently did not hold Samuel responsible even though he felt liable, probably because he was absent when the unspecified accident occurred. "We pray that you won't lacerate our hearts afresh by supposing that we would cast any blame on you on account of poor George's death," Horatio, the second son, assured his father in 1822.[10]

Some writers have conjectured that George was mentally disabled and that his accidental death was therefore particularly difficult for the family to accept without a certain amount of guilt. The demise of his son seems to have tempted Samuel to take his own life, leading Horatio, his eldest surviving son, to reassure him years later, "It is true that we greeve [*sic*] on account of [George's] death, but can't we greeve and at the same time acquit you of any blame at all. We firmly believe that it was the Lord's will he should be called."[11] Though the rest of the family accepted the loss of George, it was clear that the father found it difficult to absolve himself.

Samuel reached a crisis point a few weeks after the tragedy. The letter he wrote to his family about his breakdown has not survived, but from Selina's reply we glean several important facts. Her father seems to have fallen into a deep depression in the early 1820s that threatened to overwhelm him. His comments were so startling that Selina wrote him an impassioned letter. "You mention in your letter had it not been for the love you bore for us & the dread of offending the Almighty you think you would not have received Life so long as you have." Frightened at the depth of father's distress, Selina begged him to consider the one from whom his destructive thoughts had come and to resist the pressure. "I humbly intreat [*sic*] you," she wrote, "never to *cherish* or indulge *such thoughts* as these; as they do not proceed from above, but from the great Adversary of our souls." She feared the punishment for a "Self Murderer" and begged her father to turn to God in his despair for sustenance.[12]

Samuel did not end his life in his sorrow, but his absence from the family made the grieving process harsher. George's death, her husband's refusal to come home, and his expressions of despair seemed to embitter Ann Maria; her disposition worsened as the years passed and the separation of the family continued. Selina stepped in to care for the family, but she was not the only one to feel the burden of their father's absence. The difficult emotional state of her parents and relatives prob-ably contributed to the strength of character that she would later show.

The second son of the Bakewell family, Horatio N., was born in 1798. At the age of eighteen, since his older brother could not assume responsibility for the family and their father had abdicated his obliga-tions, Horatio became the family mainstay, a burden that weighed heavily upon him. In the late 1820s he married Margaret H. McClure, the daughter of Denny McClure, a resident of Wellsburg, (West) Vir-ginia. Margaret died on July 18, 1835, leaving her husband with a young son, James Edwin, who also died a few months later. Several years passed before Horatio remarried and had a second family. In the meantime he continued to provide the leadership for his family in his father's absence.

A prominent resident of Wellsburg, Virginia, all of his life, Horatio Bakewell served actively in a number of local organizations, but he spent most of his young adult life providing for his siblings. Horatio, probably under the influence of his mother's teaching, was a diligent member of the Wellsburg Church of Christ, the second church founded by Alexander Campbell.[13] He served two terms as elder from November 18, 1832, to June 18, 1834, and from March 5, 1839, to January 28, 1844, and also acted as trustee from March 14, 1838, to December 3, 1861.[14] He owned and operated the family business, the Bakewell Fac-tory, which sat on two lots at the southwest corner of Eleventh and Main Streets in Wellsburg. Horatio and his younger brother, Theron, had persuaded Wellsburg resident Robert Dawson to sell them the land in 1826, and the elder brother operated the business there until his death in 1865.[15] The factory produced glass, pottery, and brickware that Selina Campbell once claimed was "superior to any that ever my father ever made," even though Horatio labored "under many difficul-ties which [Father] did not—having to pay heavy rents for the shops & dwelling house."[16] Though still a young man when he began the busi-ness, Horatio experienced some success in his enterprise that enabled him to pay for his family's home and support. The *Brooke County Re-publican* on September 10, 1835, described the Bakewell Factory as "a two-story stoneware factory owned and conducted by H. N. Bakewell, employing three hands" and made of brick.[17]

On September 4, 1800, another son, Theron Hervey, enlarged the Bakewell family.[18] He and Selina, so close in age, remained good friends well into their old age. Selina was born just over two years after Theron on November 12, 1802. Another Bakewell son, Arthur H., was the first of the two Bakewell children born in Virginia. (Edwin, the youngest Bakewell, was born five years later in 1812.) Little is known about the life of Arthur beyond the fact that it was relatively short. But his experience within the family is worth mentioning for its impact on his older sister. As a young woman, Selina often expressed her concern about her younger brother and his future; she was actively concerned with the welfare for every member of the family. Arthur seemingly possessed a great thirst for knowledge, upon which his sister commented several times in her letters to other members of the family. When Arthur was a young man and had left Wellsburg in search of employment, Selina expressed her faith in his character and abilities. "Brother Arthur left this place [Wellsburg] the first of this month for Cincinnati," Selina informed Theron. She was pleased with his plan "of getting in as a clerk in some commercial House, as he had several good recommendations from this place." She described him as "a fine amiable young man, possessed of many excellent qualities—and . . . a great thirst for acquiring knowledge," but he was also "for sometime prior to his departure seriously disposed." Apparently, he longed for more than working at brother Horatio's factory could offer. Sounding much like an elder sister, Selina expressed her satisfaction that he accepted the teachings of their mother as he "read the Scriptures with pleasure & admiration & began to think that the truths therein contained ought to interest us above every other consideration." In the absence of their father, she shared a bond with her brothers that might not otherwise have been so powerful. By February 1827, Arthur had written his family to let them know that he had obtained a position at a "respectable school" in Cincinnati.[19]

An unfortunate turn of circumstances had forced Arthur to seek employment away from his hometown. As Selina informed Theron, "the reasons for leaving when he did arose from a misunderstanding which took place between him & Br H[oratio]." Apparently, Arthur felt "that he had not sufficient encouragement given him," but Horatio "thought that it was his duty to assist in supporting the family until he was of age." Assuming the role of peacemaker in the family, Selina believed Arthur did sincerely desire to help the family, but she also understood his desire to pursue his own career. Arthur had assisted his brother in running the Bakewell Factory for several years, but he soon chafed under the restrictions of supporting the family. Horatio must have shown some resentment of the burdens he carried for the family, while Arthur's constant search for a better education unfortunately clashed with the duties Horatio expected young Arthur to fulfill.[20] Two years later news reached the family that Arthur had succumbed to an unspecified illness. The family was again thrown into mourning.

The quarrel between Horatio and Arthur over the younger brother's continued obligation to the family business arose from a situation with roots in earlier events. Accompanied by his son Theron, Samuel Bakewell had fled Wellsburg and, because of debts, had wandered for ten years, seeking his fortune. One of the first stops the two made was in Nashville, Tennessee, where the father took out an advertisement informing residents of the city that he had for sale an assortment of stoneware, green glass, and other items.[21] He probably transported the goods by boat to the area and docked at a port before advertising in a local paper. His schemes all centered on the desire for a windfall that would allow him to redeem his debts and return to his family. He produced inventions of all sorts, including a plumbing system made with stoneware that he attempted to sell to various cities in the South including Nashville. He and Theron also spent time in Tuscaloosa and Coffeville, Alabama, and in Columbus, Mississippi. Letters from these places streamed into Bethany and provided the only link between the family's members. Samuel was blamed for the family's separation because he continually refused to return home and find a way to settle his debts. Instead he left the family divided and obliged his youngest children to grow up without their father.

By late 1822, father and son had settled in Washington, D.C., where

Samuel continued his experiments with new kilns for burning brick. Later he became involved in a labor dispute with the Society of Brick Makers in Baltimore, whose strike he did not support. He attempted to convince the citizens of Baltimore, especially "the exporting merchants and mechanics," that the brickmakers were trying to raise the price of bricks unjustly. He followed this argument with a request for support of his new plan for a "Brick Manufacturing & Exporting Company," which would be based upon a new type of brick kiln that he was patenting. Apparently his appeals met with little success, because in 1829 he abandoned the United States and went back to his native country in search of new opportunity.[22] He died there, never having returned to see his family, which learned of his death through a letter from relatives in England. Selina wrote to her father several times during their twenty-two-year separation and always deeply regretted not having seen him again.

At times, Selina blamed Samuel for the separations and deeply resented his absence. The long separation was painful for the entire family but especially so for the second oldest son, Horatio, and Selina, the only daughter. While Selina labored to maintain the family home, Horatio almost singlehandedly bore the responsibility of supporting his mother, his sister, and three brothers, one older and two younger. His constant struggle to make a living is evident in his correspondence with Theron and Samuel. In 1822 he longed to send his father and brother the money that would restore them to their family but lamented, "It is utterly impossible as I make no cash sales." The financial burdens that he bore in caring for his family were extensive. The rents charged for both his shop and the family's home were high. The loss of labor when Arthur decided to leave Wellsburg for Cincinnati further taxed Horatio. Selina, however, expressed great confidence in him and supported him as much as she could, maintaining that he was "honest, upright [and] just in all his dealings to a cent." His eventual success she attributed to his diligence in his business "& the blessing of Providence," because of which they now had "food & rainment [*sic*] in abundance & a comfortable habitation to dwell in."[23] She regularly expressed her thankfulness for her brother's efforts. Prosperity did not come easily for the family, but Selina never hesitated to express her gratitude to her brothers and to the God who watched over them. Although it was up to her to supply the family's domestic needs—by cooking, cleaning, and providing emotional support—she valued the connection to her brothers and her mother. To judge from her grumbling letters, Ann Maria Bakewell did little but complain and probably offered little assistance to her only daughter. Perhaps Samuel was reluctant to return because of his wife's temperament.

Even more wearisome than the financial burdens caused by their father's departure was the emotional upheaval associated with the long separation from him. In a culture that placed a premium on family life, separation meant special pain. Several letters between members of the two parts of the Bakewell family (Theron and Samuel on the road and the remainder at the Wellsburg home) attest to the problems. In 1823, seven years into the exile of his father and brother, Horatio expressed some concerns about their continued absence. He was happy to hear from them but voiced frustration that they could not return and wondered if it were by choice, as indeed it seems to have been. "It always affords us much satisfaction still to hear that you and Theron are still in the land of hope," he wrote, "but far greater would be our satisfaction were we to hear of your leaving that land of banishment to return home. Yes it would afford us joy that language cannot express. But it is a thing we look for in vain to anticipate your return. . . . Never let it be said that S. R. Bakewell became a voluntary exile from his wife and family and left them to deplore his sad fate."[24] Yet his words seem to have hit upon the truth. Horatio's father had evidently abandoned them both permanently and willfully. He left behind a grieving wife who was at times convinced that her husband and son were dead.

Eventually Selina and her brothers openly challenged their father's decision to leave Wellsburg to escape his "enemies." "O Father," wrote Horatio in 1823, "we well know the reasons, that you have, and might advance for your long absence . . . , [*but*] shall the strongest tie that ever existed in the human family a tie that was first instituted and approved by God in the Garden of Paradise be violated and broken, and that forsooth because a man cannot pay his debts?"[25]

Selina expressed serious doubt about her father's efforts to create a successful business away from his family. Nearly ten years after he left Wellsburg, she describes Samuel Bakewell's continued attempts to invent a successful method of burning high-quality brick. Glad that he kept trying to make it work, she nonetheless felt that "there is no cure for his misfortunes" and expressed her pity for his predicament. "I . . . would do all in my power to release his anxious & troubled mind . . . was I near him," she told Theron in 1826. But even though her father's actions often disturbed her and the length of his absence extended to half her life, she still claimed to be willing to "pay him every respect" and comfort him in any way she could.[26]

Selina also voiced her anxiety about the effect of her father's continued absence on young Theron. She was especially concerned about his chances of having a stable, successful career—chances that she believed were jeopardized by their father's constant wandering and chasing after "many flattering prospects" that never seemed to materialize. "When I take into consideration your unsettled manner of living & your great anxiety to return home again (to see & embrace a tender & affectionate mother whose care increases for you daily)," she told Theron in one letter, "I do not wonder that you were prevented from entering into some permanent arrangement which I have no doubt you now think would have been for the better had you done so." The careers that she thought he might pursue included carpentry (of which she knew he had some knowledge) and a clerk's position in a mercantile establishment. Her concerns may have been well founded. Theron did not marry until middle age and struggled even after his marriage to find a career that would enable him to support his family. Selina, though, never lost faith in her brother or "his honest integrity uprightness & sobriety." Indeed, she later related to Theron that Horatio would have a position for him at the Bakewell Factory the moment he returned to Wellsburg. She offered this as an inducement to bring him home as soon as possible and hoped that he would "keep your promise to do like the 'Hiberian write and bring the letter yourself.' "[27]

Ann Maria spoke to her husband more often through the letters of her children than through her own. She attempted to maintain close contact with her absent spouse but seemed resentful of his desertion and rightly worried that he would never return. Her bitterness about her circumstances may explain her somber attitude and a lack of interest in caring for her children. Samuel died while still supposedly attempting to earn the money that might allow his wife to join him. According to family legend, Ann Maria pined for her home country for most of her life and constantly complained of conditions in the United States. The circumstances of Selina's childhood were often trying and may also have contributed to the lateness of her own marriage.

Indeed, Selina shouldered many of the emotional burdens of the family that would ordinarily have been assumed by a mother or father. In many ways she seems to have held the family together. Her letters attempted to tell family members how they might best meet the challenges they faced. This role seems all the more remarkable, as Selina was the only daughter in a family with six children. Horatio certainly filled his father's economic shoes in his absence, but Ann Maria's seeming inability to accept her husband's absence and to help her children cope left Selina with the role of domestic caretaker and emotional supporter. Perhaps years later this experience helped her support her husband during his long absences, but in the short run it seemed to lessen her interest in marriage, although other factors also contributed to her hesitation about marrying.

The responsibilities that Selina assumed in her youth seem to have instilled a sense of independence and a willingness to work hard. When her father told her to beware of unsuitable suitors, she responded spiritedly: "I thank you for warning me to be ware of deceitful men. Father if it be any consolation for you to know that my affections are not set upon any mortal in respect to being united, it is true."[28] Indeed, when she later wrote *Home Life and Reminiscences of Alexander Campbell,* she described her exercise of judgment in refusing one proposal in particular. Several years before she married Alexander Campbell, she was pursued by a man she felt was not sincere in his profession of Christian faith who lacked a few other qualities that Selina deemed essential. Though a man "possessed of riches and high social standing," Selina wrote, "I could not accept of his heart or his hand, because he was not a Christian." More than fifty years later, Selina still believed that her patience and her firm refusal of this man's suit had been a prerequisite for the blessing God bestowed upon her when she married Campbell.[29] Early in her life her faith guided her choices. With the passage of time it would increasingly guide her life.

A few years before Samuel left, the birth of his sixth son, Edwin, had completed the family. This youngest child of the Bakewells, who was only a toddler when Samuel left, eventually suffered most at the loss of his father. The letters the family received evidently gave Edwin his only contact with his absent parent. The loss of his father may well have contributed to the difficulty that Edwin had supporting himself and his family later in life.[30]

One of the few activities that Selina's mother seems to have enjoyed was attending church. All the Bakewell children and their mother participated actively in the Wellsburg Church of Christ. Selina recalled going with her mother in about 1813 to hear the "great man"—a young man named Alexander Campbell—preach at what were probably special meetings held in the Wellsburg area prior to the founding of the church. Campbell's words moved her deeply. By age thirty, Campbell had already developed a reputation as a preacher of extraordinary ability. His passionate calls for a return to Scripture and an end to denominational divisions stirred many listeners.

Selina Bakewell's decision to join the Wellsburg church marked the most significant turning point in her life. She and her mother could not have guessed how the moment of hearing Campbell would dramatically alter the course of their lives. Both of them became charter members of the Wellsburg Church of Christ, which was founded in 1816, but they almost certainly heard Campbell preaching long before that date. The Bakewells had initially attended the Regular Baptist Church of Wellsburg, but this congregation soon merged with the Disciples. The involvement of George Bean, Selina's maternal grandfather, with the Baptists probably made his daughter Ann Maria and her children more receptive to the teachings of the Campbells. In contrast, their father showed little commitment to any religious faith. According to the original records for the church, Ann Maria was a member of the Regular

Baptist church when she joined the newly merged congregation. Her daughter joined with her, and her sons Horatio and Edwin later also became members.

At the age of nineteen, Selina reached her own decision about Campbell's message and was baptized by "Elder Alexander."[31] Alexander Campbell would continue to help shape Selina Bakewell's character. In the years that followed she often attended meetings at which he was the featured speaker. Once she heard him lecture for an entire year on the Book of Revelation, the last book of the Bible. When a new church was built to accommodate the expanding congregation, Selina volunteered to be one of the decorators of the new church building after the funds had been raised by Brown and Campbell.

By 1822 Selina and her brothers regularly attended biweekly services at the church when Campbell came to preach there from his home a few miles south of Wellsburg on Buffalo Creek. Selina depended on these meetings to inspire and instruct her, as she confided to her brother Theron: "Wellsburgh [sic] is a poor place and is fast declining & I should not regret to leave it only on one account & that is for the sake of the Gospel which we have purely preached by Pastor Mr. Campbell every two weeks."[32] As a girl, Selina admired his teachings. As she matured, she grew closer to the entire Campbell family.

Selina might never have developed close ties to the Campbell family had she not befriended John Brown, a prominent Wellsburg resident and an active member of the Wellsburg church. Brown, formerly a Presbyterian, became a member of the Wellsburg church after meeting Alexander Campbell in 1809. The twenty-one-year-old Alexander had delivered some books for his father, Thomas Campbell, to the Brown home on Buffalo Creek south of Wellsburg early that year. Upon leaving to return to the family home in Washington, Pennsylvania, the elder Campbell had promised to send some books to the Browns immediately upon his return. Thus Alexander made his first visit to the Buffalo Creek area to fulfill his father's promise. His biographer records that he then "formed an acquaintance" with the Brown family, which "led to important results"—his first marriage to John Brown's daughter Margaret.[33]

The story of John Brown and his family is a fascinating tale of Indian raids, frontier adventure, and family tragedy. It became a part of local legend and offers fascinating insight into many of the residents of the Wellsburg area and their experiences. The city in which Selina Bakewell lived was only a decade or so removed from a wilderness populated only by Indians. The first Mrs. John Brown was a member of the Grimes family from the Charlestown (later Wellsburg) area, but after her death, John Brown married the widow of a Mr. Glass, whose home was "on the farm immediately above, in the valley of the creek." According to Campbell's biographer, Robert Richardson, Mrs. Glass was "considerably below the medium height, energetic, industrious and intelligent." Her experience, as an early settler in the area, "had been full of privations, labor and trial."[34] She was once held captive by unidentified Indians of the region for several hours before being rescued by her husband and several other men.

Several years after her abduction, Mrs. Glass and John Brown wed. Mrs. Glass thus became a stepmother to Margaret Brown, the only child of her father's first marriage. In 1809 when Alexander Campbell visited the Browns' home, he was deeply affected upon meeting Margaret Brown. Over the next two years, their relationship deepened, and the two married in the parlor at the Brown home on March 12, 1811. The first Mrs. Alexander Campbell was, according to Selina, "taller than the generality of women, possessing a fine, expressive, open countenance, blest with an eye beaming with benignity and love." A close friendship between Selina and Margaret had developed soon after they met, not long after Margaret's marriage. When in 1815 Alexander suggested moving the entire Brush Run congregation farther west to Zanesville, Ohio, so that members would not have to travel such great distances to meet together, John Brown did not want his daughter so far away. In order to persuade his son-in-law to remain in West Virginia, Brown sold his home and 300 acres on Buffalo Creek south of Wellsburg to Campbell for one dollar.[35]

Such a gift offered Campbell independence that he undoubtedly appreciated. Accordingly, he agreed to stay and construct a new church in Wellsburg. Campbell was ordained by the Christian Association of

Washington in 1812, and his career grew quickly as knowledge of his great speaking and reasoning abilities spread around the country. For several months he divided his time and energies between the two congregations in Wellsburg. During these months Selina relished the opportunity to hear him preach.

John Brown came to know Selina Bakewell at the Gospel meetings that preceded the foundation of the second Disciples of Christ congregation. Upon making her acquaintance, Brown promptly invited the young Selina to his home. She apparently struck up a quick friendship with the first Mrs. Campbell and often assisted the older woman in her domestic chores. Selina also developed a close relationship with the Campbell children long before she became their stepmother. When Margaret fell ill, Selina came to the Campbell house and helped watch over them.

As her relationship with Margaret Campbell grew in closeness and mutual affection, Selina also formed a friendship with the man she so much admired as a teacher and man of God. In 1825 she wrote explicit instructions to her brother while he lived in Washington, D.C., about an upcoming visit that her good friend Alexander Campbell planned to make to the city. Her letter directed Theron to ensure that their father treated the visitor "with all possible friendship & respect." Selina's comments also suggest that Campbell was anxious to make the acquaintance of his friends' father while on his trip. He requested "a familiar and friendly interview" with Samuel Bakewell and planned to visit the post office after his arrival to obtain the Bakewells' address in Washington (Selina hoped that Samuel would indeed leave the address for him). The young Selina assured her father and her brother that "Mr. Alexander C" presented no danger to Samuel and could be trusted with information about his "circumstances and intentions." She also spoke of Campbell's personal integrity and his deep interest in the entire family.[36] From this letter it is clear that a close connection was developing between the two families and that there was a growing relationship between Selina and her future husband—a relationship spiritual in origin but friendly and warm in its development.

Other events further demonstrate the growing tie between Selina

Bakewell and the Campbells. While on a visit to the Campbell home, Selina noticed that a sheaf of copies of the *Christian Baptist* were being prepared for mailing to subscribers.[37] She offered to take them with her back to Wellsburg and mail them there when she returned. Since the creek separating Bethany and Wellsburg had risen quite high before she could start home, both Mr. and Mrs. Campbell urged her to stay. But Selina, who had promised to return home at a stated time, insisted that she could make the journey safely if she left immediately. It was not easy to persuade the Campbells. "I was a good equestrienne," she recorded later, "and [I] had a good deal of courage. I still proposed to start, when Mr. Campbell made the proposition that he and his farm-man, named James Anderson, would accompany me to the creek, and if I fell off my horse, they were to plunge in after me and prevent me from drowning." Her arrangements made, Selina took the saddlebags "and crossed the creek safely and mounted the hill . . . , leaving [Campbell and Anderson] at the edge of the creek." She then "rode home in safety, and sent one of my brothers to the Post office with the precious numbers of *The Christian Baptist*."[38]

The drama and concern evident in this incident attest to the bond between two people whose shared experiences had brought them and would keep them together. Selina admired Campbell from her girlhood on into adulthood. Selina's marriage to Alexander Campbell had roots deep in their past, but other factors also played a large role.

The Brown home on Buffalo Creek quickly rose to prominence in the growing Disciples of Christ. Campbell's followers expanded significantly after the Disciples' churches joined with the churches associated with Barton Stone, another former Presbyterian, and the "Christians" of Kentucky to form a combined movement with tens of thousands of members all over the western frontier and soon in the South and East as well. In 1827 Campbell applied to have a post office established near his home. He named the area Bethany and laid out the town in 1847. The Brown home, which became known as the Campbell Mansion or Bethany Mansion, remained Campbell's domicile for the rest of his life. Brown had built the original three-story structure in the 1790s. It had glass windows and glass-doored bookcases, seldom seen on the western Virginia frontier. As the years passed and Campbell's ministry grew, additions to the home changed its appearance and function. Also, as Campbell developed sheepherding, various methods of farming, and other activities, the farm's economic production rose significantly. Campbell was therefore able to devote himself to full-time ministry without searching for a source of income.

Soon after his decision to remain at the Brown home, Campbell resolved to open a school on the premises. He named the school Buffalo Seminary. It operated in the Brown/Campbell dwelling for seven years until his career entered a different phase. Some additions to the original home facilitated the operation of the school. Each year in the spring Campbell held public examinations of his students on the property. Selina regularly attended these events along with other young people in the area. They must have inspired admiration of her future husband, who was renowned for his intelligence. Selina herself attended school at the nearby "Old Brick Academy of Wellsburgh [*sic*]," which was run by Oliphant Patterson, a graduate of Washington College, Pennsylvania.[39] This experience would be her only formal education.

In the mid-1820s, Margaret Brown Campbell fell ill with tuberculosis, a condition aggravated by the cold and damp in the basement that the family occupied while the Buffalo Seminary operated upstairs. In 1823, wearying of the work involved in running a school, Alexander closed the seminary. He then began editing the *Christian Baptist* and accepting a number of preaching engagements around the country. But his wife's health continued to deteriorate. Critics of Campbell have charged that he placed the operation of the Buffalo Seminary above the health of his family and thereby contributed to their death. Still, Campbell's five daughters died from tuberculosis years after they moved from the mansion's basement, and the lapse of time suggests that other factors were involved. By 1826, however, whatever the cause of her illness, Margaret was rapidly declining. Hoping to improve her health, her husband took her on a trip to Nashville in the early months of 1827. During the trip east Margaret told her husband for the first time that she knew she would soon die.[40]

The conversation between Alexander and Margaret Campbell regarding her death, during their holiday in Tennessee, is documented by Robert Richardson and was to have a great impact on future events. In Nashville, Margaret asked her husband to choose her good friend Selina to be stepmother to her children. This request culminated a growing relationship between the two women that had roots in the network of relationships within the Wellsburg church. And though Alexander refused to believe that his wife would leave him, Margaret remained adamant.

Although Margaret asked Alexander several times, without Selina's knowledge, to consider their friend as a second wife, he denied that any such plans were necessary. The next autumn, however, Margaret's illness worsened. Further denial was now impossible. On an October day in 1827, Margaret again asked him to consider the beloved Miss Bakewell as a potential spouse if "it should prove in harmony with his own feelings." Richardson records the poignancy of the moment: "Deeply moved and unable any longer to cherish the hope that she might be spared to him, Mr. Campbell could not withhold his assent, and his acquiescence in her wishes gave her the utmost happiness." A few days later Miss Bakewell visited Mrs. Campbell, "all unconscious of what had occurred in relation to herself." The younger woman entertained the invalid by singing hymns. One particular favorite of Mrs. Campbell's began with the comforting words: "We sing the Saviour's wondrous death: / He conquered when he fell." Selina's voice with its comforting message calmed the dying woman. But Selina could not know when she left that evening that she would never see her friend alive again. Margaret called her children to her bedside and offered "them an address expressive of her hopes and wishes in regard to their future course in life." She was pleased that all of her girls could read the Scriptures for themselves. In her mind this was the most important activity of all. She left them with instructions to live godly lives, to "avoid the light, foolish, and vain conversation about dress and fashion so common among females." She also admonished them to "let your apparel be sober, clean and modest," but she emphasized above all her love and affection for them.[41] The loving mother died quietly in the evening of October 22, 1827, and was mourned deeply by family and friends alike.

A few months after the tragic death of his wife, Alexander Campbell revisited her suggestion that he remarry. Deciding that his wife's choice coincided with his, he planned his wedding to Selina for July 31, 1828, just over nine months after Margaret's death. No record tells us how Campbell presented his proposal, but it must have come at least somewhat as a surprise to Selina. She was then a young woman whose older sister/mentor had just died. When that mentor's husband then proposed marriage only a few months later, the idea must have come as a shock. To the bride, the engagement must have seemed scandalously short; she had little time to prepare physically or emotionally. The ceremony itself was a simple affair despite the momentous changes it brought in her life. It took place in the home of Selina's elder brother (probably Horatio), and guests probably came from across the region. Edward Smith, a Methodist preacher and schoolmate of Selina's, performed the ceremony. Here in her girlhood home, Selina left her childhood completely behind and embraced a new life and a new family.

Selina's emotions during the ceremony, which were not recorded in any surviving documents, were presumably turbulent. Few women marry someone they have admired greatly since childhood and a man growing in fame with every day as well. The speed of the changes in her relationship to her new husband—a mere nine months—must have left Selina breathless. Campbell's fame and intelligence would have given any young woman pause. Moreover, the regular duties of marriage, such as domestic chores and child rearing, for women in the nineteenth century were magnified in this instance by the groom's larger than average property holdings and five young daughters. These were, of course, responsibilities for which Selina's role as housekeeper for her brothers had prepared her. But as she discovered, being the wife of a prominent theologian, educator, and writer would tap all the energy and devotion she had to give.

2

The Making of a Partnership

The hurried courtship and wedding of Alexander and Selina Campbell unexpectedly produced a team that would accomplish much for the reformation of American religion, a cause each of the partners fervently espoused. Their close relationship produced remarkable fruit. The thirty-eight years of their marriage were busy ones, leaving a lasting impression on those around them. The strong partnership they developed invites close examination of how they managed their respective roles. While the husband was freed by a wife capable of managing the family assets and caring for his many interests while he was away, the wife bloomed with her new responsibilities. The volume of documents left by the Campbells allows the historian to explore the specifics of their private lives for clues about their views on key issues such as the proper roles for each gender.

The four basic factors posited by Carl Degler in the emergence of the modern family system from 1780 to 1830 provide an excellent framework for understanding the experience of Alexander and Selina Campbell. Degler found that the modern family structure, which remains largely intact to this day, was based on love, female leadership of the home life, the distinctive phase of childhood as separate from adulthood, and the sacred nature of the home.[1] This family organization resulted in part from a new conception of marriage. Women now depended emotionally on their husbands, largely because of their isolation in the home. In return, the husbands turned to their wives for emotional support. A high level of affection and companionship in marriage was not uncommon.

Alexander Campbell's role as a prominent writer and preacher entailed significant responsibility that his wife, of necessity, often shared. He traveled frequently and extensively, leaving his wife behind to take responsibility for the household. Like many American women, Selina leaned on her husband, but she was also his partner in managing their property. Even when he was home, his time was often taken up in writing for his journal, the *Millennial Harbinger;* meeting with other reformers; or preparing speeches for an upcoming preaching tour. Selina therefore had to make many decisions from one day to the next—involving management of the servants, discipline of the children, and oversight of a variety household matters. Letters from her husband testify to Selina's managerial skills. In his absence, many tasks entered into her daily routine. Alexander Campbell knew that he could not undertake tasks for his faith unless someone else could meet the other important responsibilities in his life. While he ministered to his followers' spiritual needs, Selina met their physical needs.

As an article in *Good Housekeeping* observed in 1885, "Many a man owes his fortune or his name to the sympathetic assistance of his wife, and many a one has failed because he could not have it."[2] Some have argued that the Campbell home and property, which provided the income for many major achievements of the Reformation, made the movement possible.[3] If so, indirect though it may have been, Selina's role in the growth of the Disciples of Christ was significant.

The complementary nature of the Campbell marriage applied to many areas of their life as a couple and illuminates the subject of their private lives. Their correspondence, however, adds an element that was largely absent from Degler's observations. The closeness of a shared commitment to making theirs a household of faith added a dimension to their relationship that has received little attention in discussions of nineteenth-century marriages. Certainly their kind of devotion to religious activity did not characterize every nineteenth-century marriage, but there were nonetheless millions of other families whose faith profoundly impacted their domestic life. There were 200,000 Disciples alone by 1850 who admired the religious teachings of Alexander Campbell, and many of them also read the *Millennial Harbinger* for its instructions on family life. They often looked to the family of Alexander Campbell as the most prominent preacher of the movement for a model domestic arrangement.[4] The qualities that his marriage embodied were no doubt emulated by most other believers who relied on Scripture to dictate their domestic arrangements.

Family letters as well as published sources testify to Selina's success as a hostess for a broad sector of the Restoration Movement. Frequent comments written by visitors to the Campbell home speak of her hospitality and generosity. But she elicited her husband's admiration for more than her skills and abilities. He also continually remarked on the importance of her companionship—another factor sustaining their successful marriage and one that gave their partnership a deeper meaning.

In evaluating the role that domesticity played in the life of Selina Campbell, we should ponder the words of Robert Richardson, a close friend of the Campbells and Alexander's biographer. In his *Memoirs of Alexander Campbell,* Richardson offers a vivid summary of Selina's responsibilities and describes many of the challenges she faced when she took charge of the Campbell household. Campbell "had for some time, and continued to have," Richardson wrote, "quite an extensive household, to take charge of which required no small degree of courage on the part of his second wife." Selina, unlike Margaret Brown Campbell, who "had been brought up in the country and familiarized with the details of farm-life," had to learn to manage her husband's holdings. "During Mr. Campbell's long absences [she observed] his directions for the cultivation of the fields and to engage laborers, which she did with so much judgment that Mr. Campbell always returned to find things in order, and never was known to utter a word of complaint or find the least fault with the arrangements made." Richardson's words afford a fine overview of the primary duties of Campbell's wife and hint at the nature of the Campbell marriage. Not only did Selina see to the physical and financial needs of her husband, but she also had to direct "the affairs of the family," which were "often complicated by the almost incessant visits of strangers, some of whom often remained for long periods." There was also "the presence of sickness," which "greatly added to Mrs. Campbell's cares." Yet Selina proved to be "an excellent nurse," Richardson observed, "and devoting herself assiduously to the duties she had undertaken, she succeeded in managing and arranging everything so happily as greatly to relieve Mr. Campbell and leave him free to pursue his accustomed labors."[5]

Richardson's commentary on Selina's duties speaks to the exceptionally wearying labor necessary to maintain the Campbell household. From nursing to cooking and cleaning and more, the workload would have challenged even the most capable manager. Mornings came early, and evenings dragged on interminably. Selina Campbell's dining room table, which seated thirty, was often filled with friends, neighbors, and visitors. The Campbell household itself at that time numbered more than just Selina and her children; her husband's parents also lived in the Campbell home. In addition there were Margaret Brown Campbell's four young children and another married daughter with her husband. Servants were needed to help with such a crowd, but a strong work ethic and a mistrust of the servants drove Selina to attend to most of the details herself. She quickly learned to do so.

During the first eighteen months of her marriage many of Selina's new responsibilities came into sharp relief. One month after their wedding in July 1828, she accompanied her husband to the meeting of the Mahoning Association, a collection of churches that included the Brush Creek Church (her husband's primary congregation). The churches met together as a group to coordinate their efforts and to encourage each other in spreading the Gospel in their area. While her husband and other church leaders spoke to the gathered believers, Selina most likely listened to the speeches from her pew or met with the other wives. Shortly after the couple's return home, Alexander agreed to debate Robert Owen, the famous British Socialist. The debate was scheduled to begin in Cincinnati, Ohio, on April 13, 1829, so Campbell left home in the first week of April. While her husband was interpreting the Gospel 200 miles away, Selina gave birth to their first child, a little girl. She named the child Margaret Brown Campbell after her good friend and predecessor.

In October 1829 Alexander Campbell was again called away from his family, this time by politics rather than religion. He journeyed to Richmond as a delegate to the Virginia Constitutional Convention. While his wife cared for the family and property in Bethany, he spent the fall campaigning, making speeches at local gatherings. Northwestern Virginia had been allotted five delegates to the convention, and Campbell acted as one of them. The assemblage, which met in late fall through early winter 1829–1830, included such notable personalities as former presidents James Madison and James Monroe.

Although the major issue at the convention was the growing influence of the populous western parts of the Commonwealth of Virginia, which threatened the hegemony of the East, the slavery issue was also significant. The East depended on the labor of the slaves, while the West, with fewer plantations and more independent farming and industry, for the most part did not. As a member of the convention, Campbell made a name for himself as an antislavery activist.[6] During the ensuing winter months of 1829, his other activities included editing the *Christian Baptist,* maintaining his "immense correspondence," and fulfilling numerous speaking and preaching engagements. His wife, on the other hand, remained at home, caring for their growing family.

During these first few years of their marriage, the Campbells spent much time apart, but a close correspondence, some of which has survived, reveals the nature of their developing relationship. These letters form a portion of Edwin Groover's study of Alexander Campbell and his views on family life. In a chapter titled "The Little Empire: Woman at Home," Groover makes four salient points about the union. First, Selina was not "a lady of leisure" within her marriage. On the contrary, her husband expected "her to be aware of the work that is going on in his printing establishment, in the post office and on the farm." Second, Groover described her role as Alexander's "business associate" and "trusted representative" responsible for overseeing his workers and ensuring that they exhibited the obedience the husband expected from them. Third, Selina was no "delicate being restricted altogether to the house and set high on a pedestal." Rather she must "contribute significantly to the character of the household" through her example and her teaching. Fourth, Selina was Alexander's intimate companion. Their relationship, as revealed in their private words to each other, was affectionate and loving and often overtly sexual. Though they were partners, they were more than just associates. The depth of feeling that Alexander had for his wife colors all of his letters to her and leaves no doubt regarding his tenderness and warmth toward her.[7]

Groover's four points suggest the different roles that Selina performed within the family and the expectations her husband had of her. Groover's conclusions, however, are based wholly on the eight letters Alexander wrote to his wife during his extended stay in Richmond in 1829–1830 and the only slightly larger correspondence between Selina and Julia Barclay, her close friend. The several hundred items of Campbell family correspondence collected in the Bethany College archives and the several hundred more items in the Bakewell family collection reveal the rich partnership that developed between two loving and respectful individuals. The Campbell/Bakewell documents thus depict a different kind of marriage relationship, one far richer than is suggested by Groover's more limited study. Specifically, where both Bailey and Groover tend to use words such as "subordinate" to describe the role of women in the Disciples of Christ, the Campbell/Bakewell papers more often employ the term "partner." The term "partner," and not "servant," best describes Selina Campbell's life within the context of marriage and family in the nineteenth century. While the early correspondence between Alexander and Selina demonstrates love, later letters reveal more about their partnership. This partnership relied on a shared notion of the importance of their work in advancing the Christian faith, something of greater consequence than either Alexander or Selina. Nancy Cott has observed that the deeper one looks into the primary sources, the more they reveal an active role for women in their sphere.[8] The more one reads the letters between Alexander Campbell and his wife, the more their complementary relationship is apparent.

In addition to her own correspondence, Selina also managed the heavy demands of her communication with those her husband met while on tour. From the start of their marriage, when Alexander was away from home he would often send her a list of names that he expected her to preserve. During the course of his travels he relied on his wife to record these names and to assist him in maintaining a connection with hundreds of people. It was another aspect of their partnership that allowed both people to pursue their goal of promoting reformation, for Alexander's circle of acquaintance broadened as his ideas spread his reputation far and wide.

The letters Campbell wrote home during his tenure in the Virginia Constitutional Convention attest to other aspects of the developing relationship between Alexander and Selina. During this formative time the nature of the partnership between the couple took shape, molded in large part by their commitment to the spread of the Christian faith. The relationship focused not on the superior/inferior terms of the traditional notion of separate spheres but on the premise that there were a certain number of responsibilities to be met in a marriage and that the wisest method of meeting them was to assign each to one partner in the relationship. This arrangement did rely on ideas about the nature of men and women and their abilities that were prevalent in the nineteenth century, but it also celebrated the special skills of each person. Raising a family and promoting religious reformation required active leadership at two different sites (the home and the church), making some sort of partnership necessary. The perceived emotional, nurturing nature of a woman meant that the activities associated with sustaining a family fell to the wife, in this case Selina. This work freed her husband, Alexander, to leave his home and to travel the country teaching, preaching, and baptizing. His talent, which he regarded as a gift from God, established him as the traveler and preacher, while his wife's nurturing and organizational skills fit her for the role of mother and household manager.

Groover's observations about Selina's role as business associate suggest that the wife of Alexander Campbell often performed another set of tasks in her husband's stead. The early correspondence between the Campbells reveals much about the family business. Alexander requested that Selina perform a number of tasks having mainly to do with his printing business and the procurement of household supplies. For instance, in November 1829 he wanted her to procure a thousand pounds of pork through Joseph Briant or Joseph Cabajal (both residents of the Campbell household), "to be delivered to you, at the market price—to be paid when I return or by you as the case may be."[9] He also told her who might be able to provide the pork. Later, when one of the sales agents for his publications attempted to avoid payment for goods received, Alexander asked Selina to check into the matter and to refer it to his secretary, Joseph Cabajal, if action needed to be taken. He asked her to mail books to subscribers, as he had received payment for them. He also instructed her to bury some apples for storage during the winter months, and he advised her to "have the bees taken that stand out upon the bench" and to "get your cider for apple-butter immediately and see that your fruit be saved in due time," which meant, among other things, putting away the potatoes before the frost.[10]

During the time that his wife struggled to accomplish those tasks and to keep the household running in his absence, Alexander worked diligently at the tasks allotted to him. While in Richmond, he spent his time preparing speeches for the debates being held about the Constitution and reviewed the arguments made by other participants. When not attending the debates, he preached to religious gatherings often numbering as many as 3,000 souls (hundreds were sometimes turned away due to lack of space in the meeting halls), baptizing local converts, conducting weddings, and writing articles for the *Millennial Harbinger*. His debate with Owen and his early preaching tours had established his ability as a preacher and teacher, so that he was much in demand as a speaker in Richmond and the surrounding area. In early November 1829 he seemed to tire of the constant whirl of activity in Richmond (much as Selina wearied of her many domestic burdens at Bethany): "I have just now returned from a visit to a party of ladies and gentlemen, and have three invitations for tomorrow evening," he wrote to his wife. "I preach in all these little societies for I generally get control of all the meetings. I am therefore in point of company indulged in the evenings with all, and more than I could wish." His desire to preach to any who would listen did motivate him to express his views as often as he was allowed, no matter how wearying the task. But at times he longed for the serenity of his wife's company. He once traveled twenty-three miles south of Richmond to preach in Petersburg and returned the same day.[11] He probably preached again the next day; he was never one to turn down any chance to address an audience willing to consider his words. By the same token, his wife turned away no guest who showed up at her door.

By Christmas 1829, in the twelfth week of his absence, Alexander's eagerness to return to Bethany was heightened by his impatience with the frantic pace of life in Richmond. He shared with his wife his frustration and his desire to come home. As the conference wore on, Alexander acknowledged that he was "worn out with fatigue in sitting —not going to meeting as it were and sitting in a large assembly 80 days." He likened it to going to school and expressed his growing dissatisfaction with his duties: "I am under tutors and governors and I do not like it. I need not tell you that I am homesick." The duties of participating in the convention had taken a toll on him and stretched his patience with the whole process. Politics held little appeal for him after this experience, and he was sure that Selina would "not consent to my being a politician hereafter." He told her he was equally positive that "unless you can come with me I will not consent to be a candidate."[12] Both were sorry that his service to the state of Virginia had kept them apart for such a long time so early in their marriage. One long separation seemed enough at that time, but before too many years had passed other calls to duty kept them apart for lengthier periods. Yet in the face of this first duty, Alexander did not fail to take note of the privations his wife faced. He wrote, "I flatter myself that you are resigned to your lot and willing to wait until I have discharged my duty to my country." But he hoped that she would take comfort in his assurance that "the Lord sent me here for more than political purposes, and I hope my visit to Richmond will be long remembered."[13] Indeed, his stay in Richmond was fruitful in the sense that thousands heard his preaching and were deeply moved. In its entirety the correspondence between the Campbells reveals that his devotion to the work of preaching and teaching also taught him to appreciate the woman who helped make it possible.

Though Alexander's letters to Selina contain valuable information on his instructions to her and his activities in Richmond, this is not their main focus. At the core of the letters and indeed the Campbell marriage is the true affection the two held for each other. Unfortunately, Selina's half of the Richmond correspondence has not survived, but the sentiments in Alexander's are enough alone. For instance, he often declared his joy at receiving each letter she wrote to him and "rejoice[d] to learn [her] domestic arrangements." He frequently showed interest in what was happening at home in his absence and always begged for information from the home front. "You must know," he wrote in one letter, "that I always open your epistles with a palpitating heart. When I break open the seal I think of the fingers that made it secure and of the heart that is sealed to mine, and that it is open to me as mine is to you." The tender words likewise dispel any notion that this marriage was one of convenience or dutiful obedience to the last request of a dying spouse. On the contrary, Alexander affirmed in the intimate correspondence he maintained with his second wife that "while I write for no eye but yours I can say what I feel, and how much I long to be restored to your bosom and company."[14] Alexander intensely regretted the need to be away from home and treasured the letters from his wife, as they linked him with her and the family he deeply loved.

The letters sent home from Richmond may have contained tedious instructions for Selina on mailing out books to subscribers all over the country or on harvesting the crops before the frost, but they also included passionate declarations of love and affection from her absent husband. Nearly every letter included tender affirmations of not only an emotional need for her presence but also of his physical desire for her. "I feel the want of you as sensibly as our Father Adam felt the want of a rib when he awoke from his sleep profound," Alexander wrote to his wife. "I feel the loss and you may rest assured that law which causes the spring to succeed the winter does not more certainly operate than that which will hurry me to your bosom."[15] In other letters, his feelings were even more explicit as he longed for the physical presence of his wife:

> I find privation alone teaches us the value of possession. And my want of your company has given me a new relish for it. I feel as I have lost the half of myself. I have no ear into which to whisper a secret which I cannot communicate to any other, and there are not lips I can embrace in this strange land. . . . I cannot tell what a pleasure it would give me if I could only have one hour of your company. Here I am amongst many friends and strangers but there is none can fill that part of my heart that belongs to you.[16]

Whatever the economic or professional relationship that the couple shared, at the core of their marriage there lay a deep mutual love. Alexander ascribed these feelings to the God who created them in him and affirmed the joyous nature of marriage as a gift from his Creator. He also welcomed the closeness that his union with Selina brought: "What a happy institution marriage was and is, and shall always be, so long as we are such beings, with such tender feelings, emotions, and passions."[17]

To Alexander, Selina was no paragon on a pedestal but a woman whom he could love in the flesh and also appreciate as a companion in faith and in life. When apart from her he is "reminded that there is no one into whose ear I can whisper one word of love, or upon whose bosom I can lay my head—or my hand." In a marriage not far out of the honeymoon stage, extended separation must have been difficult. Alexander obviously yearned for their reunion all the time he remained in Virginia. Four months into his absence, Alexander playfully requested Selina to "kiss my little, *our* little Margaret" and added, "I will pay you all Principal and interest too. For I am rich in love and love will be able to . . . redeem all the promises I have made you."[18] There is no record of their reunion in late winter 1830, but given the deep sentiments expressed in their correspondence, it must have been physically and emotionally gratifying to them both. For the entirety of their marriage, separation, though frequent, was never welcome.

While her husband filled his responsibilities away from home at the beginning of their marriage, Selina quickly assumed more new ones within the home. Her role as hostess, one of the most important she fulfilled, also began right away. Including her husband's parents, her stepdaughter and spouse, and her stepchildren and several servants, the household she managed numbered at least fifteen in 1829. Moreover, during the first winter of her marriage, thirteen members of the household contracted measles. It was up to Selina to nurse them all. Her strong constitution, which she attributed to her English heritage, probably prevented her from being infected with the disease herself. With so many patients to tend, probably including some of the servants, Selina quickly learned to manage domestic duties on her own and was able to sharpen her organizational skills. Her early experience caring for her brothers no doubt stood her in good stead and contributed to her ability to fulfill the obligations of her marriage.

Formal duties as a hostess demanded much of Selina's time. Visitors to the Campbell home starting in the first months of her marriage included the famous and the unknown, the wealthy and the destitute, but always visitors. They were all greeted with open arms by the master of the house. For her part, the mistress turned to prepare their beds, oversee the arrangement of their meals, and provide any other necessary comfort during their stay. "From the day of my marriage till the time of Mr. Campbell's death," Selina wrote, the house "was always open for the entertainment of friends as well as strangers, and while I knew he had the privilege of entertaining and edifying our guests in spiritual matters, I felt it a duty to minister to the body, and attend to domestic concerns." The Campbell Mansion was often viewed as the center of the Reformation, the Mecca of Campbellism, since the movement's most recognized leader resided within its walls. Most visitors expected to be well received by their leader. In the tradition of frontier hospitality, none was turned away. "Our visitors were numerous, and often their visits were protracted," wrote Selina Campbell in *Home Life of Alexander Campbell,* "but all were always made to enjoy a *home* feeling, at least that was the desire of the host and hostess." She added, "No indigent person was ever turned from our door."[19] It seems that

Selina relished her role more than one might expect. Looking beyond the drudgery, she felt that "it was the intensity of feeling and the importance of scripturally 'entertaining strangers' that lessened all the care and necessary labor" of entertaining so many guests. One can well imagine that when the stresses of entertaining grew taxing, thoughts of a reward beyond this life might have helped keep her animated.

Though she was not the center of her guests' attention, Selina took great pride in the service she provided for every visitor. Her role, though private, was nonetheless meaningful. The nature of her partnership with her husband is also evident in Selina's expressed opinion of her role as hostess: "The idea with me was, while my dear husband was feasting them intellectually and spiritually, it was my province to attend to the wants of the body."[20] She directed the servants and made sure food was ready and the house cleaned as the guests participated in daily devotions led by Campbell and enjoyed an environment of faithful study and discipleship based on scriptural precepts. Such a complementary view of the different parts played in the promotion of the Gospel sustained Selina in her labors and contributed to her good cheer.

In 1840 Alexander Campbell oversaw the construction of a guest wing for the mansion to meet the needs of an increasing number of visitors. Consisting of a large parlor and two bedrooms, this portion of the mansion became known as "Strangers Hall." According to Selina, the name came about when "an elderly neighbor, living above us on the creek . . . , was passing one day, [she] called to me in the yard, asking me to give her some of the 'seeds of those beautiful flowers—those growing by the Strangers Hall.' It was the first time I had heard it so called. I came and told the family of the name given to the new house."[21] And the name stuck. Among the most notable guests at the Campbells' Bethany Mansion were Henry Clay, the Kentucky politician and four-time presidential candidate, and James A. Garfield, Disciple, political leader, and future president. Garfield maintained a healthy respect for Campbell for many years and in his diary records reading many of the preacher's writings with favorable responses. He declined to attend Bethany College as a young man because of his feeling that the student body was too proslavery. Seeking a broader educational experience to round out his upbringing, which had occurred exclusively at the hands of Disciples, Garfield selected Williams College in New England, but he remained a faithful Disciple until his tragic untimely death only a few months after he became president of the United States.[22] Many visitors who admired the president came to Bethany Mansion and sat in the chair that Garfield used whenever he visited the Campbells.[23]

Other visitors to the Campbell home included close associates like Robert Richardson and James T. Barclay, the Disciples' first overseas missionary (to Jerusalem), and Julia Barclay, his wife, who was a close friend of Selina's. Robert Owen, the British Socialist, visited in 1829 a few months before his debate with Campbell in Cincinnati. Jefferson Davis, future president of the Confederacy, also came to meet the well-known evangelist, as did Judge Jeremiah Black, a close friend of the Campbells and later U.S. attorney general under President Buchanan. Local residents and traveling evangelists called frequently at Bethany. "Never was I anywhere received with more cordiality than here," affirmed one guest, F. W. Emmons.[24] He visited the Campbell household sometime in early 1830, and he recalled that Selina Campbell met him at the door upon his arrival and conducted him into the parlor, where he met with her revered spouse, Mr. Campbell. After making Campbell's acquaintance, Emmons moved to Wellsburg to join in the preacher's labors. He does not record what the two discussed during his 1830 visit (though it was probably the pocket edition of the New Testament that Emmons was helping Campbell revise), but he commented on his gracious reception in a letter to a colleague years later. Such a response met Selina's personal goals. After entertaining another group of visitors passing through Bethany in 1858, she reported to her daughter that she "felt comfortable that they appeared pleased with their visit" and that she "did all in my power to make them comfortable."[25] Another visitor to the Campbell Mansion, John Udell, further confirms the success of Selina's efforts to provide a home for travelers and guests. Twenty years after his visit, what he remembered most was Sister Campbell's "kindness and liberality," and he was sure he would never again "be in a society more resembling the family in heaven than Bethany."[26]

Other guests in the Campbell home included the students of Bethany College, founded by Alexander in 1840. In a letter to her eldest daughter, Margaret, Selina recounts one typical evening: "We spent a pleasant evening in conversation & singing last evening, there were several young Gentlemen from the College here. The new Hymn Books have made their appearance—they contain a variety of excellent Psalms & Hymns. I have invited them from the college and the young persons around to meet once a week at our house to improve themselves in singing—our large room you know suits well for singing."[27] The graciousness of the Campbell home comforted many students away from their homes for the first time, and the activities of this evening speak as well to the diversity of events that took place under Selina Campbell's leadership. Though many of her guests were there to interview or spend time with her husband, some of them were there because she opened up her heart and her home to them, and they responded in kind.

Many of the guests were also neighbors or servants who came to the mansion to celebrate special events, particularly weddings. The Campbell home hosted several marriage ceremonies for neighbors, such as the 1833 social planned for Mr. Hutchinson and his bride, who is identified only as "a sister of Sophronia's." Selina does not mention the couple's relationship to her family, but it seems likely that they were servants or tenant farmers who lived in their own dwelling somewhere on the farm. In a letter to her brother Theron, she boasted of giving them "a large infare" and wished he could have attended.[28] Such generosity to her neighbors formed an integral part of her role as the hostess of the Campbell Mansion.

Making her guests "comfortable" required serious planning and organization on Selina's part. Sometimes the servants provided important assistance but not always. In January 1846, in her eighteenth year of marriage, Selina was swamped with company while one of her "girls" had fallen ill and another, the cook, had recently left her employ. Selina had to complete the preparations herself and worked tirelessly to arrange a large dinner party. The level of preparations necessary becomes especially evident in the 1840s correspondence between Selina and her brother Theron, during which time the older sibling operated his own general store. During that busy decade, nearly every letter from sister to brother (and these letters make up the bulk of Selina's correspondence surviving from the period) contained a request for more household goods to meet growing needs. Like many southern women, Selina Campbell relied upon a kinship network to meet the needs of her household.[29] While many northern women lived in urban areas or had other means of accessing a general store, Selina lived in a relatively isolated area and thus depended on her brother to procure many necessary items. Theron's skill at obtaining things for his sister prompted her to lean heavily upon him. "I think there could not be a better hand to put up goods for safe carrying than you are," she told her brother in one letter.[30] Indeed the quantity of items she requested from him was quite substantial.

When viewed in total, the requests Selina made of her brother seem overwhelming. In a single 1842 letter she asked for fourteen yards of Jaconett, several bolts of white cord, "as much black sewing silk as you can spare" (probably for clothing appropriate to a family in the constant state of mourning), six boxes of hooks and eyes, a table brush, two or four brass candlesticks "if you can put them in," eight yards of blue calico, and other sundry items.[31] These items indicate the variety of Selina's activities. In addition to cooking and cleaning, she also sewed and mended all the clothes for the family, a task that must have seemed endless in such a large household.

Other letters contain requests for such practical items as 150 pounds of sugar, 40 or 50 pounds of feathers, ten yards of linen, soup plates, butter plates, common bowls, oval dishes, sauce dishes, a dozen pans, three or four larger pitchers, a dozen dining plates, a dozen small Liverpool bowls, 5 or 10 pounds of ground pepper, all the buckets Theron could spare, and other household items too numerous to name.[32] Even her children were excited about the homemade sugar Uncle Theron had promised, and their response shows that his goods were important to the entire household. Theron's ability to procure items must have seemed miraculous to his grateful sister.

Finally, after several months of frequent requests, Selina admitted that she felt "quite made up with articles I much needed—for I have so many persons to supply that it almost takes a store to do it." Her needs were at times so urgent that on another occasion she admitted to Theron, "I just put down things as they occurred to my memory and without respect to order so you must excuse."[33] Given the quantity of items she requested in each letter, it is not surprising that some of them were jumbled. Only a nimble competent mind could have gauged the needs of such a household. Yet on occasion Selina was almost undone by the daunting challenge. After sending her brother another list of urgent items she wearily wrote, "I find I shall want more than I expected."[34] Her words were probably an understatement.

Selina's gratitude to her brother for his ready assistance was obvious, and she tried not to abuse his generosity. In 1846 she urged Theron to send her a bill for the items as quickly as possible because she was "almost afraid you have robed [sic] yourself too much as it is," and she wanted to reimburse him quickly. She did not hesitate to recognize his contributions to her success. "I would not have asked you to have done it so much," she informed Theron, "if you had not appeared so willing." The items he sent her relieved her of some of the great responsibility she bore, and his willingness to help must have eased her mind greatly. She often asked him to drop off items on his way to Pittsburgh (where he regularly went on business) or offered to have her son bring them. She unfailingly complimented him for his skill in packaging items and his willingness to send items immediately. Such assistance from a family member enabled Selina to meet her obligations and marshal the resources necessary to care for her family and friends.[35]

If her family was willing to help her discharge her own duties, she understood that she had obligations to them in her husband's absence and never hesitated to fulfill them. When the second wife of her brother Horatio died in 1852, Selina opened her house to his only daughter, Emma Celestine. She then raised the girl as one of her own. The child's three brothers stayed with their father to help him run the family business. Born June 22, 1842, in Wellsburg, Emma was ten when she came to live with her aunt. She joined the Wellsburg Church of Christ at a young age. Just after her twenty-fourth birthday, Emma married Robert G. Barclay, the son of Selina's close friend Julia and her missionary husband James Barclay. After her marriage, Emma and Robert moved to north Alabama, where she spent the rest of her life. She and her aunt remained close—especially after the marriage of her cousin Decima, Selina's second daughter, to Robert's younger brother James; James and Decima also moved to Alabama. As a widow Selina often paid long visits to her daughter and niece at their neighboring homes near Hillsboro, Alabama. In 1872 Emma named her only daughter Selina in honor of the aunt who had played such an important role in her life.

Events surrounding the death of Emma's husband in 1876 further reveal the depth of Selina's feelings toward her niece. Selina learned of Robert's death in two distressing letters from her daughters, Virginia and Decima. Her response was quick and heartfelt. "I can see them in my imagination," she recorded in her answering letter to Decima, "hovering over his dying *bed*—I can hear the agonizing cries of the fond Mother for her first born!" Though unable to be there for Robert's last moments, Selina expressed her deep dismay at the loss. "And what shall I say of dear Emma the fond faithful wife so unexpectedly deprived of her kind loving devoted husband and oh the fatherless children so devoted to their good wise praying father[!]"[36]

Selina's grief at her nephew's death found an outlet in her letter to Decima. Her grief-stricken words evoke the tragedy of Robert's sudden, untimely death and attest to Selina's abiding concern for those around her. Selina recalls how she "wept out loud" upon hearing the news. She expresses sorrow for "her little name sake who so quietly climbed upon his knee" and now had lost her father before her fifth birthday.[37]

As the wife of Alexander Campbell, Selina had other occasions to show her love and sympathy for friends and family. After returning home one New Year's Eve from a tour of Washington and Virginia, she was "obliged to visit a grand daughter who was quite indisposed and needed my attention and sympathies."[38] Selina obviously believed that she needed to be present to care for her step-granddaughter and probably stayed until the child was out of danger. In a similar matter, Selina was also "called to a distance from home to attend the funeral of a dear friend with whom I had been acquainted from my earliest recollections." This person was one with whom Selina "had lived in the firmest bonds of friendship" since her childhood, and "without interruption or jar," and she felt she must attend the services as a sign of respect. Her loyalty to such friends ran deep. She showed them great devotion even after they were gone.

Her role as domestic manager was, though private and largely outside the view of most people, an active one that allowed Selina to display her organizational talents. At the same time, she made a valuable contribution to the ministry of her husband, for since Campbell was often absent on preaching tours, his wife assumed the important function of representing the family at social functions, including weddings, funerals, and other similar events. This role formed another key aspect of the partnership achieved by the Campbells.

Other activities also consumed much of Selina's time and display her active devotion to maintaining close personal relationships with her family and friends. Correspondence with those close to her also took up much of her precious time, but she never seemed to begrudge it. Though her "numerous engagements" often deprived her of leisure, so that she could "scarcely find a spare moment to put a pen in hand," when a few moments could be found, she hastened to assure her brother that "I shall ever feel deeply concerned, both for your present & Eternal welfare."[39] Such attachments to Christian friends, neighbors, and relatives were precious to a woman with a sincere interest in others and a profound dedication to service. When other cares threatened to interfere, she was mindful of the need to stay in touch with those outside her immediate family. She strove constantly to remain thankful for the benevolence of others. "Although I am encircled by a large family & many duties, and cares daily pressing upon me," she wrote Theron, "yet believe me dear brother I verry [*sic*] often think of you & your kindness & attention to my little daughter."[40]

By 1840 Alexander Campbell had extended his preaching and evangelizing activities to include the creation of a college for young men. He strongly believed in the importance of moral education based on the Scriptures, and he conceived of a school where such principles would be taught regularly. Generous donations permitted the construction of a splendid building for the college in 1841. Alexander labored to attract the best professors. Selina, for her part, helped sew linens to be used by the students of the new school. Once its doors opened, as mentioned above, she often invited them into her home. The school became important to both husband and wife as each gave time, energy, and money to promote its success. Alexander taught in the school, and it grew steadily, attracting more students every year. In 1850 Alexander spoke to his close friend R. L. Coleman about his commitment to the school. "Bethany College has paramount claims on me," he wrote, "and on all the friends of the cause to which I have consecrated my life. To further it abroad and build it up at home, in raising up men for the field when I shall be absent from this planet seems to me a paramount duty." Within a few years the cause that Campbell so vigorously supported showed new strength as numerous preachers and teachers sent out by the college in turn drew in more believers.[41] By 1857 more than 100 students from all parts of the country had enrolled to study at Bethany. After they left the school they went to churches as trained ministers providing for the growth not only of Bethany College but of the Disciples of Christ as well.

Tragedy struck in late 1857, however. On one terrible night, the school burned to the ground. Fortunately, no lives were lost, but speculation as to the cause of the fire ran rampant. The real perpetrators were never apprehended, but Selina speculated that the fire was most likely set by disaffected students who had been dismissed from the college for unspecified clandestine activities. In the new year 1858, both Selina and Alexander acutely felt the loss of this important institution in their lives. Selina described her troubled feelings in a letter to Julia Barclay that she mailed in mid-January 1858: "Still as it regards myself I am quite content and were it not that *apprehension* & *fears* steal [over?] me (ever since the burning of B[ethany] C[ollege]) I should be quite happy." The fears she felt had a deep impact on her faith. The burning of the college was a great trial for her and her husband—spiritually as well as emotionally. They both felt let down by the loss. For Selina, it challenged her to grow in her commitment to her beliefs in ways she had probably never anticipated. "My faith is called into great exercise never at any time do I remember it to be more so," she told Julia Barclay about the experience. But she refused to despair, rather taking comfort in remembering that: "the Lord knows what is best. It is certainly a good thing to feel oneself entirely thrust upon his care & protection to feel that that eye that never slumbereth nor sleepeth is watching over you. And can give his angels charge concerning you!! These thoughts console me constantly." In a life filled with tragedies great and small, the destruction of the college stood out in Selina's mind as one of the greatest. She took no small comfort in her faith that the God served by her husband would sustain him in his travels to raise the funds to rebuild the college. She feared sharing with her husband her worries, however, because she thought "it wrong to discourage him." In her role as encourager, she did not want to threaten his optimism. But she also admired the ability of her husband to bear the tragedy: "like a hero[?] Christian not a murmur escapes his lips."[42] She and her husband both mourned the loss of the college and feared for the future, but expressions of faith helped them stand firm. The faith they shared also helped them comfort each other. Selina supported her husband. Not wanting to discourage him as he tried to accept the tragedy, she sought strength within herself. As Carl Degler has observed, many women took on the role of offering emotional and spiritual support to their spouses.

For a few weeks after the fire, the Campbells were uncertain what to do next. But as donations poured in from many supporters of the school, Alexander vowed to rebuild completely. Though a large portion of the early funds sent to the Campbells were unsolicited, additional funds were necessary before construction could proceed. To save the college, Alexander and two other professors from the school, William Pendleton, coeditor of the *Millennial Harbinger* and Campbell's son-in-law, and Robert Richardson accompanied him on fund-raising tours throughout the country. The board of trustees for the college appointed the trio to raise the remainder of the sum of $50,000 needed to complete the construction of a new building.[43]

What followed was another extended period of separation for Alexander and Selina Campbell that strained them both greatly. It was not their first separation, but it was one of the longest and most trying. Alexander's health was poor, but Selina's responsibilities at home made it impossible for her to accompany him. Though both had committed themselves to the rebuilding of the college and therefore to the raising of the money necessary to undertake the project, the sacrifice of long separation wearied them both exceedingly. When her husband left, Selina did not know how long he and his companions would be gone, and she worried about him for several reasons. As she confided her situation to her good friend, "I have no idea how long they will be absent as it is of so much importance that they should prosecute the matter to the utmost extent." But even in her uncertainty about her husband's absence, Selina expressed confidence in the result: "There is I am glad to say a very considerable interest wak[ing] everywhere in behalf of Bethany C[ollege]." The future of the rebuilding seemed promising; the potential success of the mission warmed her heart. Through the coming weeks and months Selina heard frequently from her husband, who expressed his satisfaction with their fund-raising efforts. He also spoke of his great desire to see her again, but even he did not know when he might return.[44]

As her husband's absence lengthened, so did Selina's anxiety—despite his success. On his previous travels he had been a younger man capable of sustaining the often rigorous journeys by horseback or carriage over muddy roads in frequently inclement weather. In the year 1858 Campbell reached the age of seventy and experienced a continuing decline in his health that made the drudgery of fund raising more hazardous than before. His letters to his wife indicate that his work proceeded at a grueling pace. He set a goal of one speech per day and an average of a thousand dollars raised each week, a goal that he met more often than not but not without paying a price. Pendleton spoke just as often and also had good success, which boded well. The pair hoped for mostly cash contributions but received principally "subscriptions" for three-eighteen months, which satisfied Campbell, "considering the times."[45] The cost to his health, however, was substantial. Thereafter Selina rarely allowed her husband to travel unless she could accompany him to see to his needs.

In March, Selina confided to Julia that she was "exercising all the patience I can during the absence of my dearly beloved husband." Each bit of news was important to her. "I heard from him a few days since. He had taken a cold but was somewhat recovering." As long as she could not be on hand to care for her husband, news that he was falling ill hundreds of miles away must have been frustrating. But almost equally distressing was the intelligence that it was still "uncertain" when he could return "as they have not yet got the half raised though they have done wonders considering the times."[46] The monumental effort eventually paid off, and Alexander finally returned home in May having traveled through at least three states (Kentucky, Tennessee, and Mississippi) making dozens of speeches and journeying over 2,000 miles in over four months. Even before this tour, illness had plagued several of Campbell's trips. In 1853 Alexander wrote to his wife about a rather severe illness he suffered on tour in Springfield, Illinois. Knowing that she would worry, he wrote a few days later to say that he was slowly recovering: "I trust you will not be over anxious about me as I am in the midst of many brethren and friends who do all they can for my comfort." But he truly lamented her absence on this trip. He told her toward the end of 1853 in another letter, "I have much and often wished that you had been with me on this tour. But you are so much needed at home and therefore I am reconciled."[47] He seemed to believe that Selina's duties were not secondary to his but equal in importance. He sincerely respected her decision to remain at home.

The Campbells often voiced their sorrow at being so often apart. Whether fund raising for Bethany College or debating a rival, Alexander Campbell usually spent weeks and even months away from home throughout their marriage. His wife accompanied him on several tours, but the responsibilities of the home almost as often kept her in Bethany, separated from the husband she so adored. Selina was also charged with the care of several young children or long-term guests, so that she declined to accompany her husband on his journeys—but only with deep regret.[48] At other times her own activities, in particular her voluminous correspondence, threatened to keep her at home. On at least one occasion, however, Selina overcame such obstacles and acceded to her husband's request for her company.[49] By the last half of their marriage, when their children had grown and were on their own, Selina happily joined her husband on nearly all his preaching tours.

The early years of their marriage, marked by Alexander's extended absences from home for months at a time, were more difficult. His grueling touring schedule—undertaken to promote the principles in which they both so deeply believed—often kept him from those he loved the most. For example, in September 1836, he "reached home safely, having been absent ninety-four days, during which he traveled two thousand miles and delivered ninety-three discourses, averaging one hour and twenty minutes each."[50] In his absence, Selina cared for as many as ten guests at Bethany mansion in addition to her three small children. In this way, perhaps, Selina might be considered almost unique among the women of nineteenth-century America. There were probably few women who sacrificed their husband's presence at home to such a great extent for the sake of service to God. But her experience in this instance may be representative of preachers' wives, a group of women to whom Leonard Sweet has assigned a significant role in American history.[51]

July 23, 1836, found Campbell in Saratoga Springs, New York, fifty-four days into a tour of the Northeast, taking time to write to his wife about his travel plans. "We shall leave here on Wednesday, the 27th, and proceed to Vermont, where I expect to preach on the 28th," he wrote. "Then we shall pass on through New Hampshire into Massachusetts and proceed to the capital of the State."[52] Other stops on the tour included Rhode Island, Connecticut, New York City, Philadelphia, and Baltimore before Alexander returned home to Bethany. He often described for his wife the places he visited and the route he would take, but his letters to her were more than a simple travelogue. They more often than not focused on the acute deprivation he felt at the loss of her company and his desire to return home as soon as possible. "To one who so much loves his wife and children and the whole family circle and delights in making them happy," he assured her, "it is not an easy task to forsake them all for so long a time." After several months on the road, his longing for home was acute. But his letters revealed the reasons for his absence in terms as easily understood as they are eloquently expressed. The life of Alexander Campbell is as remarkable for his domestic attitudes as for his faith and desire to serve the "Cause of Reformation" in American religion. "When I think of Him who forsook the Palace of the Universe and the glory of his Father's court, and condescended to be born of a woman and to live in an unfriendly world, and to be treated a thousand times worse than I have ever been, to save us from our sins, I think but little of all I have done, or can do to republish his salvation and to call sinners to reformation and to build up the cause of life, of ancient Christianity."[53] In such a context, the pain of separation from his family could not negate his fealty to a higher call. Campbell undeniably felt a deep sense of duty to spread the principles of New Testament Christianity to all who would listen. He would suffer at being separated from everyone he held dear but counted the sacrifice as nothing compared to the love of the One he followed. The "justifiable, honorable, and useful end . . . animates and sustains me in your absence,"[54] he explained to Selina. Also, his commitment to faith in Jesus Christ was related to his belief that in his absence his duty to his family would be fulfilled by his wife, his partner in the Cause. The burden on his wife did not go unnoticed.

Early in their marriage and again later during the fund-raising trips for Bethany College, Campbell deeply regretted his frequent, extended absences from his family especially for the burden they placed on his wife. But he labored hard not to neglect his family and strove to support his wife in her work. Hardly a week went by without a letter from her "dearly beloved husband" in which Selina would find news about his travels and testaments to his love and devotion to them all. In 1838 while hundreds of miles from home touring in South Carolina, Campbell penned these tender words to his wife: "I dare not think of *home sweet home*. I am like the Swiss and the old Jews in a foreign land. I do not like to think or sing much about home. The time has not yet come for thinking much about it."[55] Thoughts of home could only bring pain to someone so far from its welcoming bosom. Such expressions of loneliness plainly indicate his desire to be at home, but his commitments kept him elsewhere. Each letter found new ways to declare his longing for home. On one occasion he likened himself to a soldier committed to a king who leaves behind his family to fight and "faithfully serve my Lord and get an honorable discharge."[56] He longed for the day when he could return home to his beloved wife (his "fellow soldier") and children, and he never failed to remind his family that "next to my own personal and eternal salvation through my Lord and Saviour, there is nothing on earth dearer to me than your present, spiritual, and eternal good."[57] Though his calling separated him often from those he loved, his emotional connection to his family remained strong and passionate.

During a tour through Illinois in 1853, Alexander expressed his appreciation of Selina's role in his labors. The recognition he accorded his wife is most notable for having been worded in scriptural terms, indicating his significant respect for her and her contribution to the Gospel. When he used the language of the Bible to frame his tribute to Selina, Campbell showed the value that he placed on her endeavors. His comments appeared in a letter he wrote for publication in the *Millennial Harbinger:*

> Inasmuch as the great Apostle to the Gentiles, and some other New Testament writers, make honorable mention of certain Christian ladies and matrons, as fellow-laborers in the primitive churches of the saints, it seems good to me, also, knowing your work of faith and labor of love in the same field of labor with some of those named in their epistles, to address to you, as John did to the elect lady, the beloved Cyria, a letter or two on some of the incidents of my present tour in the states of Illinois and Missouri.

> If Paul to the Romans, greets Priscilla as a helper in Christ; Julia and Mary, who bestowed much labor on him and his companions; Nercus, too, and his sister—being fully persuaded that you belong to that class, and fully rank with them, I feel constrained, by the authority of such examples, to address you, and through you my readers, a few notes of my tour and labors in behalf of the Bible in the College, and of a well educated Christian ministry.

> This is due to you, my dear fellow-helper in this great work, because of your many personal sacrifices of ease and comfort in ministering to the necessities of the saints, and to the entertainment

of many a sojourner and Christian pilgrim, in the rites and usages of Christian hospitality; and especially, because of your often ex-pressed desires to see the standard of ministerial accomplishments much higher elevated amongst us as a people.[58]

Her husband's praise of Selina's valuable assistance brought her public recognition for her domestic role not only as a homemaker but also as a hostess to the many "sojourners" who came to visit her husband. Certainly the separate ministries of the husband and wife were not identical and were indeed founded in definite concepts about the different male and female abilities, but this difference should not obscure the deliberate attempt of a husband to share the spotlight with his dutiful wife, whom he never forgot "amidst all the pressing cares or pleasing scenes" through which he passed.[59] Campbell's tribute to his wife shows that he was convinced of her "usefulness" and her contribution to the work he performed.

Selina's travels with her husband in the later years of their marriage eased many of her domestic worries but also created new strains. Her husband, when separated from her, assured his wife that he missed her "company more than any other privation" he had to endure.[60] Moreover, though he clearly desired her company on almost every tour, it was apparently up to her to decide whether or not she would accompany him. In a letter to her daughter Virginia, Selina commented on Alexander's regret that she could not accompany him on a tour of New York in 1856; she had evidently declined because of pressing duties at home.

Some contemporaries concluded that Campbell neglected the family he was sometimes obligated to leave behind. C. L. Loos published his perceptions regarding Alexander Campbell in the *Millennial Harbinger* just after Campbell's death. In introducing a letter written by Campbell to his wife, which she sent for publication after her husband's death, he makes some intriguing observations that hint at a less favorable interpretation of the husband's absence. "It was characteristic of him, when he left home on his frequent and often long journeys, to leave all domestic cares behind him;—these he committed to the hand of Him 'who careth for us.' His letters to his family, therefore, were in their contents devoted . . . to discoursing on the great themes of the Gospel of Christ with which his mind was constantly filled and engaged."[61] Loos's comments are an important corrective for our appreciation of Alexander Campbell's connection to his family. Though his calling was high and he paid a severe price in terms of his health for the sake of traveling the country to spread "ancient Christianity," his was not the only price. The letters he wrote home, while expressing his love, documenting the progress of his work, and expounding his thoughts, must at times have been cold comfort to a perhaps overworked wife. Though there is little evidence that Selina resented any aspect of her husband's behavior, it is possible that in a private moment or two she may have done so. Her faith certainly sustained her through the worst parts of her marriage but maybe not at every turn. Still, she rarely expressed anything that might have been a critique. The surviving documents, however, have often been in the hands of family members who may have destroyed many papers and may also have pruned the remaining material to eliminate anything even vaguely detrimental to the image of either Campbell. It is consequently difficult to determine whether there was any friction in the Campbell marriage. Furthermore, Loos admits that items of a more personal nature were omitted from the published version of the letter he introduced, and the original has apparently been lost.

When Selina was able to accompany her husband, she welcomed the opportunity to watch over his health and his mental well-being. In a letter to her son William, she described her efforts. "I am very careful of him about his eating sleeping &c&c," she began. She also made sure that he did "not speak any at night nor go out at night when Mr. Pendleton preaches." Apparently he had been sicker than Selina "ever remembered seeing him" when one journey began in 1859, but his wife quickly took charge, and his health visibly improved.[62] On several other occasions, she also worried about her husband's leaving home when he seemed ill or exhausted. But she shared his conviction that the God they served would protect them and sustain them because of the importance of their work. Illness and privation became tests of faith, spurring them on to greater trust in the God they served.

Traveling, for Selina, also required a large measure of faith. If her husband battled illness on the road, she battled weariness and depression from the constant movement on trains through the night or in carriages bouncing over deeply rutted country lanes by day. "We braved storms and wind in part of Illinois & Iowa and still were persevered on our journey," she wrote after one strenuous trip. After a while the constant privations began to take their toll. Returning home after a trip through Kentucky in the spring of 1856, she described a six-day visit with the 700 members of a church in Louisville. She was discouraged to discover that a houseful of visitors awaited her when she returned to Bethany. "I shall be in as great a crowd at home as I have been abroad," she lamented to Julia when she learned the news. How disheartening it must have been to have no break between the dual and demanding roles of travel companion and hostess. She also complained of the strain on her nervous system and of piercing headaches occasioned by the constant whirl of activity. Only the thought of "doing a little good" inspired her to "press on amidst it all."[63]

For several years, fatigue dogged Selina as she came into constant contact with the crowds that accompanied her husband's tours. She kept in close touch with her daughter Virginia, whom she left behind to manage the household. To Virginia she confided her dread of the crowds and the headaches and other discomforts of the journey. But Selina always affirmed that if any good came of it she was happy to accompany her husband and to endure the hardships.[64]

There was little, if any, conscious effort on Alexander's part to limit his wife's opportunities. Though he saw his wife's role in largely domestic terms, he based his conception of proper gender roles on scriptural prescriptions shaped by societal expectations. Such expectations had developed over the centuries and combined with Campbell's emphasis on biblical teachings to create a mindset that may have diminished many women, especially Protestant women. But at the same time the scriptural perspective allowed Selina Campbell and other women to conform their contributions to the principles they most highly revered and at the same time to take pride in their achievements: support of the Gospel they believed in so strongly and their service to others. Such activity, after all, had been modeled in Scripture by Christ himself. The scriptural view thus implicitly elevated the activities of women to the same importance as those of men. Simply because women made sacrifices did not mean that women's role was inferior. It meant only that they acted privately, outside the spotlight of public interaction. In this context, evidently, Selina evaluated her success in meeting life's challenges. Her role may have been largely out of the public eye, but it was never beyond God's observation.

Two of the most significant challenges faced by Selina Campbell, exhaustion and its companion depression, were shared with countless other women. Sometimes they threatened to overwhelm her, erasing her sense of achievement. Men sought refuge from their work outside the home in the affection of the wives they left behind each day. Though Selina Campbell's husband did not labor in a factory or clerk at a bank in town, he nonetheless left home often. When he returned from a journey, his home was his refuge from the trials of traveling and teaching. Selina, however, could not escape her duties. A woman could not find respite from her role in family life as easily as her husband did. Nancy Cott explains that a woman's "vocation" in the nineteenth century *was* domesticity, so that her "work-role imitated man's while lacking his means of escape." This situation set the stage for the larger struggle that many women faced. As Cott expressed it, "if a man could recover from his work 'at home,' woman's work was at home. She provided for his relief" but not her own. Women struggled to complete their tasks, then, and had fewer therapeutic outlets than men.[65]

Discussion of her physical and emotional state did not often dominate Selina's correspondence, but it was there—showing her susceptibility to a common problem facing women. The most obvious outlet for her distress was her friendship with Julia Barclay. The letters that survive from their correspondence center on the decades of the 1850s and 1860s, a special time in Selina's life. Her children were nearly grown or were off at school, so that she had more time free to devote to the activities of her husband. She no longer endured trying pregnancies that robbed her of her strength and plagued her with illness. Her husband's health, however, had deteriorated, and the burden on Selina to manage their active lives grew heavier in new ways. The burning of the college further added to her trials. Periods of illness and exhaustion dogged her as she attempted to maintain her household. Her friendship with Julia Barclay was a source of strength. The profound love and affection flowing between the two women helped sustain them while providing an outlet for pent-up emotions.

Carroll Smith-Rosenberg offers further background on the friendships that women developed in the nineteenth century. She points to situations of great import in a woman's life that she shared mainly with her female friends and family, such as childbirth and the almost ritual visiting of each other's homes in a complex social network of relationships.[66] Shared experiences contributed to a unique type of friendship between women. Women's culture was vastly different from that of men; it relied on different feelings and understandings. Selina's relationship with Julia Barclay illustrates many of the nuances of Smith-Rosenberg's conclusions. Their common experience as wives and mothers drew these two women together in an appreciation of the burdens both roles entailed. They were further united by their common religious beliefs. They encouraged each other to persevere during trials by discussing Heaven's rewards and the strength they received from their God.

Selina often expressed her belief that her strong constitution, which kept her healthy and able to meet the physically demanding tasks of her marriage, was a legacy of her British ancestors. But there were still moments when her health was not good, perhaps because of overexertion. In the spring of 1856, she explained to Julia that she was "of bilious habit," and in the spring she generally felt "poorly for sometime." At other points during the year the constant whirl of activity in the Campbell household seemed to wear her down. "I have been exercising rather too much and [am] a good deal excited as you know I am somewhat of an enthusiastic temperament," she admitted to Julia Barclay.[67] Such complaints are not surprising, given Selina's workload. Unfortunately, her condition was only to worsen as the tensions increased. In a July 1857 letter to "Sister Barclay," Selina admitted that her "health is very *much run down* more so that [*sic*] it ever was before." She attributed her illness to the "excitement & labour," which "has been too much for me through the spring & summer." She does not specify the nature of her activities, but at one point she lost so much sleep that she was forced to take to her bed for two or three days, finding herself "unable to attend to my domestic affairs."[68]

Probably contributing to her illness were burdens of tending to the frequent guests who came to see her husband, the yearly Bethany College commencement, held on the Fourth of July, for which she often housed a dozen or more people (in addition to her own household), and the fact that she was "obliged to change servants" that spring. Several of her domestic servants had married and left her employ, and her cook contracted the measles just before commencement, leaving Selina "without a suitable cook or indeed scarcely any but myself and one or two old persons who came in to assist."[69] Commencement that year attracted a record number of attendants, so that the Campbell mansion was filled to overflowing. The large number of guests in her care left Selina little time for herself, and the loss of many of her servants only compounded her distress.

The servants of the Campbell household were integral to the maintenance of the mansion and often became close members of the family. Their names figure regularly in the family correspondence. One of the dearest employees of the Campbell family was Elizabeth Patterson, who lived at Bethany mansion for over forty years. Eliza, the second oldest of Margaret Campbell's daughters and the one who directed the household after her mother's death, hired the young Patterson from Wellsburg just before her father's second marriage. Miss Patterson came to Bethany in 1828 to take charge of all "household affairs." She eventually nursed all of the Campbell children and grandchildren and was known as a "faithful, devoted Christian woman" and "a great reader of the Bible." In her old age "Aunt Betsey," as she was known, declined significantly in health. When she was unable to care for herself, Selina made arrangements for her to live in a dwelling adjacent to the house, where she received care from a neighbor who was probably another Campbell employee. Selina later remembered that when Aunt Betsey "died of dropsy the year after Mr. C's departure, . . . Bro. J. T. Barclay, who was at that time Professor in Bethany College, spoke at her grave, on a lovely Lord's day morning in May, before the assembling of the church."[70] The entire Campbell family relied on Aunt Betsey's affection and her diligent care for all the children.

The Campbell household also included several slaves. Just before his marriage Alexander had purchased two orphaned brothers aged eighteen and twenty. The young men, James and Charley Poole, were each promised their freedom when they reached the age of twenty-eight. According to Selina, Alexander kept his promise to the young men and also provided a public security for their good behavior, since it was illegal to free slaves at that time in Virginia. Both continued to work for the family after receiving their freedom. Jim died before his former master, but Charley attended Campbell's funeral and lived for several decades afterward. Two other slaves, Ben and Mary, also lived for a while with the Campbell family. Selina resented Mary's "bad disposition and strong will of her own" and later admitted that she "was glad for Mr. C to make her a present to her father." Ben, however, endeared himself to his owner's wife through his "wonderful musical talent." When he sang for visitors, she enjoyed hearing "the sweetness and pathos of his voice."[71] Ben also showed great talent in caring for the Campbell stable. He drove Selina's buggy for her on her frequent visits to nearby Wheeling and Wellsburg and to the various homes of the Campbell neighbors.

Though he had made a powerful case against the practice of slavery at the Virginia Constitutional Convention, his method of studying the Scripture kept Campbell from becoming an abolitionist. Since he could find no passage in the Bible that condemned slavery, he could not condemn slaveholders. But in his own life he followed a middle course. Though he did purchase several slaves, including the Poole brothers, he adhered to a promise he made each Campbell servant, slave or free, that he would provide them with an education and help in starting their own lives. His natural inclination was apparently to free his slaves at the earliest possible opportunity (usually after they had served the family for several years), but he was often constrained by the severe manumission laws of Virginia.

The Campbell household therefore contained a variety of members who lived under the same roof. Guests came and went. Servants were hired or purchased, served their terms, and left to form their own households or stayed from loyalty and worked till their retirement. Selina relied on these servants to assist her in managing the tasks necessary to care for such a large group of people, but she worked hard herself to meet the needs of the family she loved and to whom she had dedicated her service. Through her toil in providing meals, entertainment, clothing, and other household items for her family and guests, Selina fulfilled her calling as it was defined within the context of the Disciples' theology, scriptural interpretation, and prevalent social mores. While her husband preached and taught all over the country, Selina raised their family and managed their household.

The Campbell marriage provides, in many ways, an opportunity to analyze an important subset of American marriages—specifically, those between members of evangelical religious groups in nineteenth-century America. For several reasons the Campbells are a good example of such couples. First, in the early to middle nineteenth century, Alexander Campbell joined thousands of ministers who traveled the country, seeking to convert people to their theological views. Second, several factors in the context of the Campbells' relationship are outlined in Leonard Sweet's study of American ministers' wives. According to Sweet, the role of minister's wives varied from a mere shadow in their husband's wake to a full partnership in ministry. Like Elizabeth Atkisson Finney, Sweet's model for the partnership role, Selina Campbell often stood at her husband's side and worked to break down the restraints preventing women from participating in religious activities.[72] But unlike Finney, Selina did not feel compelled to abandon her domestic role in order to pursue such opportunities. Thus when Sweet identifies the women who primarily managed the domestic cares of their husbands as "the sacrificers," he arbitrarily assumes that these women found little fulfillment in their role. Selina seems to exemplify nearly all the models suggested by Sweet, but the one element uniting all of her experiences is her faith, an unappreciated ingredient in Sweet's study. When we consider faith in our discussion of women, we can see that it transcends social expectations and the sorrow of the "sacrificers" and suggests an arena of meaning for women within marriage that is hard to quantify but easy to appreciate in the case of Selina Campbell because of her prolific writing about her domestic role.

Certainly Selina was no average woman. Her marriage, her affluence, and her broad education distinguished her from most nineteenth-century women. But in some ways these very qualities make her worthy of special study. First, she represented the same group of women who have interested most historians of women: the middle-class, literate, domestic workers whose duties were centered in the home. Selina lived her entire life in western Virginia, however, whereas the women of important studies of nineteenth-century women such as those by Nancy Cott, Nancy Hewitt, and Lori Ginzberg focused mainly on northeastern women. Selina Campbell and her experience illuminate the lives of the many women who lived in the middle section of the nation—away from the urban centers of New England and closer to the American frontier. Study of her life, therefore, allow us to glimpse, if in a limited way, the role played by women in another section of the country.

Interestingly, Selina Campbell does not fit with Jean Friedman's analysis of southern women. In many ways her life combines the northern and the southern experiences. On the one hand, Cott and Hewitt emphasize the bond of being female that both kept women in the home and allowed them to develop a unique identity based on moral reform. On the other hand Friedman's corrective approach focused on southern women who relied on kinship relations rather than gender to organize themselves. Selina's approach seems to have relied on a little of each. Her isolation in the West Virginia panhandle, for the most part, prevented her from participating in moral reform associations (like southern women), but she did support the national groups that later formed under women's leadership. Her husband's frequent absence from home reinforced her more active role in the household, a situation that she shared with many northern urban women whose husbands often left the home for the industrial workplace, if only during the day.

A second factor making Selina Campbell worthy of study *is* the relationship she shared with her husband. As she traveled with him, she often became his model of proper female behavior—a model to which she was able to contribute. Richardson confirms that Alexander Campbell often read his many essays and sermons to his wife for her opinion before he published them or read them publicly.[73] At the same time, she often suggested to him a number of items for his perusal that also shaped his opinions.[74] It is hard to quantify the extent of this interaction, but the evidence is enough to show that it existed.

But beyond Selina's support of her husband's work, the Campbell marriage also left Selina room to develop several of her own talents outside the domestic circle. These include the promotion of missions, the development of her own writing career, and the expression of her own opinions on matters of spiritual and temporal interest. One of her most deeply felt interests, and one she shared with millions of American women, was the promotion of missions efforts at home and abroad. In this unique area Selina first provided significant overt leadership for many of the women in the Disciples of Christ. Though she supported many of the popular ideas of nineteenth-century womanhood, she found little to limit women's activities. Specifically, she agreed with her husband, who found women "constitutionally, legally, and religiously, modest and retiring in the presence of him whom God made first." Yet it is important to note that even in her support of many of the traditional notions of female piety and proper activity, Selina never believed women should completely disappear from sight or perform only passive functions. Indeed she advocated some prominent roles for women in evangelism and service—believing that the interests of the private home could be preserved only through public action. Family life, the appropriate center of a woman's life, should not excuse a woman from responsibility for promoting the cause of missions within her own circle of friends and, through her financial contributions, to the entire world. In this way Selina Campbell agreed with Mrs. Lydia Sigourney, a well-known nineteenth-century writer whose comments appeared in the *Harbinger:* "If she share not the fame of the ruler and the blood-shedder, her good works, such as 'become those who profess godliness,' though they leave no deep 'foot-prints on the sands of time,' may find record in the 'Lamb's Book of Life.' "[75] Such an interpretation suggested that private actions, though accorded almost no recognition, were not insignificant.

After her husband's death, Selina's concerns changed little. Though she found more time to write essays and interact with her friends as a widow, her approach to issues of faith and gender hardly changed. Now without her husband, she traveled less and therefore interacted personally with fewer people, but her published articles gave her an even broader audience. The only major shift in her thinking was one that she shared with the rest of her Disciple sisters—the rising postbellum concern that something more needed to be done for the soul of America.

One of Selina's most enduring interests, and one that she shared with so many of her friends, was the development of missions efforts both in the United States and abroad—especially through the work of women. She often expressed her great excitement "in all that appertains to the furtherance of the blessed gospel that comes within their sphere of work!"[76] Since her earliest days, when her mother had taken her by the hand to lead her to church, Selina had learned the importance of the salvation message. Her own efforts to promote the Gospel began in small ways. The friendships she developed with large numbers of women provided her with her first opportunities to share her faith. During her constant travels accompanying her husband on preaching trips and at home, where she received hundreds of visitors each year, she came in contact with a host of women. She often used these occasions to share her faith and urge women to consider scriptural prescriptions for their life. While the men met to discuss church business, the women often sat and discussed their own issues. Her leadership in promoting the Gospel through methods other than preaching demonstrate an active role for women that, though it was private, was not passive.[77]

Like many nineteenth-century women, Selina often attended sewing societies. She valued the society meetings as opportunities for developing sisterhood among the women of the churches. The women who gathered together learned to support and depend on each other while they sewed quilts and discussed issues that were close to their hearts. In 1856, Selina served as president of the Bethany Sewing Society. One of her most important duties was choosing the book that would be read to the women at the meetings as they worked. Through her position she encouraged others to embrace the cause so dear to her heart. Under her direction the society read the biography of both the first and the third Mrs. Adoniram Judson. Both accompanied their husband as missionaries to Burma, and Selina considered their stories inspiring for anyone. No one interacting with Selina on the subject of women in missions could fail to note her deep support for the activity. Many of the women attending these meetings were deeply affected by her dynamic leadership on the issue.

Though she did not support public preaching for women, Selina did not absolve women of responsibility for work in support of spreading the Gospel. For this female evangelist, evangelism did not consist of public preaching and teaching. There were other active roles for women apart from public proclamation. These included collecting contributions for missions work, letter writing, setting moral examples, and speaking directly with friends about their faith. All these avenues were open to women, Selina believed. She herself never missed an opportunity to reach out to anyone with whom she came in contact. To one female guest who stayed in her home briefly, Selina gave some tracts written by her husband and Robert Richardson, his colleague at Bethany College. She also talked to the woman about her faith and in the course of the conversation learned that she was a Methodist. Fearing that her allegiance to this denomination might hamper the woman's reception of the simple Gospel message, Selina nevertheless mentioned how much she admired the woman's courage in seeking truth so openly. Both she and Mrs. Barclay maintained a relationship with the woman with good results; the visitor later joined one of the Disciples of Christ churches.

After observing women in the churches, Selina concluded that many felt discouraged at not being allowed to preach publicly as the men did. But this, she assured them, was not the proper attitude to take: "If we can not do some great work, we can certainly find minor things to engage our *hearts,* and employ our hands in matters of usefulness in the Master's house, the church, which is the 'pillar and support of the Truth.'" She also suggested examples from Scripture that could serve as inspiration to them all, reminding women that "the poor widow, who cast her two mites, has been distinguished over the whole world, or to the extent wherever the gospel has been preached, inasmuch as she threw into the treasury of the Lord 'all her living.' Can not we as Christian women deny ourselves something to have to give to the Lord?"[78] Through their generosity, then, women could serve the cause of Christ without preaching.

A move to open the pulpits to women had been growing within the Disciples ever since the close of the Civil War. Many were influenced by the concept of the "new woman," for whom preaching would be yet another skill to contribute to the church.[79] Selina, however, allied herself with the true woman's more private role. She believed women's preaching was in no way supported by Scripture, but she found plenty of evidence for women's participation in other areas, such as teaching children, in the New Testament.

The suggestions that Selina offered to women about the need for sacrifice (rather than preaching) for the cause of truth applied to many groups of women. These ideas also required what might be small sacrifices for some but perhaps large privations for others. For all women, they were couched in terms as persuasive as they were impassioned. From her broad reading Selina identified several things other than preaching that women could do to promote the cause of Christ in their own way. In 1832 a *Harbinger* article written by Ann Judson, a well-known missionary in Maulmien, Burma, expressed concern about many women's desire to array themselves in fancy attire that only drained their finances and limited their contributions to more worthy causes. "Let me appeal to conscience, and inquire, what is the real motive for wearing ornamental and costly apparel? Is it not the desire of setting off one's person to the best advantage, and of exciting . . . admiration of others?" she asked. Judson then made an impassioned plea to the women to rid themselves of such artificial outerwear. "O! Christian sisters, believers in God, in Christ, in an eternal heaven and eternal hell! And can you hesitate, and ask what you shall do? Bedew those ornaments with the tears of contrition; consecrate them to the cause of charity; hang them on the cross of your dying Lord. Delay not an instant."[80] Persuaded by Mrs. Judson's dramatic opinions, Selina was probably the one who urged her husband to publish the essay. Women could now show their devotion to the Christian cause by donating their jewelry and sacrificing unnecessary "fripperies." But Selina found other ways in which women might serve.

With her increased free time as a widow, Selina considered many of the ideas to which she had been exposed and often suggested strategies women might develop to support the cause of missions. One of her articles in particular, published in the *Christian Standard,* called upon women to make specific changes in their lives for the support of the Gospel effort. "Can not *our pride* or *our avarice* be curtailed?" Selina asked her sister. Then she suggested, "Let us look at our wardrobes; could we not have spared something from the decorations of our bodies, that might have been thrown into the Lord's treasury . . . ? Could you not deny yourself of a fine piece of jewelry, or the multitudes of gloves so extravagantly worn nowadays . . . , Christian women, to have something to put into the missionary box?" She was especially concerned that "mothers teach their children and the younger ones to give something." Thus, even in small ways, Selina urged women to support the church. The great need to evangelize the country demanded the efforts of every church member. Though hardly any of the women had an income of their own on which to draw for contributions, Mrs. Campbell nevertheless called upon them to go without some frippery in order to further a greater cause. Certainly this type of privation fell more heavily on some, but other suggestions may have struck nearly every woman equally. Fans especially received Selina's censure. She described in vivid detail their senseless use by women of her acquaintance. She turned the issue into one of great importance for women as a distracting influence in the church and counseled against their use in worship:

> This is the season for the *use* of *fans*. How many fans of various descriptions will be purchased, and carried to the house of worship to relieve the mortal frame of a little unpleasantness. Yes an infinite number will wave, almost keeping time, and I have thought, quite enough to *distract the speaker* with the annoyance of beholding them. They are well enough for the drawing room, but surely anything but sanctifying in the house of worship. If the Bible was carried to the church as it was wont to be by the disciples fifty years ago, they would find a useful employment in turning to the passages of scripture quoted by the preacher! I was struck with a remark of a traveler in some foreign country who attended a worshiping [*sic*] assembly, that although the climate was warm, not a *fan was seen waving in the congregation,* but a most solemn aspect pervaded the assembly. I was so penetrated with the propriety of the thing that I have never used a fan in public worship since, *nor ever shall.*

To a modern observer it may seem trivial to disparage fans, but in Selina's mind they represented the tendency of many women to focus on their comfort and appearance in places of worship rather than reviewing the state of their soul. Yet at the same time she did not condemn other women for their behavior without observing that they were all "poor weak frail creatures," and she routinely included a prayer asking the "Lord [to] teach us and lead us by the Spirit till we reach thy courts above."[81] Selina did not use her prominent position as a soapbox. Instead she shared her views with other women, hoping they would find truth in her words.

The widow of Alexander Campbell also responded directly to those who advocated that women preach. The more conservative Selina was horrified at the prospect and developed a reasoned analysis of why such activity was at best unnecessary and at worst socially destructive. In 1880 she composed an engaging letter arguing against the practice of female preaching that Isaac Errett published in the *Christian Standard*. "I would ask," she began, "Were there women preachers in Jerusalem in the days of our Saviour and his apostles? . . . Did he select women preachers when he inspired the holy twelve and sent them out? And did he ever take any with him to aid him in his labors when he traveled? These are grave questions and ought to be asked, as it is evident such was not the case." She thus denied any support from Jesus Christ for women preaching, asking "Can a 'thus saith the Lord' be adduced for the practice? If it can, where is it?" The ultimate authority for women's preaching must rest on the Bible. Drawing upon her study of Scripture, Selina presented her views on how they established the role of women: "The apostle positively says 'women must be silent in the church,' and nowhere does he bring them forward as co-laborers in the gospel."[82] Her search for a scriptural basis for women's preaching left her convinced that there was none. But to Selina, the lack of scriptural precedent was not the only reason to reject the practice. Indeed, after presenting the scriptural bases of her argument, Selina quickly moved to reveal the basic flaws in many of the common arguments put forth in support of the practice.

While Selina mistrusted the arguments used to support the role of women in preaching, she especially questioned motivation. "At this late date,' she wrote to Errett, "many of my sex are seeking notoriety by coming forward without being *called or sent to do the work*." Such independent actions did not conform to Selina's notion of the divine mission. She also suggested that "the descendants of our mother Eve" are "always trying to do something EXTRA, something, too, both what they are not bidden to do, and *forbidden*." She worried that the women had forgotten the teachings of Scriptures and pursued only their own ends. But far from being surprised at the actions of the women, Selina knew that their behavior merely stemmed from their nature, the same sinful, rebellious nature shared by all humankind. Only "keeping close to the teaching of our divine Savior and his inspired policies can keep them right," she believed, and the fact that they pursued extrascriptural actions hampered their service. "It is a fearful thing to add or diminish from the word of God," she warned her readers, "and surely it is risking the displeasure of Him who had left on record what is the work of the children in the church."[83] Both the Presbyterian General Assembly and the Methodist Conference had recently voted down allowing women to preach, and their decision received Selina's support. She continued to use whatever influence she had to steer women away from careers in preaching and into other careers of service.

Selina's comments, even when critical, sought less to censure than to avoid committing error. She continuously supported women in a variety of activities and urged them not to limit their opportunities to engage in public activities. "You know that I make but little pretensions to appearing before the public in any way," she wrote to Julia Barclay. "Still I am of the opinion that a person should not withhold his or her might of doing good even by the pen provided they have the ability." This was especially directed at those individuals who denied their ability because "of pride or false delicacy." No woman was excused from writing, speaking, or serving merely because she was a woman. Only preaching violated the private basis for women's active participation and that only for very specific reasons. Selina reminded her readers that there might be terrible consequences for their families if they demanded the right to preach. Her husband's career having left her only too well aware of the sacrifices necessary to sustain a successful preaching career, Selina cautioned her sisters and proposed alternative courses of action. "I am happy to think that the sisterhood are anxious to find work to do in the Church," she began. "But it is certainly not their duty or province to gather up their *cradles* and *babies* and take a three months' tour in preaching the word." Leaving their families would violate their charge as the "keepers of the home" and would threaten the centrality of the home in child rearing. Selina instead shared with her sisters her own experience as an evangelist—not of the pulpit but of the servant. Drawing upon her childhood and the early years of her marriage, she made specific reference to activities that promoted the "kingdom of heaven" without requiring women to assume a new role. Though "there was not in the church of which I became a member a single youth of either sex . . . , I found plenty to employ my time even then—visiting the sick and the poor, etc., etc.—

and I have been preaching ever since according to what I *learned from the word*—that is, telling the good story of the cross." She reminded women of the opportunities to share their faith, "yes, to the washer-woman at the tub, to the cook, and to my visitors in the parlor; and when in stage coaches, on railways, on steamboats, indeed, in the house and by the way, so as to enlist some in leading them to Jesus that they might be 'saved from sin and its terrible consequences,' as dear old Father Thomas Campbell well used to express it." But she concluded, "I never found my way into the pulpit. It was not *commanded*."[84] A woman's connections, then, went beyond her family and relatives. Though not "commanded" to preach, women could influence an entire community of relationships and therefore did not need a more public expression of faith. But the overarching principle in Selina's thought remained obedience to the Scriptures—which she felt forbade women to preach. The remainder of her suggestions to women were meant to clarify and support scriptural injunction.

Selina Campbell demonstrated a heartfelt concern for those she perceived as "lost" or "unsaved." These were the people who either had never heard the Gospel of Jesus Christ or had not believed when they had heard. She shared this concern with women of many denominations.[85] Women of nearly every Protestant group organized themselves in the late nineteenth century into missionary societies. Selina Campbell's approach to the issue reveals how this concern affected women on an individual basis.

Selina especially grieved for women who she felt "lived their brief lives in error." She called it a tragedy and never missed an opportunity to influence anyone with whom she came in contact. One particular example is her correspondence with Mary Bell Tomlinson Bakewell, the wife of Theron. When Selina's brother married a woman who was not a Christian in 1841, the sister worried that it would bring him only unhappiness. She assured her brother that his marital choice was a good one but expressed her disappointment that his chosen wife "has not professed to be Religious."[86]

Selina did admire her new sister-in-law for not making "a bigoted confession" but instead remaining honest. She welcomed the younger woman into the family even though her responsibilities precluded attending the ceremony. Leaving nothing to chance, however, Selina established a regular correspondence with Mary and often made appeals to her sister-in-law to consider developing a faith of her own. Just after the fifth anniversary of Theron and Mary's marriage, one letter from her sister-in-law asked Mary to consider a particular request: "I often think of you & would wish from my heart that I could see you & have an affectionate conversation with you upon all the important matters of Religion & our eternal interests." Selina's request required a delicate approach if she wanted to maintain open lines of communication. Selina did not want her own zeal to push Mary away from God. Her deep faith in the importance of a close relationship with Jesus Christ caused her to worry about people who lacked such faith, but she did "not wish to be obtrusive or appear to dictate to you in the least," as she assured Mary. "I know you have a mind of your own and have not the least doubt but that you think often and think deeply on these vastly interesting subjects." Selina admired her sister-in-law and never failed to show her the utmost respect. Her letter to Mary also addressed a particular concern that she had about her sister-in-law. She felt that all the duties of a wife and mother required strong faith to be performed well. "You have the charge of a family to engage you," she wrote in 1846, "the cares of a mother and anxieties attendant on a married life calls for the supporting of religion to enable us to discharge the various duties encumbent [*sic*] upon us, as wives & mothers. I know you make a good wife & mother, although you have never professed to be a follower of the Savior but how much happier and how much more would you enjoy yourself if you felt that you had obeyed the Lord & Master in his ordinances and had the approbation of your own heart in confessing him before men."[87] Here we see Selina offering advice to her sister-in-law, linking success at women's vital tasks to a dynamic relationship with a living God. Not only did the elder woman offer her own guidance, but she also encouraged Mary to seek advice from her Creator.

Her deep concern for her sister-in-law found further expression in sincere hopes for Mary's conversion. The approaching millennium left little time for a decision, so Selina's request was urgent. Mary's decision needed to be made before the Savior returned, which could be at any moment. There is no direct evidence that Mary heeded her sister-in-law's appeals to profess her faith, but there are some indirect clues to her eventual response. Mainly, in a 1848 letter to Theron, Selina declares her joy that Theron has "made the blessed choice" to acknowledge his conversion. More than likely, Mary joined in her husband's decision, because Selina did not mention any opposition from the wife. Theron and Mary, in fact, eventually entertained several visiting evangelists and joined local efforts to found a congregation in their town.[88] Such personal activism further supports the conclusion that Mary Bakewell shared her husband's decision of faith.

Selina also emphasized the importance of sharing the Gospel in what she termed "her neighborhood." For Selina, this neighborhood included the students of Bethany College who spent significant time in her home. In 1858 she expressed her enduring interest in the "young folks" of Bethany. She feared that there was too little effort to "further the Cause of the Gospel" among them, so she encouraged the students of the college to attend special functions at her home that would help introduce them to the Christian life. Through songs and Bible studies conducted in her front parlor, Selina maintained her efforts to reach the youth of her acquaintance with the Truth. With opportunities to reach so many people without ever stepping up to a pulpit, Selina expressed her trust that "the knowledge of God's word and obedience to it will lead *our sisters to abandon the practice* [of preaching], and consider it as *rebellion* against God's will."[89]

Though she did not, in common with her sisters of many faiths, support women's preaching in public, her skill at writing letters and essays worked in much the same way, if on a smaller, more private scale. Only by protecting the home could the United States preserve certain traditional values from the challenges of a rapidly advancing technical world. Christopher Lasch has pointed out that many in the late nineteenth century entertained a strong belief in progress through technological and intellectual development. When the complexities of urbanization and industrialization such as poverty, crime, greed, and self-interested competition began to undermine this belief, consumerism served to glaze over most of the anxiety.[90] Americans in essence accepted these misfortunes in exchange for the new products of an industrial society (from electricity to sewing machines). Women sustained the optimism of Americans by protecting the home (which became the center of consumption) from these destructive values of the public realm.

A letter she wrote to a "young brother" reveals an approach to promoting the importance of spreading the "Gospel." Appearing in the November 1858 *Millennial Harbinger,* the letter articulates many of Selina's concerns about the faith of the young. She prefaced her remarks by reminding the unnamed recipient that she had witnessed his baptism and was anxious to guide him in his journey of Christian faith. "Allow me then, in all kindness, and, as one having some experience in the Christian religion, to make a few further suggestions to you, for your benefit personally." She went on to encourage him to attend churches where exceptional preachers would speak the truth and to spend his time regularly with those who also enjoyed such activity. "I regard such preaching as necessary everywhere," Selina informed the young man. "Immortal beings should not be allowed to slumber over the burning pit!! They should be aroused to a sense of their danger, their duty, their honor, and their happiness. It is unkind, it is worse than unkind, to speak words of 'peace' when there is no peace."[91] She believed in the power of the spoken word to bring the Scriptures to the mind and persuade the young to develop a faith of their own. She was probably strengthened in her view by the emphasis of Scripture on the importance of participating in worship with other Christians.

"A Letter to Young Converts" also offered advice intended to bolster the resistance of the young to the opinion of their peers. Selina reassured the recipient of the letter that his faith was not "strange" but a quality of true worth and gratification. She encouraged him to nurture that faith even when those around him did not. Such a faith should be sustained through regular attendance at church and committed study of the Scriptures.

From the early years of her life as a Christian, Mrs. Campbell strongly supported efforts to spread the Gospel abroad. She traced her interest in missions to reading the biography of the first Mrs. Judson, Ann Hasseltine Judson (1789–1826), a missionary to Burma about whose life she had learned at her sewing society meetings. The book, published in 1823, read almost like a popular novel. Judson's life encompassed illness, war, and extreme deprivation as well as abundant evidence of the difficulty of preaching Christianity to people of such a radically different culture. Selina greatly admired the courage with which Judson faced the trials involved in living in a "heathen" land. The memoirs of Judson's life left a clear picture in her mind. "Her husband's suffering and patience was so imprinted upon my mind that I have never forgotten the christian heroissm [*sic*] & fortitude they manifested under their trials," she told Julia. The image of their suffering would not allow her to ignore their example; indeed, she could not "see how any one professing to love the cause of Christ can be indifferent to it." In the case of the Judsons in particular, she meant to do more for their cause: "I have often felt a spirit impelling me to write for the good of society something more about them," she told Julia. "Although so much has already been said—I would especially like to hold them up to my Christian sisters and indeed to all of all denominations as pure Models of piety and devotedness in the Master's Cause."[92] She never fulfilled her desire to write about Ann Judson, but the activities of the Judsons inspired her to begin a crusade of her own to bring the issue of missions before her sisters and ask for their help in supporting the cause.

Selina's first public attempt to promote the cause of missions among women appeared in the *Millennial Harbinger* in 1856. She prevailed upon her relationship with her husband, the editor, to publish an article entitled "An Appeal to the Sisterhood." The article was short and simple but nonetheless represented the first public notice by a woman attempting to raise funds in support of foreign missions among the Disciples of Christ. "To my Christian Sisters in the Common Faith," the article began, "my object in addressing you, my dear sisters, . . . is to appeal to your sympathies and warm benevolence in behalf of our only missionary at present in a foreign field—Sister Mary Williams, now in great need."[93] Mary Williams was a close friend of Selina's whose work in the Holy Land was threatened by a lack of funds. Selina, though hesitant to begin a public campaign, nonetheless published a request for Williams's support. It was a prime example of Selina's belief in the ability of women to contribute even if only in a small way to the cause of Christ in the world, but she apologized nonetheless to her readers for the use of such a public forum.

Selina probably first met Miss Williams when the woman was teaching instrumental music at Fall's Seminary, the school for women run by P. S. Fall, a prominent Disciples educator in Kentucky. A native of New England, Miss Williams was one of the favorite teachers of Selina's daughter Margaret, who attended the school. From this beginning, the two women developed a close friendship and pursued a common interest in missions in the Holy Land. Both were born in England and had an affectionate relationship. Indeed, Williams remained close to the entire Campbell family; Alexander, Jr., even named his daughter after her in 1862. When Selina learned of her friend's predicament, she felt she must act.

In 1851 Mary Williams had decided to relocate to Jerusalem and begin working among the people there as a "self-constituted missionary," one not connected to any missions organization. Upon arriving in the Holy Land, she quickly organized classes for children and at one point had the charge of over sixty Jewish children. In observing the hard work of Sister Williams, Selina concluded, "such a manifestation of zeal and perseverance, under such disadvantageous circumstances, most certainly calls upon us, as Christians, in this highly favored land, to cooperate in manifesting our sympathies and benevolence."[94] Since she had gone on her own, Williams did not fall under the oversight of Disciples' only foreign missions organization at that time, the Missionary Board of the American Christian Missionary Society. Initially she was supported by other women in Philadelphia, Cincinnati, and Bethany— all communities where she had lived and worked. The funds obtained from these sources, however, proved insufficient, according to Selina. Seeing her sister's great need, Selina quickly volunteered to direct her fund-raising efforts. She first applied to the Missionary Board but was

turned down. This quick rejection of her request did not sit well with
Selina. She later expressed great frustration with the board, which turned
deaf ears to many of her requests for assistance in raising funds for
female missionaries. Forced to turn to the pages of the *Millennial Harbinger,* Selina then wrote the article that her husband published.

In the following years Selina published several pleas for money in the
pages of her husband's journal. In this medium she found a means of
raising support for women working in the cause so dear to her heart.
Even though she believed strongly in the cause for which she pleaded,
she had serious reservations about her chosen method. An 1856 letter
to Julia Barclay revealed her shame in presenting "before the public the
brief Appeal I made in the Feb. [Number] of the M.H. in behalf of our
neglected sister Williams." Her strong support of women's private role
in the home made such a public action problematic for her, but she also
believed that "nothing but dire necessity impelled me to do so." Prefer-
ring to raise money individually, she had, before writing the article, "for
more than one year raised all I could privately and had turned over in
my Mind every plan I could devise and still failed of doing what I
thought ought to be done for her."[95] The letter in the *Harbinger* was
the last of several attempts to meet Williams's needs. In her private
efforts, the concerned Selina had written dozens of letters to friends
and family asking for money to support the missionary. One letter to
Alexander and Mary Anna, for instance, asked them to solicit funds
from their rich friends. Selina turned to a public appeal for funds only
when she learned of her missionary friend's serious illness. She had
hoped Miss Williams would use the money to come home and recuperate but allowed her to use the funds as she wished.

Two months after the first published request for support, a chart of
funds received along with the names of the donors appeared in the *Harbinger.* In just a few weeks, the appeal had raised over $125. Though
pleased with the progress, Selina knew much more was needed. She
continued to appeal intermittently to all her acquaintances and to the
readers of the *Harbinger.* But she also knew that it might be better if
Miss Williams returned home soon, in light of the woman's advanced
age and frail health. Williams's supporters continued to urge her to ac-

cept their funds and use them to pay for her passage home, but she persisted in postponing her return.⁹⁶ Admiring her devotion, her friends supported her as best they could.

Also, though Selina eventually raised several hundred dollars for the support of Mary Williams, she did not offer her sister financial support alone. In a letter to her benefactor, Williams thanked her not only for the money she received but also for Selina's prayers and emotional assistance. "Your letter of December 14th [1856] was received by me yesterday, with great pleasure indeed," the sister wrote. "It is impossible to say at this distance from home, how we long for letters, when they come not, how we are again and again thrown upon our dependence upon God, without the intervention of human help and comforts." "The fresh rays of brotherly love beam in your communication and I am again stimulated," Mary told her friend. But most important, she understood "I do not work alone, for you pray for me, and give my poor name a warm place in the hearts of the dear children of God." Thus, in addition to monetary support, Selina understood the importance of including Williams in her prayers and offering her the encouragement and the support of caring friendship. Though grateful for Selina's efforts to arrange her journey home, Williams still remained in Jaffa, working to spread the Gospel for several more years. Selina's letters to Julia Barclay reveal the tremendous emotional and spiritual support both women offered their "sister in Christ." In one letter to Mrs. Barclay, Selina said she had opened her home to Sister Williams for her use after retirement. But the offer was never accepted. Unfortunately, Mary Williams died in Palestine on December 17, 1858, never having returned to her adopted homeland. Unaware of her final illness, Selina was greatly saddened when she received the sudden notice of her sister's death. In a short article commenting on Williams's obituary in the *Millennial Harbinger,* the grieving friend nonetheless reminded mourners that they could "have the fullest assurance and consolation in the confident hope in her departure, that she has gone to a land of perfect blessedness."⁹⁷ Selina had stood firm in the support of her steadfast friend, even when organized structures had failed.

The American Christian Missionary Society had been formed in

1849 to coordinate the efforts of individual congregations in supporting missions. Selina Campbell's relationship with this organization is of particular interest because many Disciple leaders argued over the nature of her husband's support for it. The establishment of the ACMS, however, had inaugurated what would become a long-lived controversy that centered on whether or not the ACMS enjoyed the full support of Alexander Campbell.[98] Early in his career Campbell had decried denominational organizations as destroying local autonomy and encouraging tyranny over the individual Christian. He had equated them with denominational hierarchies, which he regarded as unscriptural and injurious to the vitality of the "Church."[99] On the other hand, Campbell had always supported group meetings of churches interested in organizing their domestic missions efforts, so that many believed he would support the ACMS.

Nevertheless, when the first society meeting took place in 1849 and elected him president in absentia, many of his supporters were outraged. They charged that he had betrayed one of the fundamental principles of the movement: congregational autonomy. Prominent leaders emerged on both sides of the issue. Some, such as David Burnet, a preacher and journalist from Detroit, thought the society the only logical means of marshaling all the resources of the movement. But others, such as Nashville preacher Tolbert Fanning, feared the concentration of too much power in the hands of the few who would control such an association. Selina Campbell's role in the controversy is intriguing because of her relationship to both the proponents and the opponents of organized missions efforts.

The issue of the missionary society represents the only potentially definable conflict between Selina and her husband. As Selina became more involved with her fund-raising efforts for Sister Williams, she became increasingly frustrated with the lack of support from the ACMS. Her husband was president of the society and thus a focus for her dismay at its actions. On one occasion Mrs. Campbell was overwhelmed with guilt to learn that important funds had been delayed in reaching Mary Williams because of the hesitancy of the ACMS to release the money. Selina learned of the delay only when she received a letter from

the missionary that she described as "appropriate in manner and matter." The letter complained of the consequences of the failure to receive
the promised funds, and she shared this with her husband, who also
expressed his sorrow at the situation. But Selina, in a burst of emotion,
accused him of feeling too little. "I almost felt like blaming him as being the President of the Society that such had been the neglect," she
admitted to Julia Barclay, who was home on a break from missions
work herself. Alexander Campbell defended his decision not to interfere in the conduct of the Missionary Board by shifting the blame onto
the shoulders of D. S. Burnet, the board's apparent chair and the person
responsible for coordinating overseas missionary support. Selina speculated that Burnet had been distracted by issues facing the Publication
Society, another arm of the ACMS, and thus had not been sufficiently
sympathetic to Sister Williams's predicament. She vowed to right the
situation herself if necessary. "Immediately on perusal of Sister Williams letter I *determined* not to let *another* Post go out without *sending*
all that I had collected for her." She prevailed upon her husband for the
check and sent it immediately.[100]

The distraction of the Missionary Board also apparently extended
even to the work of the Barclays, their most prominent missionaries.
Given the board's history of neglect, Selina quickly expressed her concern to Julia about her returning to the mission field: "If they do not
promise to do more than they have ever hitherto done," she warned her
friend, "I *feel* dear sister that however determined that you are in going
& doing good in that distant land that it will be a hazard."[101] Worried
about what might happen if the Barclays were stranded in the mission
field, she cautioned Sister Barclay to think again before committing
more of her own resources to the work—an option Selina felt the missionaries should not have been forced to pursue.

Selina's frustration over the lack of support for the Disciples' overseas emissaries did not end with the leaders and supporters of the Missionary Board. She also disagreed with its detractors. Tolbert Fanning,
the prominent Tennessean, especially drew her ire. He was, at first,
strongly opposed to missionary societies on the ground that although
they had begun as an aid to local congregations, they had quickly begun

supplanting local authority and "were in fact seeking to legislate procedures." His interpretation of Scripture found no precedent for such organizations. As an "Alabama farm boy," Fanning feared the social elite that he felt gained power through them. For him, all the work that needed to be done could be accomplished through the local church without a larger superstructure that would attempt to dominate all missionary activity.[102]

In 1857 Selina took on the task of enlisting Fanning's support for the ACMS and its programs. Hoping to win him to her side, she took every opportunity to influence him. Whenever she encountered the man, whether it was while traveling with her husband or during Fanning's visits to the mansion, she spoke with him on the subject. In March 1857 she updated Julia Barclay on her progress, "I am truly sorry to say that [Fanning] is opposed to our Missionary Society he thinks it ought to be conducted by the Church but I cannot enter into his views likely [*sic*] you have seen them. I tried to say all I could to inlist [*sic*] him. Though I have understood that he is firm and rather *self-willed* and not easily moved." Selina quickly learned that all she had heard about Fanning's personality was more than true.[103]

Even though she disagreed strongly with his views, Selina nonetheless found a few things to admire about Fanning. She found him, as she told Julia, "social & pleasant and I have no doubt *very good* in his own way." Hoping to be able to work with him, she wanted to mitigate his dislike of missionary societies. In this, Selina showed her grasp not only of the source of Fanning's opposition to organized missions society efforts but also of the facets of his personality that might present a challenge to anyone trying to persuade him. But she could not conceal her disappointment when he and others could not be persuaded that it was important to support missions efforts. "Really sister Barclay," she wrote of the missionary society controversy, "I am so *distressed* & *disgusted* both with those who oppose and those that they say they favour them, that I scarcely know what to say in regard to the matter!!"[104]

Meanwhile, the situation had deteriorated as opinions hardened to such an extent that compromise proved impossible. As division arose, Selina could not "imagine how christians can oppose such benevolent [societies] so critic[ally] that they will not coopperate [*sic*] with one another." She expressed her further despair at the actions of those who, at least nominally, took the same side that she did in the debate. She accused the leaders of the ACMS of neglect, mismanagement, and failing to act in a Christian manner especially concerning Brother Denniss, another Disciples missionary in the Holy Land. "Neither can I understand," she wrote, "how a band of brothers united in these matters as our Board of Missionary cooperators [*sic*] at Cincinnati can aquit [*sic*] *themselves.*" She objected to their treatment of "*our beloved Martyr like* sister *Williams* and [other] pious laborers, *and devoted brother Denniss* and also their noble self-sacrificing bro[ther] Barclay." "I do not think matters could be managed *worse than they are,*" she declared to Julia. "I cannot comprehend matters in any way. All I can think & let me *think* as charitably as I can *that they cannot have* right views of their duty else their *souls* are well too *constructed.*"[105]

Clearly Selina was disappointed and puzzled at the lack of commitment to missions among the male leaders of the Missionary Board. But her defeat was not total. She sent letters similar in tone to Benjamin Franklin, Fanning's coeditor of the *American Christian Review,* to enlist his support. Working together with Julia in writing individual letters to persuade Franklin of their viewpoint, she found a listener more willing to hear their pleas than Fanning and the others. In fact, Franklin eventually became one of the most prominent supporters of the society and published favorable reports of its activities in the *American Christian Review.* The women asked him to address the board regarding Brother Denniss, a missionary who had not received his promised support and was then at work overseas. Perhaps the journalist could succeed where the women had failed and could influence the board to take some action. Neither Selina nor Mrs. Barclay recorded Franklin's response to their request for support, but historian Richard Hughes notes that David Lipscomb, another vocal opponent of the Missionary Society, felt that Franklin had succumbed to the influence of friends and associates and, against his better judgment, had changed his position to favor the Missionary Society.[106] The vigorous letter-writing campaign of these women may have tipped the scales and enlisted Franklin's support.

In 1859, the board, after reviewing Denniss's situation and after hearing from Brother Franklin, was convinced that money should be allocated for the missionary, so they voted him $200 in board support. Selina later explained that Denniss's situation had apparently occurred as a result of a misunderstanding stemming mainly from the board's mistaken assumptions about the circumstances of Brother Denniss's hiring. "They thought that Bro D—— was not a regularly employed missionary and that they were not under obligation to pay a regular salary," Selina wrote to Julia. "I do feel very much for Bro D—— but it appears that there was a misunderstanding in regard to his engagement by the Board." Thus, though the board had at first seemed negligent, she was heartened by their efforts to rectify the situation by allocating a generous sum of money for his support. Still, she wished "that much more could have been spared to him" to reward his "devotedness."[107] But still in her efforts to support Disciple missionaries, Selina outpaced many of the men who were supposedly responsible for such activity.

Selina Campbell had much in common with many other nineteenth-century women and is therefore a figure worthy of careful analysis. She is perhaps most interesting, however, because of the respects in which she was unique. Though she married hastily, true affection quickly developed between Alexander and Selina Campbell. This affection sustained them both and gave additional meaning to the duties each assumed in the relationship. Theirs is a fascinating story of marital devotion. They both had their own interests and abilities, but they ably functioned as a team in the cause that both supported. While some of the details of their union may not necessarily speak to the experience of the majority of American women, to the extent that this information advances the reader's knowledge of the character of Selina Campbell they are included to enhance the total picture of her life.

The marriage relationship into which Selina Campbell entered in 1828 is one of the most common standards that have led many to regard nineteenth-century American women as inferior and subordinate to men. Most studies have found evidence for this conclusion in property laws, divorce laws, and the like. But as Selina Campbell's life shows, this is often but half the picture. For many women, giving up property rights was not an equality issue but a public leadership issue. The "nasty" business of asset management and wage earning was left to the husband, while the wife, though expected to be thrifty and a good manager of the family resources, reigned supreme over the moral and spiritual atmosphere of the home. Nominal equality rather than a strict legal equality characterized many nineteenth-century marriages and explains why the feminist movement did not appear earlier than it eventually did. Women were willing in many instances to sacrifice their financial and political independence to serve their families. Such a role was valued in the nineteenth century and offered many women significant fulfillment. Certainly to some women such a system was a prison, trapping them in a life of few choices, but for the majority it appears to have permitted a life of meaning and contribution.

A close analysis of private sources allows us to understand the partnership between Alexander and Selina Campbell. Nancy Cott noted that the more one looks at private sources, the less harsh the separate spheres appear to have been for women. The severe proscriptions regarding female behavior that Welter, Lerner, and others have posited in a way resembled the advice and ideas displayed in fashion magazines of today. The literature may have been purchased and consumed by many women and may even have encompassed a well-developed, ideal picture of womanhood. But in the day-to-day existence of many women, the reality of life may have taken over, whether their faith in God shaped their worldviews or their devotion to their husbands and children.

Marriage, however, was not the only determinant of Selina's domestic role. As a wife, she not only assumed a duty to her husband but also entered into another set of relationships. Her life was profoundly shaped by motherhood. Selina's role as a mother entailed far more than just feeding, clothing, and loving her family. It also meant significant emotional and spiritual responsibilities that merit special consideration on their own terms.

3

"An Abiding Interest and Love"

Motherhood stands as one of the most fundamental defining roles of women throughout the ages. The fascinating aspects of nineteenth-century motherhood include its religious dimension and its meaning to women themselves. Selina Campbell took motherhood seriously, and the ministry partnership she shared with her husband hinged on her abilities as a parent to raise godly children in his absence. In the context of the partnership that Selina and her husband Alexander developed, her role as mother was a key element and another realm in which her faith played a major role.

Most of the evidence regarding Selina's relationship with her children surfaces in the exchange of letters between them. She maintained a vigorous correspondence with a number of relatives and acquaintances, but the letters to her children came first with her. She once affirmed that she could not "think of foregoing the pleasure of addressing myself to my children if every thing else should be neglected or if I should deprive myself of sleep!"[1] No consideration of Selina Campbell as a nineteenth-century woman would be complete without consideration of the role that maternity played in her life.

Selina's letters illuminate both the place of motherhood in her life and her private thoughts and feelings about the role. She wrote to her children about a multitude of topics, especially including her daily activities, such as calls she had made and received from friends and neighbors and news of births and deaths. But most of all she wrote to the children about her "abiding interest and love" for them and her responsibilities in raising them. The responsibilities mainly reflected her Christian faith, which formed the foundation of the Disciples' notions about parenthood. We can begin to understand the nature of the relationship between a mother and her children and the role of that relationship in the lives of women in the nineteenth century by analyzing Selina Campbell's interaction with her children. Moreover, Selina Campbell's connection with the founder of the Disciples of Christ allows us to regard her life as a meaningful example of motherhood within that body of believers.

On her wedding day in 1828, twenty-six-year-old Selina Bakewell acquired more than a new husband to love and sustain and a household to manage; she also became the mother of the five surviving daughters of Margaret Brown Campbell, her close friend. The care of these girls, ranging in age from seven to sixteen, represented a new stage in Selina's life, one that would require her to develop some of the most common skills of nineteenth-century women. Giving birth to six of her own children further increased the demands that motherhood placed on her time and energy. Indeed, childbearing and child rearing formed such a central part of the experience of the majority of women in the nineteenth-century United States that the character of women came to be closely identified with this role. As mothers, women assumed a particular identity that in turn shaped the part they played in American society. Motherhood was a vortex of social change for women that had been accelerating since the Revolutionary War era (1776–1789). An understanding of motherhood in the life of Selina Campbell necessitates consideration of the larger changes affecting women in the half century before her birth. The debate about the nature of motherhood in the postrevolutionary era provides a backdrop for comprehending the importance of motherhood within the Disciples of Christ and more specifically in Selina's life.

Character loomed large in the Disciples' worldview as part of faithful living, and the home as well as the church was charged with its maintenance. In this way the home became a specific dimension of the church as the locus of religious instruction and the place where good character was to be inculcated. In the nineteenth century, women were believed to be more naturally suited to the duties of this unique classroom. An article in the *Christian-Evangelist* explains how many Disciples viewed the connection: "The mother associates with the children more than the father, knows more of their wants and can have more influence on their lives and character. She bends the 'tender twig,' shapes the spirit, implants principles. John Randolph could never shake off the restraining influence of a little prayer his mother taught him when a child. It saved him from infidelity."[2] Alexander Campbell also believed that women had a special ability to communicate knowledge about God and could describe "the wonders of creation" better than "any Doctor of Divinity that ever lived."[3] For Campbell, the role of motherhood carried with it eternal importance in the lives of the children. Through this medium women exerted their influence on the world. As one article declared: "Like a pebble thrown into a pond, which produces an influence from centre to circumference, so your influence, mother, will be on the great sea of human thought and action, through the characters you set afloat on that sea in the person of your offspring." Fred Arthur Bailey initiated modern discussion of the topic of motherhood in the Disciples of Christ. In his reading of the published material on the subject, he concluded that in the post–Civil War era motherhood was a part of the defense against "the so-called revolution in morals, the rising number of divorces, the falling birth rate among 'the better sort of people,' and the changing position of women in society."[4] Motherhood was thus integrally connected to the Disciples' fundamental preconception about the organization of society.

Though most of the factors cited by Bailey occurred after the Civil War and therefore after most of Selina Campbell's children had reached maturity, these influences had begun during Selina's life and thereby provide important background for an examination of the significance of motherhood for the Disciples. The growth of cities and the rise of factories seemed to threaten the American family even before postbellum factors of divorce and falling birthrates presented new hazards. In the decades before the country divided, Christian values such as temperance and simple living seemed threatened by the frivolous amusements of the new industrial society. One of the strongest lines of defense against such decay was the lessons that mothers gave their children in resisting the temptations of the new culture and upholding the values of their parents. The antebellum challenge for the Disciples and others was to build frontier societies based on cherished values that avoided the excesses which modernity seemed to encourage.

Articles in most Disciple newspapers furthered the maternal ideal and celebrated the influence of mother upon child: "Beside the cradle, in the nursery, at the fireside, woman may gain victories for God, and man, and virtue, and liberty before which all those gained by bloodshed on the tented field pale into absolute significance," read one article. The republican concept of "virtue" that Jefferson and others had articulated translated into the Protestant concept of righteousness. A woman's influence, exerted in a haven from the anarchy of the world, would sustain goodness in her children. Recognition of women's effort often appeared in the pages of Disciple newspapers—affording women public recognition for their private activities: "To woman is given many opportunities of helping in this great battle of right and wrong, nor do you find her faithless to the duties lying in her pathway; for all over the world you find noble women working in every sphere of life for the good of humanity."[5]

The correspondence of Alexander and Selina Campbell indicates that his public statements regarding the role of women found concrete expression in the Campbells' own family life. Alexander's partner in this family life received his coaching together with his commendation on her role through his letters. "My Dear Selina," he wrote in 1837, "I need not enjoin upon you the religious and moral training of our dear children. . . . I have all confidence in your maternal as I have in your conjugal affections." He also made some observations he considered supported by Scriptures about the close relationship between mothers and their children. "The Lord has wisely, kindly and deeply planted in the maternal and paternal heart—but more deeply in the maternal than in the paternal heart—a paramount affection." This "paramount affection" meant "mothers have more generally a deeper and a more enduring natural affection than fathers." Because, as Campbell expressed it, "we presume, they need it most . . . , Children generally love their mothers more than their fathers; and so methinks they ought; for a mother's affection is generally stronger and more enduring than a fathers [*sic*]."[6] The role of mothers, then, was established by the same God who created the world and inspired the Scriptures. Campbell interpreted the things he observed in his life as having been ordained by God and having been included as part of his plan for humans. In this plan, mothers played the largest part in the spiritual and emotional development of the children entrusted to them.

From the above statements about the role of motherhood within the Disciples we can readily identify some of Selina Campbell's beliefs. First and foremost was her belief in the mother's role in the salvation of her children. Selina joined her husband in stressing her role as spiritual adviser to their children, but at least two other issues bring the image of Disciple motherhood into clearer focus. First, motherhood had a dual nature. For many women, it was a source of both joy and recognition, but it also had a more somber side that involved deep pain and constant, selfless service to others. Second, the primary concern of a mother is the salvation of her children. As a mother, Selina Campbell assumed the responsibility for the primary objective of the early instruction of her children: a lifelong commitment to Christian service. This was one of a woman's more important functions within the Stone-Campbell movement. On women rested the responsibility of training the next generation of religious leaders. A mother's special relationship with her children was vital in teaching them about salvation. It was a particular contribution that women made to the spread of their faith. While men preached publicly, women preached from the private pulpit of the home.

The correspondence between Selina and her family describes only the relationships between Selina and her natural children, since most of the offspring from Alexander Campbell's first marriage died quite young. There is thus a gap in our knowledge, but other sources provide several clues to her feelings toward her stepchildren. Specifically, she records information about her inherited family in the book she completed about her husband in 1879, *Home Life and Reminiscences of Alexander Campbell*.[7] The first marriage of Alexander Campbell, to

Margaret Brown, lasted fifteen years. When Margaret asked her husband to marry her good friend Selina Bakewell, Margaret was appointing Selina as a stepmother to the five young girls. Selina clearly embarked upon her role as mother with a glowing recommendation from her respected predecessor. Her fondness for her stepchildren, though, was quite evident from the start. Indeed, in the years to come, it was always her habit to refer to them as "daughter," and they referred to her as "mother." The use of such names was common in the nineteenth century but is nonetheless very important.

In the first chapter of *Home Life,* Selina introduces five new daughters. Jane Caroline, the eldest, married Albert Gallatin Ewing, a native of Nashville. The wedding took place several months before her father's second marriage and two months before the bride's sixteenth birthday. She married Ewing in the old parlor, the same room where her parents had taken their vows more than seventeen years earlier. After their marriage, she and her husband were "inmates of the family" for several months. A confessed Christian since her early childhood, Jane died of tuberculosis (just as her mother had) in 1834 at the age of twenty-two. Buried nearby in the Bethany cemetery, she left behind three children, Margaret, Sarah, and Henry.[8]

Selina describes Eliza Ann, the second daughter, as the "most attractive in person and character." It was the enterprising Eliza who hired "Aunt Betsey" just before her father's remarriage. She married Dr. John C. Campbell, a lawyer and "a gentleman of high intelligence and standing" from Wellsburg.[9] Sadly, Eliza's only daughter, Victoria Huntington (who took her middle name from her stepmother), died only a few months before her mother succumbed to illness on July 9, 1839.

The third daughter of Margaret Brown and Alexander Campbell, Maria Louisa (pronounced Ma-RYE-ah) was thirteen when her father remarried. Her stepmother called her a "very thoughtful child, mild and gentle." After her marriage in early 1831 to Robert Y. Henly, the son of a close associate of her father's, Maria remained near Bethany. Her husband purchased a farm for the family from the Campbells. Maria's daughter Caroline often visited her grandfather at Bethany after the death of her mother, and her own son Thomas later attended Bethany College.

The two youngest daughters of Margaret Campbell who survived infancy were Lavinia (born January 17, 1818) and Clarinda (born July 14, 1821). Both Lavinia and Clarinda often traveled with their father as young women and attracted numerous suitors wherever they went. Selina relates that as "a small child [Lavinia] was delicate," but by the time her father remarried she was "a sprightly, affectionate, and interesting girl, not quite grown, and inclined to be tall like her mother." Like her sister Maria, Lavinia also married a close friend of her father's (and a subsequent president of Bethany College), William Kimbrough Pendleton of Virginia. They had one daughter, Campbellina, known to her family as "Cammie." Lavinia also died of tuberculosis just after her twenty-seventh birthday.[10]

Margaret Brown Campbell chose the name of Clarinda (her fifth daughter) from a pseudonym her husband used in writing several essays for the *Washington Reporter* of southwestern Pennsylvania. Selina Campbell later described the essays, which began in 1810, as "criticisms for and against 'Old Maids,' and . . . most amusing and entertaining." Some time after the death of Lavinia, Clarinda married her sister's former husband. Apparently after the marriage there was some talk about its propriety, but Selina defended it as "a very natural thing, and not a word in the Scriptures can be found against it."[11] Only a few years after her marriage Clarinda succumbed to the same disease that had taken her mother and her sisters.

While Selina watched her five stepchildren die in the prime of their lives, she was at the same time beginning anew the responsibilities of motherhood with the birth of her own children. She and her husband rejoiced with the birth of her first child in the first year of their marriage. The girl was named Margaret Brown Campbell in honor of her father's first wife. Little Margaret was a busy, affectionate child well loved by her four uncles as well as her parents and stepsisters. In 1848 she married John O. Ewing, the nephew of Albert Ewing (who was the husband of her stepsister).

Alexander Campbell, Jr., the first son, was born October 24, 1831. As an adult, he became a well-known Confederate colonel, fought bravely in the Civil War, and remained a prominent figure after the conflict. Through his wife, Mary Anna Purvis, whom he met when she attended his Aunt Jane McKeever's Pleasant Hill Seminary in nearby West Middleton, Pennsylvania, he inherited a plantation in Concordia Parish in southern Louisiana. Alexander often accompanied his father on his preaching tours and saw to his parent's needs in the absence of his mother. His mother and father supported him and his wife until they moved into their own home in 1854. He is the oldest of the Campbell children to outlive his parents; he died in 1906 and was buried in the Bethany cemetery across the road from his parents' home.

After Alexander, Jr., Selina and Alexander had another daughter, Virginia Ann, on January 24, 1834. Selina's second oldest daughter often traveled with her father. Many of his surviving letters from the trip to Europe in 1847 are addressed to her. In 1863 she married William R. Thompson, a businessman from Louisville, Kentucky, near where she attended school. Her husband, however, proved irresponsible, and she lost nearly all of her possessions to his creditors. Her mother offered some help, but financial difficulties remained until eventually she secured an appointment from President Garfield as postmaster for Louisville. Before her death in 1908 she also served in the Library of Congress.

In 1837 the family rejoiced at the birth of another son, Wickliffe, named after the great translator of the Scriptures, John Wickliffe, who was much admired by the baby's father. Less than three years later, the tenth daughter of Alexander Campbell was born and received the name Decima Hemans. Her father chose her name and often "laughingly remarked that the Romans only went as far as octavia, but he went as far as Decima."[12] Her middle name came from the surname of a poetess well admired by the entire family. Decima, like her sister Virginia, traveled often with her father. She had a pleasant personality and was attractive in appearance, so that several suitors asked for her hand in marriage. She eventually married John Judson Barclay, son of James and Julia Barclay, close friends of the Campbells.

William Pendleton Campbell, Selina's youngest child, entered the world on March 11, 1843. The birth of this fourteenth child of Alexander Campbell was celebrated by the entire family. On his twenty-eighth birthday, his mother wrote him about the great fuss after his birth. Beloved ones such as his Grandmother Bakewell and Lavinia were still alive at the event. Selina fondly related to William one humorous incident that had occurred immediately after his birth, when Sister Clarinda and Lavinia were sitting "by the fire in my room." "Lavinia had you on her lap," the mother began, "when you took a spasm and she and her sister gave a loud *shriek,* thinking you were dying." Though he was not ill, the incident shows that the youngest Campbell baby was adored by the whole family. Indeed, so much attention may have spoiled "Willie" a little. But the scene that Selina describes from his infancy reflected love for this tiny child that would continue for the rest of his life. His mother ends the story with the simple observation "but you soon recovered."[13]

The correspondence between this fourteenth child of Alexander Campbell and his mother dominates the collection of Campbell family papers, accounting for over a hundred of the approximately 400 letters. William attended school in Wheeling (just a few miles south of Bethany), which seemed to be as far as his mother would allow him to go. He then studied law in Louisville, where in 1870 he met and married Nannie Meaux Cochrane, the daughter of Mrs. Jeanette and Dr. P. H. Cochrane. He eventually settled in Wellsburg, where he opened his own law practice.

Selina's close relationship with the mother of her five stepdaughters before her marriage spawned her love for her stepdaughters. Her frequent visits to the Campbell home had furthered her acquaintance with the girls and laid the groundwork for a new relationship with them after her marriage. Over fifty years after the death of her friend and predecessor, Selina comments that in her relationships with her new daughters, she "ever took an interest, and it was my sad privilege to be with them all in their sickness, and in death's trying hour."[14] Indeed a common theme in Selina Campbell's remarks about being a mother is the twofold nature of the role. At the same time that she loved and took pride in her stepdaughters, she also lamented the "sad privilege" of watching them die. Unfortunately, she experienced the death not only of her stepchildren but also of some of her own children.

Before the death of her new daughters, however, there were years during which they developed close relationships. Love bound mother and child together. "I have thought often of writing you to express a mother's interest for you," Selina would write to her youngest child, William. "An abiding interest and love (for you my youngest born) is engraven *deep down* on my hearts tablet and that can *never* be *erased*, through all the changing seasons of earth and time!" The language used by Selina Campbell was exalted and heartfelt, expressive of her emotions: "O the depth of my love can never be known or appreciated only by Him who created the relationship of Mother and child."[15] These sentiments flowed through her letters to all her children. To Selina, the role of mother was all-encompassing, a solemn responsibility ordained by a wise Father God to ensure the proper development of children and society in general. And it required her greatest effort. She believed that since babies are born helpless and need parents—unlike animals who within moments can seek their own food—mothers had a sacred responsibility to care for their children both physically and spiritually. Motherhood demonstrated the interdependency of humans in a cycle of life sustained by a loving and active God who ordained the precious relationships between his created beings. The role of the parent thereby becomes critical to the Christian (especially the mother) in the preservation and improvement of life.

The love and concern that Selina felt for her children found further expression in the advice she offered them on a variety of subjects. Since the majority of her extant maternal letters are addressed to William, it is easiest to reconstruct their relationship and appreciate its nuances. The bond between this mother and her youngest child reflected many of the aspects of nineteenth-century motherhood. The chief thrust of her advice to William was to seek faith in God and avoid things that distract from this pursuit. She consistently importuned him regarding his activities, for it seemed that William acquired many habits offensive to his mother.

Selina's efforts to guide her children began with the critical relevance of prayer for her children's instruction and benefit. She regularly identified the importance of the "Mercy Seat" in her efforts to solicit divine guidance on behalf of her children. The Mercy Seat was a metaphorical place where many Disciples believed God listened to the requests of his followers. His followers enjoyed this opportunity, which had been made possible through the intercession of His Son, Jesus Christ, as the part of God that once assumed human form and continued to work on their behalf. Selina Campbell strongly believed that her prayers, offered at the Mercy Seat, reached their object. "As an Eagle her young ones upon her wings bears her young . . . towards heaven," she told her son William, "so do I *bear* you night and day before the Mercy seat of my Father in heaven. . . . The angels that nightly guard my bed hear my supplications on your behalf and they carry the *undying agonies* to their kindred angels! But above all my adorable Saviour heard my *cries* & sees my *tears*."[16] Selina's regular letters to her children constantly spoke of such a belief in God's concern for his creations. Selina's deep emotional investment in her children is also evident, as the letters record several incidents that attest to Selina's prayerful, motherly devotion. Her regular references to approaching the "Mercy Seat" demonstrate her commitment to the spiritual well-being of her children.

The letters also record pleas when the children's values did not appear to match her own. Selina's belief in the influence of early instruction in a child's life suffuses her letters and underlay her attempts to persuade them to move toward a deeper faith. The Scriptures promised that if a parent "train[ed] a child in the way he should go . . . , when he is old he will not turn from it."[17] This biblical promise formed the basis for many Disciples' emphasis on parental instruction, and mothers became the specific agency through which the promise was realized. Selina believed that her early instruction would guard her children when life took them beyond her direct care and influence. Though her children did not always follow her instructions once they reached adulthood, Selina nevertheless worked hard to remind them of the things they had learned as children.

The advice she received from her husband reinforced her goals in parental instruction. Though often away from home, Alexander Campbell frequently affirmed his interest in his children. He also gave several instructions to his wife that further reveal his thoughts on her role as mother. Most of these instructions centered on Selina's critical role in introducing her children to the Gospel that their father promoted so assiduously. "I trust you are all attention, my dear," he wrote in 1836, "to . . . the education and improvement of our dear children. Remember, this is the great business of life: to transmit to those, and through those to whom you have given birth, the knowledge of God and of his Anointed for their sakes and for the good of others yet unborn." Other instruction also showed his concern that his children live a proper life. At times a sense of urgency underscored Campbell's exhortations to his wife on the subject, as when he urged her to "say to his children flee, flee, flee from the wrath to come, and seize the proffered pardon before the uncertain moment, and yet certain to come, overtakes them." This pursuit by the children of a pardon for their sins included living a life that emphasized laboring "not for food that perishes, but for that which endure[s] to eternal life."[18] These instructions from her husband reinforced Selina's deep convictions about the critical nature of her child-rearing role.

Coupled with his frequent advice was Alexander Campbell's regular affirmation of his belief in Selina's competence. Parenting was a shared activity. At times, Campbell would briefly but firmly state his belief in her competence as a mother and move on to other topics. In other instances, his letters resembled discourses on the importance of parenting more than they did personal correspondence. It would seem that he intended these letters for publication in the *Harbinger*. In both types of letters, Campbell's respect for his wife's ability remains clear.

But Alexander's travels presented one of the greatest challenges that the Campbells faced as parents. Some have charged that Campbell's sons chose not to follow in their father's footsteps from resentment of his constant absence. There is no direct evidence to support this assertion, but it seems likely. For the young William, the enticements of the city proved irresistible. It was a challenge for the mother to guide her youngest son even after he left home. During his school years in Wheeling, Selina warned William to beware of schoolmates who would induce him to start smoking or using tobacco. She reminded him that such a "pernicious habit" did not contribute at all to his "usefulness." When she learned of his use of the substance several months later, she did not hesitate to pen a stinging letter to her son begging him to drop the habit. Later, she spoke of her hurt that he continued despite her concerns.[19] Interestingly, other letters from the Bakewell collection seem to indicate that Selina's parents both indulged in the tobacco habit. Selina must have found it difficult to buck the tide within her family.

Selina, however, did not focus on a religion of negation. Rather she took direct steps to teach her children the importance of a dynamic faith. To protect them from "evil company and evil habits," Selina advised them not to follow a strict regimen of do's and don'ts but to read the Bible every day. In her letter of January 24, 1858, Selina gives William passages of Scripture centering on the resurrection of Jesus Christ from the dead. She hoped he would study such things and order his life accordingly; her desire for her children to read Scripture reflected her goal of raising committed Christians. The message of Scripture's importance was especially familiar to the Campbell offspring because of their father's career. Alexander Campbell sought to make the Bible the basis of all religious faith. It is not surprising, then, that Selina should have showed such concern when her sons and daughters appeared to have forsaken the preaching of her husband. She reminded William on one Lord's Day in 1858 that Jesus' role as intercessor (after his death and resurrection) made it possible for William to approach God asking forgiveness for sins, and she hoped he would take the opportunity to receive forgiveness. Selina's interest in saving her children from divine retribution never flagged.

Selina also emphasized to her children the importance of honoring the Sabbath, or, as the Disciples celebrated it, the Lord's Day (Sunday). William especially seemed reluctant to attend church without fail. Through letters and poems that Selina composed, she hoped to use the

power of language to persuade her children to pursue more spiritual
things. One short poem about observing the Sabbath clearly reflected
the importance of the practice in Selina's mind:

> A Sabbath well spent, brings a week of Content
> And health for the toil of tomorrow
> But a Sabbath profaned, whatsoever be gained
> Is a Certain forerunner of Sorrow[20]

Most Disciples regarded the Bible as providing a clear blueprint to follow in living one's life. The consequences of ignoring its commandments were severe and plain. Obedience to the commandments would
bring each believer blessings. These blessings did not necessarily trans-
late into material possessions or good health but signaled a special relationship with God that emphasized eternal meaning over present suffering or gain. Selina wanted her children to believe, as she did, in the
utility of pursuing the things of God.

Since only a few letters still remain from Selina to her youngest
daughter, it is difficult to discern any difference between her advice to
her daughters and that which she gave her sons. Yet there does appear
to be some contrast. Selina's advice to her sons had an emphasis on
righteous behavior. Her advice to her daughters, on the other hand, expressed a mother's concerns for the physical well-being of her children
apart from any inappropriate behavior. While attending school in Kentucky, Virginia was warned not to go out much at night and was reminded to preserve her health. In another missive, Selina instructs Virginia to economize, because her mother has many bills yet to pay. In her
husband's frequent absence from home on preaching or fund-raising
tours, Selina took charge of many of the material needs of her children.
She apportioned their spending money, and she also monitored their
progress in their studies. Selina's tasks seemed easier in the case of her
daughters, who apparently stirred much less anxiety.

Alexander, Jr., caused his mother some concern in his younger years.
He appeared attracted to many of the worldly things she had warned
all her children against. In 1847 Selina engaged the prominent preacher

Moses Lard to travel to Elizabethtown, where her brother Theron lived, to conduct a protracted meeting. The town as yet had no Disciples' congregation and relied on traveling speakers for instruction. Young Alexander asked to accompany Lard and visit his uncle. The mother agreed, but in a letter informing Theron of the arrangements being made, she asked her brother to keep an eye on his nephew so that he would not "go through town too much especially by himself." She was concerned that he had "grown very much & is too much a man for his years." But she took some comfort that he was "improving some," which she attributed partially to the fact that he was reading more than he had at one time.[21] Her brother's agreement must have eased her mind. She still worried, however, about young Alexander's tendency to neglect his studies both in school and in church.

William continued to resist following the teachings of his parents for much of his life. Nearly every year his mother composed a letter to him on his birthday, exhorting her wayward son to return to the instruction of his youth. To mark his thirty-fifth, she penned "A Birthday Remembrance." The main theme of this four-page essay was her great interest in his spiritual condition, the interest of "a fond mother *whose heart* has been ever set upon the Salvation from sin of her offspring." She was especially concerned about William's and his brother Alexander's susceptibility to worldly distractions: "As the Good Melancthon said, when he went forth to Preach and endeavor to Save a world lost in Sin, 'It was too strong for him'. . . . So say I the world, with its whiles [*sic*], and sinful snares, has been too strong for my beloved son—or may I say *Sons*. For I have two, that although brought up at the feet of Jesus, & early instructed in the knowledge of God's will . . . how little proof have they given to the world!!"[22] The essay ended with an expression of her wish that her sons might return to the teachings of their youth. There is little evidence that they ever did, but their mother never gave up hope.

Unfortunately, conflicts over their father's estate exploited the intergenerational conflict and later degenerated into accusations from the children, who challenged their mother's financial management. This would be the saddest quarrel between the mother and her children. One incident in this affair suggests some of the difficulties that Selina faced in proving her goodwill toward them. During a dispute over ownership of the Bethany Mansion following the death of Alexander Campbell, Selina's devotion to her children was questioned by her daughter-in-law Nannie Cochrane Campbell. The full circumstances remain unclear, but surviving documents suggest that William felt entitled to ownership of the mansion and began to consider selling it or using it as collateral to pay his debts. Alexander, Jr., also wanted his mother to put up the house to cover his debts. Selina, then, was caught between her two sons, each wishing to use the equity of the house to pay his liabilities. The actions of Selina's children indicate a seeming lack of trust in their mother's motives. They seemed reluctant to respond to her love and affection in kind, and Selina's disappointment in them was evident.

Yet even in her disappointment, she was always quick to maintain an open relationship with her children no matter what their indiscretions. Though she repeatedly pleaded for her sons and daughters to repent and seek after the things of God, she also desired them to "bear with" her and give "most serious consideration to the *deep concern* [and] affection of an anxious and devoted mother's *heart!*"[23] She held up her good intentions before her children as a shield against any resentment they might feel against her intrusion into their lives. She seemed to fear that her repeated entreaties might have the unintended effect of alienating the very ones she sought to draw near, so she kept the communication lines open by consciously refraining from moralizing with her children and instead spoke openly and with understanding. Letters between Selina and her children that have not survived (and there must be many) may have revealed dissension between mother and children that the surviving letters do not so clearly indicate.[24] It seems reasonable to conclude, however, that though the constancy of Selina's appeals may have carried a danger, she was aware enough of such a possibility to try to forestall it and maintain a close relationship with her children even when she disagreed with their decisions.

Perhaps the biggest tragedy in Selina's role as mother was the sudden loss of her fourth child, Wickliffe, in 1847. No other incident in Selina's life so challenged her in her faith and service to her God. In *Home Life*,

Selina described her ten-year-old son as "a child of great hope to father and mother, and giving promise, from his early piety, of being a bright and useful worker in the Lord's vineyard." Though so young, Wickliffe had already attracted a great deal of attention from many who met him. In many ways Wickliffe was the spiritual hope of both parents. He delighted in memorizing Scripture, which greatly pleased his father and grandfather, and he was often seen carrying a Bible to the fields to spend an afternoon "reading and studying." He was described as a "remarkably polite, obedient and affectionate child—always serene, always happy." To his mother, he had a future which "promised all that was good and noble."[25] Everyone expected him to follow in his father's footsteps and take up the cause of reforming American Christianity. Moreover, the relationship between Selina and Wickliffe was especially close. Wickliffe's father recognized that "his mother's heart was bound up in him, and he was, as I often said to her, 'like her shadow,' always by her side." The boy's sudden death by drowning shocked all who knew him, caught the family unprepared, and affected the parents deeply.

Wickliffe had gone swimming in Buffalo Creek with two of his father's grandsons one sunny afternoon in the first week of September 1847. His father, before leaving for Europe in the spring of that year, had told him that he could not bathe in the creek until the end of the summer. September brought the end of the "dog-days," so his mother gave him permission to join his playmates—unaware of what was to come. She later wrote: "They were all diving off a small skiff when Wickliffe disappeared and became bewildered under the apron of the mill-dam—for it was near the mill-dam and in sight of the house, and a short distance from it where he was drowned."[26] Immediately after the calamitous event, "the alarm was given, but it was some time before he could be recovered. I was soon at the place. Many gathered around on the beautiful green banks of the Buffalo, near the spot where multitudes had been baptized, and the voice of exhortation, prayer and praise had resounded. . . . The agony of that hour can never be forgotten. . . . the idol of my heart lying lifeless, speechless before me!"[27]

Far away across an ocean, the father of the deceased child experienced a puzzling agonizing night of worry for his family that mirrored his wife's distress. Initially unaware of the cause he later discovered the reason for his torment when he returned to the United States and found a telegram awaiting him. This incident seems particularly unusual because of the lack of a mystical element in the Disciple worldview. In their rational approach to scriptural interpretation, the Disciples had no mechanism for interpreting Alexander's experience the night of his son's death. Not until his ship arrived in Boston did Alexander learn of his son's death. The loss of Wickliffe was "a sad bereavement, an almost insupportable shock, too much for flesh and blood," wrote his father. Furthermore the tragedy was ever more difficult because, as Alexander wrote, "although inured to all afflictions, with loss of many children, on all former occasions our minds were gradually prepared for it, by the slow and doubtful advances of a lingering decline."[28]

It is difficult to overemphasize the importance of the death of Wickliffe in shaping the whole perspective of Selina Campbell. Richardson observed that her recovery from the loss was slow even after her husband returned from Europe. Campbell came home to find his wife mired in grief. Her "unhappy stand of mind . . . pressed very heavily upon him as he was naturally of a cheerful and even joyous temperament," Richardson recorded. Several months passed before Selina showed any sign of improvement. Her health suffered. "Overwhelmed with sorrow" she was "unable to take any longer her accustomed interest in the household affairs." Her husband did all he could to aid her recovery, seeking her out every day upon his return from the college, and spent as much time with her as he could. "Often, in the dusk of the evening, missing her from the family circle, and suspecting that she had stolen away to weep at the grave, he would hasten to the cemetery to find her, and accosting her in the kindest accents, 'My dear,' he would say—my dearest Selina, the loved ones are not here. They have passed beyond these earthly scenes to happier abodes'; and taking her arm with the most touching expression of sympathy and love, would lead her gently home."[29]

Under her husband's ministrations, Selina improved, but her progress was slow. In a response to a letter of condolence received from the Coleman family, close friends of the Campbells, Alexander records the struggle both he and his wife faced four months after Wickliffe's drowning:

> She is . . . still very much grieved and dejected. She thinks she never can cease to grieve that the Lord was constrained from anything in herself to lay his hand so heavily upon her. Being constitution-ally of very strong affections and feelings, and of a very sensitive and delicate conscience, and withal being at the time very much debili-tated in her health, she has been greatly dejected and afflicted in this case . . . I fear it will be some time before she be herself again. I have suffered much in the loss of my children. Yet the last loss—so unex-pected, and as such a special providence—has been more oppressive than any one case or trial through which I had passed. Many a fond hope and promise clustered around Wickliffe. But he was destined for another field of sovereign good pleasure I desire to bow with the most devout submission, praying only that the Lord may make it a blessing to myself and to all his relatives.[30]

Grief brought Alexander and Selina closer together and challenged them to understand the will of God in the death of their child, but Selina would face further tragedy before she developed a reservoir of emotional and spiritual strength to deal with her heartbreak at the loss of Wickliffe.

Eliza Davies, a guest of the Campbells at Bethany Mansion for sev-eral months in 1847–1848, describes the difficult months in the house-hold that followed Wickliffe's death. Her narrative of life in the Camp-bell home in late 1847 records in particular detail the high price Selina paid. A short time after the tragedy, Mrs. Davies, a distant relative of the Campbells, arrived at the Bethany Mansion for a visit. She wrote of Selina, "I did not see Mrs. Campbell when I went to the house at first. Her mind was deeply afflicted for the loss of her boy. Her affections had been placed on this boy supremely. She had thought he would live and follow in the steps of his illustrious father to honor and renown, and fill, or take the place of, the great man when he had passed away." Davies's insight into the impact of this tragedy on Selina also merits close examination. "Her hopes and aspirations for Wickliffe were dashed to the ground. Her idol was broken, and she was inconsolable. The family were in deep distress on her account, as well as for the loss of the child." Davies also wrote of her first meeting with Mrs. Campbell. "When Mr. Campbell came home from college, he asked: 'Where is mother?' After he had kindly greeted me, and bade me welcome to Bethany House, he passed out of doors. I saw him after a while leading a tall, thin, melancholy looking lady, dressed in black, with her clothes dripping wet, and clinging to her spare figure. This was Mrs. Campbell, who had been to the creek where her boy lost his life, and who was so gently led to her own room, and tenderly cared for by her noble husband."[31]

The loss of her beloved son seems to have prompted a nervous breakdown in Selina. Several months passed before she showed any signs of improvement. Grief for the dead—especially children—was a prevalent theme in the experience of nineteenth-century women. Selina's family, feeling deep concern for her in her distress, must have wondered whether she would ever regain her equilibrium. "Grandma Campbell is in much better spirits, than when you was [*sic*] here last," little Margaret C. Ewing, daughter of Selina's oldest stepdaughter, Jane Caroline, wrote to her great uncle Theron Bakewell, "but still, she never can forget dear little Wickliffe, how could she. I am sure I never will and much more must she feel for indeed he was the most —— child I ever saw, of his age. And if he attained to such a state of perfection, so young, what might he not have been if he had lived?"[32] The lost promise of the beloved child prompted an outpouring of grief and sympathy from the entire family.

Later, Selina came to believe that the experience of losing her child had taught her that "often such children the Lord, in his mercy, removed from the 'evil to come.'"[33] Special children seemed to be drawn back to their creator as if their very nature caused God to bring them home early. At the same time, Selina's faith in God assured her that "her Heavenly Father" had not deserted her in her hour of need, a belief that stayed with her and that she often reiterated throughout her life.

On one occasion when her grief lay heavily upon her again, she took comfort in "repeat[ing] the words of the good John Newton: 'And soon or late, that heart must bleed, which, idols entertain.' "[34] Selina often feared that her love for Wickliffe had interfered with her devotion to the God whom she served. Perhaps, she reasoned, that was why God had taken him away. One might also ask whether this was not simply the natural tendency of a mother to blame herself for the premature death of her son. But Selina seemed sincere as she sought to explain the death of her son in terms of her faith in a God whose wisdom surpassed her own. In this way she hoped to find an outlet for her grief. Acceptance did not come easily.

Selina shared her hard-won understanding of her son's death not only with her own family but also with others who experienced a similar loss. Even should a child survive infancy, the struggles of living in a developing area such as western Virginia often resulted in fatal injuries. Many women lost children. In 1860 Selina, in a letter to her close friend Julia Barclay, asked Mrs. Barclay to send her condolences to Sarah Barclay Johnston. Sarah, the daughter of Julia, had recently lost two infants. Selina asked Julia to remind her daughter that she would see her babies again in heaven and to draw strength from this future promise. So much of a woman's life was bound up in her children that losing them touched every woman deeply. Selina and her friends looked to God for comfort in the face of such sorrow. The support women offered each other in times of adversity often reflected their spiritual beliefs and their faith in God's loving care.

Such faith and confidence did not come easily, however. Selina, in fact, never completely recovered from the loss of Wickliffe until another great loss pulled her back into the reality of her responsibilities. Even after the death of her beloved Wickliffe, there was more for her to learn about the somber side of motherhood, for on October 22, 1848, tragedy struck again. Only a few weeks after giving birth to a son (Selina's first grandchild), Margaret Campbell Ewing, Selina's eldest daughter, learned she had contracted tuberculosis, the illness that had killed all of her stepsisters. Though her husband called in several doctors for consultations, the verdict was that she had only two months left to live. "I could not realize that the lively, bright, black-eyed Margaret was doomed to an early grave," wrote Mrs. Davies.[35] The family had just begun to revive from the loss of Wickliffe and now so quickly faced another enormous loss. Margaret's husband, John O. Ewing, took her to Pittsburgh, hoping for a miracle, but she soon returned to Bethany resigned to her death. Yet Selina found a new lease on life in this second tragedy. Eliza Davies describes the importance of Margaret's passing in her mother's life:

> I was taken into the room where lay the slender form of the fair girl, beautiful even in sickness. I watched the working of the nerves of her pretty face, and oh, how sad I felt, when I saw in it the convulsive throes of death. I left the room. Her mother followed me. . . . This brave old Christian lady spoke calmly about her daughter. It was the calmness of a desolate heart. My heart wept for her, the grief-stricken mother, as she was about to part with her darling child. She needed all her Christian philosophy to bear up under heavy trial . . . After Mrs. Ewing's death, Mrs. Campbell regained the lost equilibrium of her mind, and she seemed a very different woman. She took an interest in her household duties.[36]

Unfortunately, Davies did not, and likely could not, explain exactly why Selina recovered her equilibrium after Margaret's death. Her brother Edwin expressed relief at the perceived changes in Selina: "I am rejoiced to learn that Sister is becoming more reconciled to the loss of dear Wickliffe. I wonder not at her agony of soul—an aching void within her will no doubt be ever present—but all things will work together for good to those that love the Lord. It is therefore our duty and our happiness to be resigned to the will of him who can give & take away."[37] With the death of Margaret, who left a newborn grandson for the grandmother to care for, perhaps now Selina could see new meaning in her life and steeled herself for new responsibilities. She never explained how she coped with the loss of her eldest child, but it was probably the culmination of her struggles to accept that God could take her children away for his own purpose. Selina Campbell had passed the first critical test of motherhood. She faced many trials in the sacred task entrusted to her by her husband and her God, but losing her children to the sting of death always challenged her most. Both the joys and the sorrows of motherhood came home to her, and though more trials followed, she faced them strengthened by this difficult experience and able to guide other women (especially those younger than she) in their solemn responsibilities.

Selina relied especially on the instruction of Scripture regarding sufferings that included not only death but also illness, poverty, and loneliness. In each case Selina turned for comfort to the words of the Bible. The serious illness of her daughter Margaret in 1848 was just such a circumstance. "Oh! What a consoling hope the gospel brings with it," she wrote to her brother Theron about Margaret's affliction, "the thought that when these poor careworn & sin-worn bodies are laid in the dust—that they shall be freed from pain." The knowledge that her daughter's pain would some day be eased was a great source of comfort to her during Margaret's protracted illness. The mother was especially distraught to see her daughter bedridden for several months, unable to join her family in their daily activities and finding surcease only in her faith. "She suffers a good deal from constant lying, her bones are almost through the skin," the mother wrote.[38] In the face of such hardship, Selina clung to the Bible's promise of life after death; someday her daughter would no longer suffer.

From Scripture and her own experiences, Selina developed a view of the world in which suffering had a particular, if temporary, place. "We journey here a few short years of toil and care—our pilgrimage cannot be otherwise than marked with care, and endless anxieties!!" Suffering was thus an unavoidable part of living. Moreover, it was not something fearful or disheartening, for "at the same time the ten thousand mercies of the Lord call for our hearts to rejoice in Him and to overflow in strains of gratitude adoration and praise!" She firmly believed that suffering, though difficult for anyone to bear, did not mean abandonment by God. Selina especially cautioned those who were not prepared for the inevitable trials of life. "Oh! That we could realize that . . . all we have belongs to the Lord & that he has a right to take back the gifts & loans, at any time He pleases. If we could only say at all times, with all our hearts 'Thy will not mine be done' Oh Father in Heaven how happy we would be."[39] The only way to meet the challenges of sorrow in life, therefore, was to understand them as the will of a God who promised victory in the end and a reward to those who persevered. True happiness rested not on prosperity and the absence of trouble but on an understanding of the nature of the world and a hope for the future. For many women, such beliefs must have offered some solace. In the death of a child or in the constant whirl of daily activity, the serenity of deep spiritual acceptance fortified many women just as the moments of quiet spent reading Scripture and praying served to energize them.

The happiness of trusting in an omniscient God to see to the interests of his people, however, did not preclude deep sorrow. The death of Wickliffe, though Selina claimed to understand the "why" of it, nonetheless troubled her deeply. Understanding did not stifle her emotions as much as it allowed her to work through them and see them for what they were. Though she believed strongly in the Lord "Who sees and knows what is best for His children, both for those taken above, and those afflicted by their removal, who remain on earth," years passed before she "could feel my 'sorrow turn to gladness.'" Ten years after the tragedy, her sorrow remained fresh but was tempered by hope. "Ah! me how I think of your beloved brother Wickliffe who passed away in the creek!" she wrote to William in 1858. "But I must not dwell upon this subject. I trust his spirit is with the Lord injoying [*sic*] happiness. . . . therefore I must not grieve as those who have no hope. I think of dear Wickliffe, now being a pure spirit, freed from all temptation and from sin!"[40] The hope of life after death sustained her.

In Selina's view there was no call for complaint by any Christian, no matter their circumstances. Instead, all "should be resigned & not repine no matter our lot." Challenges would come, and dark times were unavoidable. In any case, the suffering would not last long, for soon the Savior would return to take his followers to Heaven with him, the living and the dead. Such sentiment sustained Selina in trying situations, including separation from those she loved. In 1846, for example, she expressed her "regret" as being so far from her brother Theron, who then lived a substantial distance away in southern Virginia. She worried about what might happen to him and how she could help him if it did. "How happy I would be to visit you often especially in times of sickness what a comfort it is to receive the consolation of friends." The only consolation for the separation was her trust that "the hour draws nigh when we shall be separated in this world—may we meet in a better & happier clime."[41] Selina took heart from assurances in the Bible that all Christians would be reunited in heaven either after their death or after the return of Jesus Christ to bring all believers to God. Selina believed that though she and her brother might be separated in this life, they would spend eternity together. Such Christian doctrines comforted many women.

The core of the private daily experience of motherhood, then, was unsurprisingly complex. Though Selina was charged with the moral upbringing of her children, she did not automatically succeed. Neither of her adult sons ever demonstrated any deep commitment to moral living or church membership. The absence of their father surely contributed to the antipathy that the children felt toward the cause that had kept him away. The surviving evidence supports no other explanations. Selina's disappointment, however, was evident.

Motherhood required the deepest energies of a woman but did not confer automatic rewards. For Selina, the emotional investment in her children—her love for Wickliffe, her guidance of Alexander, Jr., and William—did not guarantee that they would respond. Despite her best efforts, her children often rejected her advice and pursued their own desires. Her concern for her offspring, like that of many other mothers, remained strong throughout her entire life. And she never neglected her role in teaching her children about the Gospel and its promises for their lives. Alexander Campbell wrote about the crucial importance of a mother. Yet even his own wife, who shared his belief that her influence was powerful and who prayed continuously for her children, was deeply chagrined at their lack of devotion to the faith of their parents. Though motherhood had great potential for women, it did not always bring them joy and fulfillment. The close relationships between a mother and her child were central to most women, but their frequent, abrupt disruption could represent a deep trial in a woman's life. Though her "abiding interest and love" for her children was often a source of joy for Selina, the rewards for the sacred responsibility of motherhood were not always realized in her life on earth.

The second Mrs. Alexander Campbell reached maturity in a society whose understanding of motherhood had recently shifted in ways that reflected new concepts of domesticity. This shift was shaped by events that fundamentally altered the social and economic landscape of the United States. Ruth Bloch describes the changes as prompting a move from an eighteenth-century view, which deemphasized mothers generally, to the Victorian image, which exalted the maternal ideal and regarded mothers as exerting a seminal influence on the direction taken by society.[42] But other factors were also promoting change in the American social landscape.

Driving such developments was a shift in the locus of wage employment, which impacted the family and domesticity in several ways. Prior to the Revolutionary War, the family generally worked as a unit in a farm-centered household. As new industries grew that depended on wage labor, however, many fathers abandoned the farm for the factory. Mary Ryan has suggested that this development served to make households less patriarchal and contributed to a new domestic ideology that reinforced the influence of women in daily household affairs.[43] With the male authority figure largely removed from the household, women found new opportunities for active leadership of the family reflected in Selina Campbell's pivotal role in her home.

The transition created two different worlds in which the two different genders were expected to live and rule. The world of women was based on domesticity—caring for the home and its interests. The post-revolutionary Republic, with its emphasis on each man's role in governing the country, contributed to a new public sphere (separate from the home), in which men would be active participants. They worked for money by clerking, manufacturing, and producing goods for sale. Women ruled over the home, the private arena of each individual family, where their labors centered on household chores without remuneration.

The two worlds engendered different values, goals, and ethics. The male world of competition required less emotion and interpersonal cooperation; the female world, in contrast, remained largely outside the competitive marketplace and centered on forging close interpersonal relationships based on affection and love.[44]

Several factors enhanced the maturation of the role of motherhood in this environment. First, the new republic needed educated, virtuous citizens to perform their civic duties, including voting and serving on juries, for political leaders such as Thomas Jefferson realized that unreliable citizens would threaten the integrity of a fledgling democracy. To create good American citizens, mothers had to raise their children to be competent participants in a new nation. Whereas women had previously been regarded by many clergymen as irrational, unduly sensitive, and therefore easily discounted, women's emotional, nurturing nature was now viewed as suiting them for the new role: "No longer grounds for disparagement, the supposedly natural susceptibility of women to the dictates of 'the heart' now grew to be considered as the foundation of their superior virtue."[45] Those concerned with the advancement of women looked not to sexual equality to improve women's status but to this new arena of virtuous dominance for power. Rather than seeking parity with men in the public sphere, women maintained their power and influence in the domestic arena, where their emotional and spiritual nature seemed natural and appropriate.[46]

The perception of women in the home as more sensitive and caring than men formed the second reason why the role of mother blossomed into a powerful ideal in the early nineteenth century. The revivals of the immediate postrevolutionary era stimulated respect for the worth of piety and righteousness and also contributed to a longing to preserve traditional values, which became associated with true morality. The new industrial world and its focus on aggressive self-interest expected men to compete with each other in the public arena to produce material goods for sale and consumption. Such competition contradicted revivalist Protestant values, which focused more on the small town as the ideal of a community of cooperating believers. The home, staffed by women and free from the corrupted industrial world, remained separate from the men's world and therefore preserved the supposedly "traditional" ideal. In this way the separate spheres ideology was born. Motherhood was the linchpin of this ideology and provided for the inculcation of private, traditional values removed from the corruption of the public domain.

Although theological issues ordinarily assumed prominence among Disciples adherents, church people remained a part of the culture and reflected many of the national concerns of the early republic. The Disciples' emphasis on motherhood often resonated with the events surrounding them. The literature of the Disciples of Christ reveals more specifically how various issues shaped the environment in which Selina Campbell acted. In many ways the Disciples reflected the values of the culture as a whole, for example in their view that women were responsible for children's education as part of their duties at home. But the life of Selina Campbell further demonstrates that motherhood played a vital role in Disciples ideology and constituted the major contribution that women were expected to make to church culture. The instruction of children assumed a pivotal position in the church's development: "Without this school no system will ever meet the expectations of the world, the predictions of the Prophets, or qualify human beings for the high destiny, spiritual and eternal, which awaits them who walk in the paths of wisdom and virtue," wrote Alexander Campbell.[47] In a church that required each soul to choose between the Gospel of salvation and eternal punishment, the home was the crucible for salvation. Women gained great stature as mothers and consequently the head of the home: "Upon them depend the earliest education and first impressions of their children," wrote one Disciple. "They regulate or materially influence the principles, opinions, and manners of their husbands and their sons. Thus the sound and healthful society depend on them."[48] Such emphasis on the home as the center of values was consistent with many Americans' view of the importance of counteracting the evil of "the world." If parents instructed their children properly, then they did not have to fear that the children would fall away when they entered the "kingdom of the enemy." Thus motherhood became an important part of the evangelistic efforts of a dynamic movement within American religion and offered women true status within the church.

Selina Campbell may have made her most lasting contribution through her daughters. In addition to all of her comments on the proper public role for women and the importance of studying Scripture, she instructed her daughters on the proper character of a woman in her home. On this occasion she could pass on to her children her understanding of the opportunities available to women for service and salvation. Her views on the proper role of women appear most clearly in the advice she offered her eldest daughter after the young girl left the family's home to go to school. In 1843, Margaret Brown Campbell, Selina's eldest child and barely fifteen years old, enrolled in P. S. Fall's Seminary in Kentucky. Like many parents, the mother agonized over the absence of her eldest child. She probably feared the influences that might enter her daughter's life or worried that harm might come to her so far from the bosom of her family. Most of all, Selina apparently missed constantly expressing her love for her daughter and her pride in Margaret's accomplishments. "When I think of our long separation & you so very young," Selina wrote in a letter to Margaret, "I find a kind of overflowing Love, come over me & desire to give scope to my feelings & tell you, how much I love you, & the pleasure I have in thinking, that you have ever been a dutiful & an affectionate daughter."[49]

Separated from her daughter by so many miles, Selina found that her influence on the child had necessarily become less direct. But she openly expressed her love and concern by offering a mother's wisdom through her regular letters. One letter in March of 1843 reflected this practice. Selina's advice to her daughter began with the topic closest to her heart: "I . . . hope, sincerely hope, you will persevere in doing well & ever seek the approbation & love of the Wise, & good, & *unceasing desire* to enjoy the love & approbation of your Gracious & Adorable Heavenly Father." Selina accepted the same mission with each one of her children, and it continued even after they left her home. The mother further reminded Margaret that, though young, she had thus far ably demonstrated her "love of *Truth*" and her "affectionate disposition."

But Selina did not wish her daughter to rest on her laurels. Building a strong character required constant attention. She entreated her daughter to continue in her efforts to keep the love of truth and her affectionate disposition "still more deeply embedded in your nature & practiced in your every day intercourse with your fellow beings." And in a warning against overemphasizing her studies, Selina told Margaret she should "let no literary or intelectual [*sic*] attainments eclipse the nobler feelings of the soul." This was especially crucial for a woman because "no acquirements of art . . . no Embellishments, whatever, or however, desirable they may be can never supply the deficiencies in *Woman* of an amicable sympathizing *affectionate Truth loving* & *Truth telling* disposition." Thus Selina reached the essence of her communication with her daughter. Though the mother valued the education she had pursued and the one now available to her daughter, she also believed that learning could never be more important than a woman's character and example in the home. Writing eloquently to her daughter about the significance of avoiding "the semblance of *vanity* or *affectation* which can cast a shade over your behavior," she suggested that, instead, a woman's actions should be "*plain, simple, modest & unaffected practicing true* Politeness." More than just adopting a polite and simple disposition, a woman should cultivate her spiritual nature as well. She should weigh her decisions "on the principles which the Bible teaches that of making our happiness consist in denying ourselves, & seeking to promote [the] happiness and welfare of others."[50] This was the sacrifice that Selina had willingly made for her family. She urged her daughter to do the same.

Selina also warned her daughter of the dangers of developing habits unacceptable for a woman. "Ever study, my child, to avoid all selfishness, no one can be an acceptable companion who possesses it—it is less excusable in woman than in man, to be selfish. It is expected of her to make all around her happy, in order to do this, she must lose sight of herself & be wholly absorbed in the good of others."[51] A woman's life was one of service—a quality modeled by the instigator of their faith, Jesus Christ. Thus, while the encouragement that women received to sacrifice themselves for others often diminished their individuality, in a culture based on faith and service to others it often drew the highest praise. Selina's advice to her daughter revealed many of her ideas regarding the role of women in the home and reflects her own marriage and the literature she consumed.

Her teachings seem to have taken root with her daughters. Decima married John Judson Barclay, a son of the first Disciples missionaries. The two were fully committed to the spread of the Gospel. Judson, as he was known, also edited a religious journal for several years.[52] Decima and her husband were dedicated Christians all their lives and opened their home to Selina in northern central Alabama during her widowhood. Emma also married a Barclay and was an active Christian throughout her life. Thus, in two of her daughters and her niece, the mother could feel that she had had some success in her mission to educate her children in salvation.

4

"Usefulness in a Wilderness"

Early in the morning of March 12, 1862, Selina climbed the stairs of Bethany Mansion to the second floor with more than her usual haste. She quickly entered one of the bedrooms, awakened her daughter Virginia and her niece Emma, and told them that this was "the anniversary of the first wedding day of my dear husband, fifty years ago." She was referring to Alexander's marriage to Margaret Brown. The girls' eyes widened with awe at the momentous occasion. Throughout their marriage, Selina's husband, if away from home when the time came, would often write a letter to her on that day to remind her that this was the anniversary of his first marriage. In the 1839 letter, he also told her that he had found her "worthy of all the affection and esteem which were due to her who designed to bless both you and me by nominating you to be her successor."[1] But the day was often celebrated by the entire family in honor of the life of Margaret Brown Campbell. It was a time to recall a woman whose life had touched many hearts, and Selina, too, participated in the formal remembrance of her friend's life. In 1862, while many had urged Selina to plan a golden anniversary party, others pointed out that her own thirty-third anniversary was the following July, so that a silver anniversary would be appropriate.[2]

Alexander had often been away from home on the anniversary of his first marriage, but because his health was precarious, the seventy-four-year-old evangelist was at home in 1862. Virginia and Emma hastily planned a fitting celebration of the golden anniversary of his first marriage. Guests were invited, and preparations were quickly made. "The evening was propitious for their coming together," Selina later wrote, "and as they had been invited with reference to the eventful day, all assembled with a cheerful, good heart, and many were the pleasant sayings and congratulations."[3] The event marked the beginning of many changes for Selina that would culminate in a new life for her—a life in which domesticity would no longer dominate her actions, in which she would choose many new activities that more fully reflected her varied interests.

The evening of the fiftieth anniversary party involved several activities including a formal supper, but the most important was an informal ceremony that was called "the transfer of affection." Selina described the memorable scene:

> A short time . . . previous to the supper, my daughter Virginia informed me "that I was to go into the parlor, and seat myself in a certain place, that father was going to make me a present, a *golden present.*" So in I went and seated myself, according to a concerted plan made by my daughter and Sister Pendleton. I had been seated but a short time when my dear husband arose, and in a grave, but happy manner, approached towards me. I arose to meet him. All eyes were upon *him,* when, in a style most dignified and gracious, he presented me with a ring: at the same time sealing the presentation with a loving kiss. . . . The whole was intended as a continuation and a transfer of that connubial attachment from the first to the then present time. As Mr. Campbell had often been heard to remark, "that it was a transfer of his affections entire from his first to his second wife."[4]

The ring that Selina received was fashioned from a lock of Mr. Campbell's hair "with twisted gold over the space in which the hair lay."[5] It symbolized the deep love of a husband for his wife. Though it may seem strange that Campbell waited until the thirty-third year of his second marriage to honor his wife in such a way, the lapse of time in no way showed a lack of esteem for Selina, nor was the 1862 ceremony the first time he ever honored his second wife. Rather, significant changes taking place within the Campbell family found expression in this special event.

The changes began with the aging preacher's severe illnesses, which seemed to follow one upon the other, starting before the beginning of the Civil War. Alexander's years of traveling and preaching ended with the deterioration of his health, and he returned home to a new relationship with his devoted wife. He spent the twilight of his life at his mansion in Bethany, where he received visitors and spent hours in the company of his life's partner. The "transfer of affection" commemorated by the fiftieth anniversary party crowned the long marriage of the couple and launched a new phase that had actually begun with Campbell's retirement from public life. But their life together took new meaning from this event. The family tutor, E. K. Washington, a respected teacher in his own right, described these years before Campbell's death in moving terms: "For some two or three years before his death the world heard less of him. His essays were less numerous in the Harbinger,—his labors in the pulpit more rare than before. Where was he now? He was at length restored to his family. The heart of his companion now claimed him as all her own, and he was permitted some years of rest— of sublime, beautiful and happy old age, 'ere his change come.' "[6] These years of rest were a special time for Alexander and his wife. Campbell never lost the respect of his followers, who admired him and gloried in his last few years, but at the same time the aged evangelist enjoyed every moment spent with his wife, to whom his devotion was now completely directed. Selina more than anyone rejoiced at the return of her husband to the home on a more permanent basis and welcomed the opportunity to take care of him.

With his retirement, Selina gave free rein to her concern about her husband's mental health and physical well-being. She hovered over him, fearful of any threat to his health. His memory of dates and places failed often during the last years, but Selina remained nearby to fill in any gaps. David Lipscomb, the prominent Nashville preacher and editor of the *Gospel Advocate,* publicly questioned Campbell's state of mind in 1849 and particularly attributed to senility his acceptance of the presidency of the Disciples' first missionary organization. When the American Christian Missionary Society formed in 1849 in Cincinnati, Campbell was chosen as its first president, an office he held until his death. Lipscomb and others objected to granting any authority to institutions outside the local church. Since the missionary society received funds from church members and made decisions on how they should be allocated, it especially warranted their censure. Selina rushed to defend her husband's connection to the society. She particularly objected to their derogatory comments about her husband's mental faculties in 1849 and penned her own written vindication of her husband's soundness of mind in 1887. "I feel it to be my imperative duty to make statements (that can be proven and substantiated) to the contrary. . . . In regard to my husband's failures of mind and memory, . . . the statements in the Gospel Advocate are *incorrect*. I admit that his extensive labors, had bourn [*sic*] upon him and for a length of time his memory had failed, but . . . *not* at the time spoken of by the Editor of the Advocate." She then included several statements from her husband's speeches and essays after that period and up to his death that testified to his mental ability. Many of these public utterances had previously been praised by Lipscomb. Unfortunately, her defense did not end the rumors; as long as the debate remained alive within the Stone-Campbell movement about the desirability of missionary societies, so did the controversial nature of Campbell's support for them.[7]

Though Selina remained concerned about Alexander's welfare, in 1863 she did acquiesce to her husband's request to address students at Bethany College occasionally and often sent for a chair to convey him to the Bethany Church so that he could preach. But when he expressed his desire to take up responsibility for lecturing on a regular basis again, she convinced him that "it was too much for him to undertake now that the winter is setting in." She suggested instead that he could speak on an occasional basis instead and no one would be offended.[8] Perhaps the approaching weather conditions were a convenient device that obviated the need for more adamant objections, but whatever her reason, Selina urged her husband to ease his labors in any way she could. Campbell traveled only rarely now, and when he did, his wife nearly always accompanied him. The two settled into a quiet life on the Bethany farm, where they lived until his death. Now that Alexander Campbell had retired, he led the life he had formerly given up to serve his Lord.

Late in Alexander's life, in the midst of the Civil War, the Campbell family celebrated the marriages of both of Selina's surviving daughters. Soon after her marriage to J. Judson Barclay in 1863, Decima accompanied her husband to Cyprus, where he was appointed U.S. consul. Virginia and her husband William Thompson settled in Louisville, Kentucky, after their marriage in 1861. The family had come full circle; the letters flowed into Bethany from the children to the parents rather than vice versa. Alexander delighted in receiving letters in which his children spoke of their adventures abroad or in another area of the country. Alexander, Jr., had married into a Louisiana family and spent much of his time in that state, while William studied to be an attorney in Louisville, Kentucky, with his sister. Campbell was known for his Union sympathies, but with Alex fighting as a colonel in the Confederacy and his wife living on their plantation in Louisiana, the conflict was rarely discussed in their home.

Death was not long in coming for Alexander Campbell. In February 1866, a serious illness confined him to his bed. His lungs were congested, and his breathing became labored. The entire household plunged into taking care of him. Occupants of the mansion at the time of his death included Mary Anna Purvis Campbell (the wife of Alexander, Jr.), Emma Bakewell, William Campbell, and Judson and Decima Barclay. At the request of William Pendleton, a son-in-law and replacement editor of the *Millennial Harbinger*, Mary Anna began keeping a diary on February 24, a week before Alexander's death, and records her observations of the events of those seven trying days. They become a "death narrative" documenting the important events of the final moments of a great man. While Mary Anna intended the journal only for her husband, Alexander, Jr., so that he could be a part of his father's last days even though responsibilities in Louisiana kept him away, the diary nevertheless stands as the most comprehensive record of the events surrounding Campbell's death. Her chronicle began with

Selina's sad comment that her husband's death would surely come soon and she must prepare for it. Alexander, Jr., aware of his father's dire condition, left for Bethany but did not arrive until the day after Campbell's passing.

Feeding and preparing medicine for the patient while caring for the entire household was a heavy burden that drained the energies of every member of the family. Overcome at the prospect of losing the beloved patriarch, Mary Anna saw to the preparation of Campbell's food and administered his medicine while Emma managed the housekeeping for the rest of the family. Judson often read to the patient speeches from Congress about the progress of Reconstruction, so that Campbell remained informed about important events right up to his last moments. Selina sat with him nearly every minute, afraid to leave him lest his condition worsen without warning. Concerned about her health, family members often forced her to sleep, change her clothes, and eat, but her sorrow sometimes made even the small things impossible. As her husband's illness worsened, so did Selina's anxiety.

Mary Anna's comments in her journal also offer insight into Selina's emotions and activities during her husband's illness. Many of these were most evident at her husband's bedside. Her sorrow at losing her husband affected her deeply, but she took heart in his buoyant attitude. Her husband viewed his death as the reunion with the Savior he had served his entire adult life. Throughout his illness, he remained particularly aware of his wife's grief and made every attempt to ease her mind. Once when Selina leaned over him to ask if he was in pain, he answered softly, "No, no only sorry for you, *sorry for you.*" His love for her remained ever present and obvious to those to who witnessed their final moments together. "Through the entire sickness," Mary Anna wrote on February 26, "he never forgets to say pleasant things to those around him & particularly to Mother. He misses her all the time when she is out of the room & last night when she came in from taking a nap he kissed her, kissed her hand & was so glad to have her beside him & said 'why Mother I was just about to advertise you to find out your whereabouts.'" Pendleton later wrote in the *Harbinger* that the last person to comfort Campbell before his death was his beloved wife, and she was also the one to whom his last intelligent words were directed. "When his voice had almost left him, and he was struggling for breath," Pendleton remembered, "his wife said to him, 'The blessed Savior will go with you through the valley of the shadow of death.' He looked earnestly into her face for a moment, and then, with a great effort, said emphatically—'That he will! That he will!' And this was about the last intelligent and pointed expression of his deathless confidence that we can now recall."[9]

Campbell's condition worsened early on March 2, 1866. Mary Anna awoke that morning to hear her mother-in-law calling her to the sickroom, sure that he could not last much longer. His breathing was so labored that they thought the end would be only hours in coming. The entire family gathered around, but Alexander improved enough after daylight on Saturday to play briefly with the children and kiss them before he again slept. Before his nap, he expressed his hope that Alexander, Jr., would arrive soon. By midnight that evening, however, his son had not yet come and Campbell's breathing had once again deteriorated. Too weak to cough, he struggled to breathe despite the congestion. Saturday, March 3, passed slowly in a dramatic bedside vigil. All who watched feared that each breath would be his last, and hours passed with little change. Selina stayed by his bedside, refusing to leave him alone lest he should die without her at his side.

Sunday morning, March 4, 1866, dawned clear but chilly, according to Mary Anna. The patient could consume only a few drops of tea and lukewarm water for nourishment. "His mind is gone now," Mary Anna wrote, "& he is now like one in a feverish prostration & perfectly insensible." To ease his mind, Selina read two chapters of Scripture to him but was saddened that "he could not value & think & talk about the precious things they contained as always before."[10] The wife now knew it was nearly time for the final goodbye. She probably wondered how she could accomplish it best. In the late morning, surprisingly, Alexander rallied enough to read Scripture to his family and friends for several minutes in a hoarse, weak voice. Still he lingered, but just before midnight several people crowded into the room to hear his few final breaths. Then Alexander Campbell died peacefully on the Sabbath he loved so well.

Mourning began immediately. Notices of the beloved preacher's death were sent far and wide. Little is recorded about Selina's activities in these last few hours of her married life and during the next several months apart from notice of her profound grief. Her life did not regain a semblance of normality for some time.

Alexander, Jr., arrived the day after his father's death. In February he had written of rumors flying around the country that Campbell had already died, but he waited to hear the news from his family first. When the death did come, all shared in the sorrow, but Selina's life changed the most profoundly. While the children lost their father and mentor, she lost her partner, the man with whom she had spent nearly every minute for almost ten years and whose life she had shared for nearly four decades. With her children now grown and caring for families of their own, Selina's activities changed drastically in the transition to widowhood. But even after the transition, many things remained the same. Her faith remained the center of her life and her domestic role continued to be significant. These two elements provided continuity in Selina Campbell's life.

The bedside vigil illustrates the great burden that Selina often assumed in her marriage. Her decision to serve her husband's domestic needs demanded significant labor and attention. While he lay ill in the sickroom, she oversaw the preparation of his food, read to him to soothe his pain, and at times went without food and rest to care for him. The domestic role absorbed so much of her time and energy that she had little left to care for herself. This is the somber side of the separate spheres observed by Leonard Sweet and others.[11] It is the challenge that many women faced in ministering to their families while striving to care for themselves as well.

After Alexander's death Selina's role in her husband's life and career received significant attention. E. K. Washington's comments in his tribute to Campbell are an important example. A tutor to the Campbell children, Washington gained a deep respect for the role of Mrs. Campbell in her husband's career. After Alexander Campbell's death he observed, "There have not been wanting numerous and able eulogies on him. The heart of the brothers has been deeply touched, and it has sent forth throbs of agony for the great loss." But he was "astonished" that "certain notices of his life" appear "in which all allusion to the companion, help-mate and partner of his bosom for thirty-seven years, has been omitted, and we are constrained to say, that could he now from his glorious home in heaven look once more on the scene of his labors, he would say he could NOT have been what he was but for *her.*"[12] These powerful statements are some of the first public comments on Selina's contributions to the cause she shared with her husband. Acknowledgment of her achievements appeared in several other articles scattered among the papers of the brotherhood of churches. These articles show that Alexander Campbell was not alone in understanding the significance of his wife's contribution. They also told Campbell's followers of the family's importance in his ministry and spoke of the respect that Selina had received from the associates of her husband.

There was also recognition of another, more sympathetic kind. As with many other widows of admired prominent figures, church members approached Selina with heartfelt sympathy. They all deeply mourned the loss of Alexander Campbell's leadership, and conferred on his widow some of his stature. Tributes flowed into Bethany Mansion from all over the world, expressing the great sorrow of thousands. Selina responded warmly to their sympathy. "No language at my command could adequately convey to you the high regard and warm appreciation, I place upon the consoling words of sympathy and remembrance, you have so kindly and considerately addressed to me," she wrote in the *Millennial Harbinger* and then affirmed her unwavering confidence that she would some day be with her husband again.[13] At the time of Alexander's death she thought the separation would be brief, since she assumed that she had only a few more years to live. No one could have predicted that she would live thirty-one years after her husband.

Even with an increase in the burdens of domesticity after the death of her husband, the thirty-one years of Selina's widowhood presented her with a new frontier. She lived quite independently after the death of her husband, her activities regulated more by her own interests than by her duty to her family. This phase in Selina Campbell's life is especially informative because it demonstrates so much about her own thoughts and the facets of her new personality. Though she gloried in her duties as a wife and mother, she now found great satisfaction in pursuing a writing career, visiting her grandchildren, and developing her reading habits. But as much as her activities as a widow represented a departure in her life, they also evinced significant continuity. Her love for her children persisted, and her attachment to her home also remained. She nursed her sick grandchildren using the knowledge she gained from her own study as well as many treatments she developed on her own.

Although her freedom expanded as more of her time became her own, so did her vulnerability to circumstances, especially financial troubles, which threatened her and her family. With her husband's death, the income of the Bethany farm dropped precipitously as his assets were spread among his heirs. Preserving the mansion and her husband's memory consumed much of Selina's time. Providing for her children and the causes to which she was devoted further drained her resources. In all, the new freedoms and opportunities of widowhood presented a great many challenges for Selina, but at the same time they drew her more deeply into the faith she shared with her husband.

Much as Alexander Campbell had enjoyed his retirement from public life because it allowed him to reunite with his family, Selina welcomed widowhood as a kind of domestic "retirement." Now she could pursue interests she had previously sacrificed. While she was grateful for the new opportunities of widowhood, she did not regret at all the years of service to her family. Rather, her final years gave her a special time after her years of domestic devotion had ended.

But Selina Campbell's commitment to service did not end entirely with the death of her husband. She spoke often of maintaining her usefulness. Although the concept of a "useful life" had arisen frequently during the years of her marriage, it became a favorite topic of her writings as a widow. She shared this concern with many other women. While men most often measured their usefulness in economic terms, for nineteenth-century women the concept translated into a focus on moral and spiritual activity.[14] Guarding the home from the forces threatening to undermine its centrality, such as urbanization and its companion challenges of poverty and religious diversity, demanded their full attention. Other women emphasized these moral and spiritual challenges, but like Selina, they also faced significant challenges in economic matters. Yet she always affirmed that it was her "privilege to work" before she joined her husband in Heaven; she was happy to meet the challenges as they came.[15]

For Selina, one of the greatest challenges concerned her husband's will.[16] The estate granted to him by John Brown early in his first marriage had prospered under his care and left the family quite wealthy. This estate was augmented by other interests such as the hymnbook published by Campbell in 1835, which went through several editions. Though Bethany College consumed much of the family resources, it did not deplete the whole, and some of the money was repaid. At his death Campbell's fortune remained significant, approximating $275,000. In the will, which he wrote himself and signed on March 11, 1862, he left legacies ranging from $1,000 to $3,000 to the grandchildren of his first marriage. The remainder of his estate went to Selina and their four surviving children. Alexander, Jr., received two tracts of land totaling nearly 200 acres in addition to the 270-acre Bryant farm he had already received. To William was willed the homestead farm (excepting the mansion, of which his mother would have the use for the remainder of her life) and an adjacent tract of land. The provisions of the will generally favored Campbell's second family over the first. Rumbles of discontent from Margaret Brown's grandchildren surfaced immediately. The will entered the public record June 26, 1866, and the named executors included Alexander Campbell, Jr., and William R. Thompson (Virginia's husband) with court-approved sureties George Miller, Lewis Applegate, J. E. Curtis, W. P. Campbell (Selina's youngest son), J. Judson Barclay, and Thomas Everett. Since a challenge was expected, testimony of the subscribing witnesses was included with the original filing. But this testimony would not be enough.

Two of the main instigators of the challenge to the will were Robert Y. Henly, the surviving husband of Maria Louisa (the second daughter of Margaret Brown Campbell), and his cousin by marriage James H. Pendleton. Henly in particular remained a thorn in Selina's side for many years, with his constant claims—even five years after Alexander's death—that Campbell had owed him money. Apparently Alexander Campbell had feared that the family from his first marriage would attempt to make large claims on his estate, so in 1864 he added a codicil to his will tying the cash bequests left to them to their relinquishment of all future claims on his estate. He basically distributed among the heirs of his first family $14,000, estimated to be the original value of the estate that John Brown had left to him. The rest of the income Campbell himself had gained for his second family, and this he left to Selina and the children.[17]

Henly and Pendleton quickly charged that Campbell's mind in the later years of his life had failed, leaving him open to undue influence, and the will was thus invalid. Pendleton charged that in the codicil of the will "the hand & the Language of the lawyer [William Thompson] is patent"—evidence that Thompson had improperly influenced over the aged man. Though the codicil was "in Mr. C's handwriting," he was "made to copy it of course," Pendleton claimed. He was suspicious of the fact that the codicil came soon after Virginia's marriage to Thompson. If the codicil were set aside, an additional $50,000 would apparently come to Pendleton and Henly. Pendleton also spoke of testimony anticipated from Mrs. McKeever that Campbell could not even recognize his sister during one visit in the mid-1860s. Evidently no one from the family would speak to him about the matter as the case came to trial. He affirmed his belief in the ability of Alexander, Jr., to act rightly, but he mistrusted the control that Selina and Virginia exerted over him. He believed that they might have convinced Campbell's eldest son "that their honor & (I add) their work require his defence [*sic*]," indicating that they wished to retain the money of the estate against the claims of the other descendants.[18]

Within a few months of widowhood, Selina moved to Kentucky to stay with her daughter Virginia and her son William. During her visit, Virginia gave birth to Selina Huntington Thompson. She was some time in recovering. By July 1866 the trial over the validity of the will was under way. It would last for nearly two years. Returning to Bethany after several months, Selina was wounded by all of the accusations surrounding her husband and his mental state. There is no conclusive evidence on the condition of Campbell's mind when he made out his will and the attached codicil. Some of his associates, such as the prominent preacher and editor David Lipscomb, had expressed doubts about Campbell's faculties.[19] But Selina maintained her belief that while he had both good days and bad days, he was fundamentally of sound mind. In January 1867 back at Bethany, Selina received "*some* 12 or 14 interrogatories" that she believed "contrary to the law." Decima was copying them to be sent to Mr. Thompson for his advice on whether a public response was required. Selina felt that her husband's grandchildren "are going to try & wring out the patience to bring to a compromise."[20] She quickly acted to prevent this from happening.

Alexander, Jr., visited Judge Jeremiah Black and former Union general James Garfield about representing the family in the case. The two had already agreed to act on the family's behalf, and the issues were discussed. Selina meanwhile attested to her innocence of the charges made by her stepchildren's heirs and reiterated her faith that all would work as God intended. "I trust in the Lord who will ajust [*sic*] all things aright," she told Virginia. "I feel so Confident that I *never* influenced to wrong that I cannot for a moment feel unhappy." Indeed she believed, in speaking of the heirs from the first marriage, "it was *their* own doings for years that caused their Grandfather to draw in his generosity if he did." She also quoted W. K. Pendleton, who had advised Campbell that if he did not make his grandchildren equal with his children in the will, the grandchildren would challenge it. "This was a threatening that *did* not sit well upon the magnanimous spirit of the departed man of God," his wife declared, and so Alexander Campbell had taken no action to rectify the supposed imbalance.[21]

The arbitration of the will took place in Brooke County Court during February 1868. For ten days witnesses testified, and "the circumstances surrounding the making of the will were fully ventilated." The courthouse was packed with spectators anxious to see the outcome of the challenge to the will of the area's most prominent man. W. H.

Lowrie and W. J. Robertson were the two arbitrators who assumed responsibility for deciding the will's validity. Garfield remained as attorney for the Campbell family through the entire process, while Judge Black had to resign after the second day of the trial because of other commitments. At least eight attorneys advised the two sides in the dispute and were present at the trial. According to the terms of the arbitration agreement reached several months earlier, the two families were to split all court costs. On February 28, the arbitrators reached their decision. They concluded that the original will and its provisions were valid (including the codicil) and that the will should be filed as originally written.[22] The long ordeal had come to an end.

For Selina, the months preceding the trial prompted great misgivings amid growing responsibilities at Bethany. The notorious court case exposed her to the speculations of a number of people. In February 1867 she wrote to William of her anxieties. "The return of the season that your dear father took his last illness (just this week) and the near approach of the anniversary of his death has a most peculiarly heart saddening effect. . . . Add to that all that is now unfolding—the deep dark shadow that ungodly men are endeavoring to cast upon the beloved memory of your honored godly father, you can in a small degree imagine the deep waters of affliction through which your mother is passing." Even with the end of the trial, Selina still faced the challenge of maintaining the mansion without her husband. She spent the winter of 1867–1868 visiting Decima and her family before returning to her home. Judson had recently purchased a farm just east of Huntsville, Alabama, which became known as Ingleside Plantation. He and Decima lived only a few miles from Robert and Emma, who had also purchased a large farm. While in Alabama, Selina especially enjoyed deepening her relationships with her grandchildren. Before she returned to Bethany, she also met a young woman who agreed to come and work for her to help take care of the mansion. This woman was probably Pleasants (the only name by which she was ever addressed), a servant who remained in Selina's employ for several years during the 1860s and 1870s.[23]

The pair returned to Bethany in mid-February 1868. Selina once

again took up the tasks of preserving her home. The previous year
Emma, her niece, had married and moved out, further increasing Selina's
burdens. Selina was now charged with the tasks that Emma had formerly performed. The commencement season for Bethany College also
meant arduous labor for Selina. The mansion housed at least a dozen
guests in town for the event. The beds needed to be made, the food
prepared, and the yard cleaned—and these were only a few of the necessary tasks. "My time is occupied with duties I can not avoid," Selina
admitted to William during her preparations for the event.[24] After the
commencement, Selina wrote Alexander that she wanted to shut up the
house. Though she wished to leave, she feared abandoning her home
for the winter with only the "colored servants" to care for it. She worried that they were too careless and heedless of the risk of fire. In a
letter to William, she does not mention the specifics of her uneven relationship with many of her black servants but speaks openly about her
low estimation of their character. Selina was not unaffected by the prevailing notions of race in the age in which she lived, but she did strive
to be fair to those in her employ. Though she never fully trusted her
servants, she did nonetheless always provide for their education and retirement.

To relieve his mother's burdens, Alexander hired John Dowdell and
his mother, local white residents, to care for the grounds, the house,
and the farm animals for the winter while Selina wintered with Decima
in Alabama. Unfortunately, Dowdell died on the very day when he was
to begin work, July 20, 1868, and Selina was forced to postpone her
departure for Alabama. She never recorded what arrangements were
made in the end. Probably either William or Alexander agreed to keep
an eye on the mansion, for she did eventually arrive at Decima's plantation.

Although Selina was eventually forced to leave her home and to live
with her children, she thought often of the mansion during the next
twenty years. Selina undoubtedly felt bound to the house by her happy
memories of events that had taken place within its walls. During her
marriage, she was so fearful of fire that she refused to allow her husband to insure the mansion.[25] Even as a widow, she expressed concerns

for it, frequently reminding William (who lived there briefly one winter in his mother's absence) to beware of certain fire dangers. During one of her early absences from Bethany, she admitted that while she had "everything to comfort" her in Alabama with Decima, and at other times in Kentucky with Virginia, she still longed "to visit 'The Mouldering Urn' again." She especially missed the spot where she "spent so many blessed days in the society of one so pure, so excellent, so devoted to the worship of God." Her memories of her husband were always bound up in the home they shared. There was to her a "sanctity" about the Bethany Mansion and its "holy atmosphere" that she could find nowhere else.[26] Though she enjoyed watching her grandchildren grow, being away from the home where she had lived so happily for almost forty years was difficult.

In 1871, two years after she was forced to reduce her time at her old home to a few weeks each year, she openly acknowledged that the mansion was too much for her to care for on her own. Still she deeply regretted being away from it. Even the summers she often spent there exhausted her, so she eventually resigned herself to the continued absence from her home. But as the years passed, she began to wish that she might return to her home for her final days. "I do long to be back in my home again," she told Nannie, William's wife, in 1876. "I feel as though I could not die so contently anywhere else. I have felt almost superstitious about it. My dear husband expressed the wish I should *live there*."[27]

Her devotion to her children escalated when she became a widow. Presumably the loss of her husband's companionship caused her to rely on her children even more for love and affection. She was often dismayed when she received no letters, and her anxiety grew when it seemed that any of her own letters might not be reaching them, for "it is a great comfort to write & receive letters," she told William. The widow also valued the letters to her friends, and they too seemed to increase after her husband's death. "I have many letters to write to friends from whom I have received them," she told William in 1869. But even with her new freedom from the responsibilities of caring for her family, she struggled to find the time to correspond with her friends.

"I have been trying to keep pace with my correspondents for I do not like to keep any in suspense but really I am almost despairing of being able to clear the docet [*sic*] as we say."[28] The freedom of widowhood had also brought an interest in renewing ties with the friends on whom she had often relied for comfort and companionship. But her time remained filled with activity of many kinds, and as the months passed, the chores necessary to keep Bethany Mansion in good shape lost some of their meaning and became more like drudgery, especially with the loss of a family to care for. They also interfered with her correspondence with friends and family.

While Selina enjoyed preparing for and receiving the visits of her friends to the mansion, she more often expressed her desire for her children to visit. In late 1869 she asked William to help her persuade the ailing Virginia to come with her family for a visit so that she could care for her. "I shall be too happy to be like good Old Naomi who was nurse to her daughter-in-laws [*sic*]," she confided. "I shall be still happier to be nurse to my *dear* daughter." The grandmother also attested to her competency as a babysitter to her grandchildren. "I will not go to sleep or let *baby* fall and I can get up at any hour of the night to tend to it," she promised.[29] Her great desire to remain involved with her children's lives continued through all of her years—a testament to the continuing importance of domesticity in her life.

Selina Campbell played other significant roles as a widow. She had already proved her nursing skills several months prior to Virginia's illness when she tended Decima's eldest daughter Virginia Huntington Barclay, born in 1866. Selina seemed especially taken with little "Virgie" and did some quick thinking when the child suddenly fell ill in late 1868. Selina dramatically and lovingly told the story of Virgie's illness in a letter to William. Apparently one of Decima's servants, Josephine, accidentally left a bowl of poisonous cherries within the toddler's reach. When Selina arrived on the scene, Virgie had consumed a number of the cherries and "was on her mothers lap *insensible*." The child had already vomited some of the "fowl berries," but "her teeth were *set* & foaming at the mouth." Selina feared what would happen if she did not act quickly. "Her father came & we gave her to him to hold whilst I called for *Mustard* & *hot water.*" The treatment that followed was apparently recommended by Selina. "We pried her teeth open and her father succeeded in holding her mouth open whilst I poured in the mustard water. I then gave her one teaspoon full of Lobelia diluted with water—all of which made her vomit several times." Selina also "had her feet bathed in hot water to keep up the circulation" and "put a mustard plaster upon her stomach . . . ancles [*sic*] and wrists." Within an hour Virgie recovered enough "to open her eyes & . . . speak . . . saying 'I am sick.'"[30] The crisis passed, and the members of the family slowly returned to their normal lives, shaken but grateful. Selina expressed her great anxiety at the close call. "There was danger of convulsions as well as the poisonous nature of the berries. I thought at one time we should not be able to get her teeth open again," she recorded in her letter to William. So many things could have happened to take the child's life; it was viewed as something of a miracle that she survived. Selina attributed the success of their efforts to cure the child to the Father who "had mercy on us & restored her to consciousness & life again!"[31] It was to Him that she went to offer thanks as she did throughout most of her life.

The grandmother had occasion to demonstrate her nursing skills again and again. Her knowledge of medicine and treatments was probably gained from years of caring for sick children and servants, for she mentions no source other than treatments suggested in newspapers. Selina played this role during the years she lived with her children. Decima once experienced a serious illness after childbirth that required Selina's serious attention. In December 1875, she walked "to the far side of the peach orchard to gather Mulle[i]n leaves to boil in water to scatter the inflamation [*sic*]"—the last remedy she knew that might ease Decima's symptoms.[32] Her treatment appears eventually to have succeeded.

In 1875 she reached her limits. Little "Virgie" had contracted another serious illness. Selina had grown especially close to those of Decima's children with whom she spent the most time, and Virginia, who was born in Cyprus, was a special favorite with her grandmother. She first entered the United States as a toddler just before the death of her maternal grandfather. The sickly Virgie received a good deal of her grandmother's special attention, especially after the incident with the cherries. In 1869 Virgie's grandmother requested Decima's permission to take the little girl to Bethany for a few weeks before the arrival of the girl's parents. Decima did not wish to be separated from her daughter for so long, but she eventually yielded to her mother's pleas. Selina greatly enjoyed spending time with her young granddaughter.

Selina's fondness for Virgie probably stemmed at least partly from the child's resemblance to her aunt Margaret. The grandmother's concern for the child became even more obvious when a serious illness left Virgie severely crippled at the age of six. Little description of the illness itself appears in the family letters, Selina identified it as a "Spinal disease" (perhaps a version of polio) that seemed to attack the muscles of Virgie's arms and legs, interfering with her ability to walk and requiring severe treatments. Selina described some of the lasting effects of the illness in detail.

Decima also lay ill during most of her daughter's illness, slowly recovering from a difficult childbirth. It taxed her energies greatly to care for Virgie after the crisis had passed. Selina's heart nearly broke observing the situation, and she poured out her sorrow in another letter to William. "I wish you could see the process that the Mother of the little *afflicted child has* to *go through every day* in dressing & undressing her," she wrote of Decima's distress. "I had not (nor anyone else) the slightest idea of the time & care it takes to keep from hurting in placing the steele [*sic*] brace on the Neck and tighting [*sic*] the Jacket and screwing the chin cup upon the dear child—and she is so patient & can direct where & how to fix it to be comfortable." Her grandmother's heart went out to the young child who suffered so much at such a tender age and to the weakened mother who labored to care for her. The bonds which developed between Virgie and Selina, who often cared for her in her mother's absence, lasted a lifetime. The family letters say more about Selina's relationship with Virgie than about any relationship Selina sustained with her other grandchildren.

Selina often remarked that Virgie's illness did not dim the child's radiant personality. From all accounts, the girl was the light of the home in which she lived. Even though often bedridden, she still sang hymns and remained "cheerful and happy." Moreover, even in the midst of significant pain and discomfort, the six-year-old remained "bright, lovely and interesting," her grandmother attested. And just as with her own children, Selina taught her grandchildren the importance of faith in their lives on earth and in their eternal destiny. As she went about her daily chores, the grandmother often told her precious grandchildren stories from the Bible. Virgie especially delighted in hearing "the history of the Saviour how he was carried into Egypt" and how King Herod had eventually died and worms ate his body. The exchanges between Virgie and Selina over stories from the Bible hint at their growing intimacy. Selina especially enjoyed having her granddaughter sleep with her while her mother tended the little baby brother. To a sick child, the soft voice of such a loving grandmother must have soothed many a hurt. And Selina treasured the opportunity to "tell [her] about the Saviour."[33]

Her love for Virgie prompted Selina to search diligently for a cure for her condition. At first she hoped Robert Barclay, the child's uncle, could offer a solution, but he proved unable to do so. Selina then vowed to seek an institution that could help, no matter what the cost. She promised to use all of her resources, especially while Virgie was still young, to cure her; she would consider the money well spent no matter the outcome. Immediately she began writing to infirmaries seeking information on available treatments. Unfortunately, there is no record of what became of all Selina's efforts on her granddaughter's behalf. Perhaps she was successful in her quest for a cure, because Virgie did survive to attend Hamilton Female College in Lexington, Kentucky. Later, in June 1882, the young woman arrived at Bethany to attend her cousin Mary Campbell's graduation from Bethany College. But though Virgie surmounted her handicaps to become a beautiful young woman, she fell victim to an attack of what Selina termed "a congestion of the brain." Her illness lasted two weeks before she died at the home of her uncle, Alexander Campbell, Jr. The Campbell and Barclay families and all who knew her mourned her loss deeply. Selina expressed her sorrow in an obituary she composed for the *Christian Standard*.[34]

Other articles that Selina wrote for publication attest to her concern with preserving the memory of her husband and his career, labor that reflected her love for God as well as for her husband. Preserving her husband's memory had a personal aspect as well as a public one. In private, Selina treasured her opportunities to visit the grave of her husband and to mourn his loss. When she visited her children she deeply regretted being away from the mansion largely for that reason. But in a more public fashion she also commissioned his memoirs and later sent copies of his writings to friends and family. In so doing she sought both to commemorate his life and to identify herself with his work, which she had supported to her utmost ability.

On April 3, 1866, less than a month after Alexander Campbell's death, Doctor Robert Richardson announced in the *Millennial Harbinger* his intention "to complete the Lord willing, as soon as practicable, a memoir of this eminent servant of God." He intended the public notice to solicit material and "any important facts or interesting incidents" regarding Campbell's life from any who knew him. Though Richardson undoubtedly received several usable items for the memoirs from this announcement, the largest contributor to the work was Selina herself. Selina not only commissioned Richardson to write the book but also provided him with boxes and boxes of letters she had saved, claiming that she had never thrown away anything connected to her husband. From these materials Richardson crafted a two-volume work, *The Memoirs of Alexander Campbell,* which met with lavish approval not only from Selina and other contemporaries but also from historians of every generation since. No biography provides the same quality of analysis and explications of the significance of many aspects of the life of Alexander Campbell.[35]

On a late spring evening in 1868, Selina sat at her writing desk in the parlor of the mansion and wrote to Dr. Richardson. "Allow me to thank you *over* and *over* for the *very* beautiful copy you presented me with of the 'Memoirs' of my beloved husband!" Selina was deeply satisfied with the result of more than two years of research and writing. She hastened to assure Richardson that she was "*more* and *more* convinced of the *propriety* & *importance* of having selected you and desired you, to be the Author of the Memoirs of him whose life & labors, are so *precious* to my memory and heart." She felt that no friend "living or dead" could have "given to the world such a volume of interesting facts and incidents relative to the Beloved departed." Affirming the accuracy of his conclusions, she also felt her role in the compilation of the volume was significant. "The letters I kept for years show the inner life of the Grand-Man and show his toils and labors on his journeys better than anything that could have been told," she expressed to William. But after her comments on her role, she recognized Richardson's superb effort in "both matter & manner."[36]

Selina's profound appreciation for the written word shows through in her desire to commission a fitting biography of her husband. She firmly believed that the cause served so wholeheartedly by Campbell would be greatly advanced by publicizing the facts and circumstances of his life as a reformer. Selina did not doubt that people would be persuaded by the dramatic events of his life to seek the faith he so ably promoted. "The clear & able presentation of the truths he taught, cannot fail to carry conviction to the minds and hearts of thousands who shall have the privilege of reading them," Selina declared to Dr. Richardson, "and thus it may be truly said of him 'though dead he will still speak'!" Thus Selina's first act in promoting the faith of her husband was promoting knowledge about his life. Taking an active hand in spreading as many copies of the memoirs as possible throughout the United States, Selina mailed volumes to many friends and relatives. Moreover, her involvement permeated many aspects of the project. Her contribution to the biography transcended her domestic role and demonstrated again the commitment of this "fellow soldier" to the cause of her husband's (and her) Reformation.

In 1882 Selina demonstrated another aspect of her respect for the written word in general and her husband's writings in particular. Anxious to make her husband's thoughts more available to all, she purchased a copy of Campbell's debate with the Socialist Robert Owen to be placed in the New Harmony Library in Indiana. Apparently she had visited the library previously and discovered that it possessed only a few speeches by Robert Owen and none of her husband's writings. So she sent them a copy of the debate bound in red morocco. In return she received a "very complimentary return of thanks from the librarian."[37] Her commitment to spreading her husband's writings remained strong her entire life.

Selina also made personal comments about the preaching and teaching of her husband in her *Home Life and Reminiscences of Alexander Campbell,* intended largely for her grandchildren but also for anyone else who was interested in the life of the great man. Her memoir of her husband recounts one public incident in great detail. In 1874 the editors of the *Memphis Appeal* published an article that she felt contained some unfair accusations against Alexander's teachings. Her reply to the article, which she also reprinted in *Home Life,* refuted many of the challenges made in the *Appeal.* The article had included some comments referring to Campbell as a sect maker. Of all the characterizations of Alexander Campbell, Selina probably objected to this one the most. "I desire simply to say," she wrote,

> that Mr. Campbell never intended to inaugurate a sect, and that he never did inaugurate a sect. His grand and sole object was to enlighten his fellow-men upon the teachings of the Saviour and his apostles, and to bring them back to the simplicity of the original gospel (Luke xxiv., 47,) in order to the union [sic] of all Christians upon the one foundation, and thus to annihilate sects, sectarianism, and schism in the Church of God. I respectfully submit that this is not the work of the sect-maker.[38]

She maintained her husband's commitment to eradicating denominational conflict and uniting all Christians under the banner of Jesus Christ's life and death.

The *Appeal* in an admiring response affirmed Selina's capable defense of her husband's memory and teaching. After noting the essential correctness of her position and the corresponding error of the newspaper, the responding editor voiced his approbation of the author of the critique:

Mrs. Campbell during [her husband's] life, was the able coadjutor and assistant of her husband; and . . . in every sense she was worthy to be the helpmeet of such a man. She speaks as one by authority, and, so speaking, places her husband right before the world, justifies his great efforts at reforms, and elevates those who worship according to the Scriptures, without other rule or guide, to a dignity which sects never can reach. We are glad, then, to be the medium of publication of a letter so full of interest to the religious world, especially to those who call themselves "Christians."[39]

Selina's reply by its competence gained the respect of her readers. Though they knew the abilities of her husband and associated her with him, they also recognized that her writing showed her own capability. Certainly, her relationship to Campbell and her gender required a polite response from the *Appeal*'s editor, but the public nature and the content of the article indicates his desire to acknowledge her ability.

A striking factor in Selina's remembrance of her husband is her awareness of the faults that others often noted in his character and behavior. Many charged, for example, that he often turned his acidic pen on those who disagreed with his opinions. Though not blind to his tendency to attack his enemies personally, Selina did not allow this characteristic to cast a shadow upon her husband's life. To those who called Alexander Campbell resentful in disposition, she declared that he "sought to correct falsehoods and misrepresentations" in fierce terms but only in "as strong a manner as such an *unhallowed course called for*."[40] Her defense of her husband reflects her devotion to his memory. She does not describe him as others saw him but nonetheless exhibits an awareness of aspects of his character that others found troublesome.

Selina also commissioned several monuments to her husband. One of the most important is the bust of Alexander Campbell that has sat at Bethany College for over a hundred years. The story of its construction involves several twists and turns. The original plaster was taken by Joe T. Hart during Campbell's debate with Nathan L. Rice in Lexington, Kentucky, in 1845. After the debate Hart took it with him to his studio in Florence, Italy. Years after her husband's death, Selina co-incidentally learned of the existence of the plaster from a friend whose son studied under Hart. She quickly dashed off an order for the artist to execute the bust in marble. The finished product arrived in time to be presented to Bethany College at the 1875 commencement cere-mony.[41]

Such generosity became increasingly difficult for Selina with the passage of time. Like many widowed women, Selina faced growing financial worries. Added to these worries was the growing indifference of her son William to his ownership of the mansion. The trouble began with Campbell's will, which parceled out his substantial possessions into such small portions that none was as profitable as before. Two aspects of this problem merged in the mid-1870s, creating discord within the family. Selina had been given lifetime use of the mansion, and her son William, the homestead farm. William proved a poor manager. In need of money, he proposed selling the farm in 1876. In September of that year Selina received a letter from him telling her of the upcoming sale. "I have *grieved* and *agonized at heart* ever since I heard of the contemplated Sale of the dear Old Homestead Farm! It was the *earnest wish* of the now sainted father, it should remain with his name in the family and he no doubt thought it would for many years after his decease. But it is not to be so." The letter to Nannie was strong in its tone. Reading between the lines, we may safely conclude that Selina regarded Nannie as unfeeling about the sale of his house and farm to a stranger, possibly because Nannie had not known Alexander Campbell. William claimed that his mother had signed the house over to provide collateral on a loan he needed several years previously. The farm and the house therefore had to be sold to cover the note. Selina denied ever taking any such action. "I have never said *here* nor *there* that I had given it up!" she claimed. She told William and Nannie "years ago that I thought I would occupy it and live by myself, but they would not hear of this." The sale, however, had already been scheduled before she learned of it, so she could only express her extreme dismay at William's secrecy regarding the transaction. She attributed it to his "aberrations of heart from the right path" and quickly sought a way to retain possession of the mansion.[42]

Selina informed Nannie in her next letter that Decima intended to bid for the house and the surrounding property. Since Decima could not leave her home or take her baby with her, Selina resolved to go herself and act on her daughter's behalf. She planned to journey to Bethany in late September 1876 just before the sale of the mansion was scheduled to take place. She also wanted to move into the house and prepare living quarters so that Virginia, who was then very ill, could come and recuperate under her care. Apologizing to Nannie for any misunderstanding, she offered to share the house with her and William after Decima purchased it. William and his family had been living in Bethany Mansion for several years. Selina assured them that she was guaranteed possession of the house by the will, and she invited them to choose a wing in which to live. In the end, Decima proved unable to purchase the homestead in 1876. But three years later the family did regain possession of the property from a subsequent owner. Campbell's widow moved back into her home in 1879 in time to begin her book about her husband.

Throughout her widowhood, Selina made few public appearances. The main reason was her belief that a private, retiring role was more proper for women. But her fear of crowds probably reinforced her reluctance to attend large events. In addition, however, she remained in deep mourning for her husband and associated large public meetings with his memory. This was especially true in the case of church gatherings.

Large gatherings of Disciples were controversial for many who feared that they would lead to a denominational structure and would thereby betray the origins of the movement. But Selina took a more moderate approach. While some church journalists and preachers decried national conventions of the Churches of Christ as belying the movement's antidenominational origins, Selina once wrote that "political men have their large meetings and why not Christians?"[43] Even given his reluctance to attach too much importance to such gatherings, Campbell often supported assemblies as ways of combining the efforts of individual congregations to create a group effort for evangelism. His endorsement of membership in the Mahoning Baptist Association early in his career and other similar decisions throughout his life thus presaged his later acceptance of missionary societies. Elected president of the American Christian Missionary Society in 1849, Campbell, together with his wife, gradually accepted the goals of the society and often attended the annual national conventions. The couple came to look forward to the conventions as an opportunity to see old friends and enjoy a time of uplifting prayer and singing with a large crowd of fellow believers.

After her husband's death, Selina could not decide whether to attend the conventions alone. In 1869 the convention met in Louisville, Kentucky. William attended the gathering and reported to his mother all of the goodwill messages from her friends and those of her late husband. Grateful to be remembered by so many, Selina nonetheless decided against going to the convention because there would be too many memories. "I was with the brethren convened in spirit," she wrote William after receiving his letter in Bethany. "I fear had I been present in person, there would have been so many associations with the Memory & life of your sainted father that I fear I should have exhibited much weakness of my nature and almost a want of faith."[44] Though settling into her life as a widow, she still found living her life alone a struggle. She could not bear attending the convention: "it would have been so painful to not have seen *your father* amongst *them*." Mourning remained a difficult period for her. Her expressions of grief reflect both sincere feelings and the sentimentality of Victorian American culture.

As with nearly everything else, she expressed and shared her sorrow with her children through her letters. "Oh my dear child," she wrote to William one day a few months after Alexander's death, "how I long to be in his society again tongue can not give utterance to." Even two years after his passing, the depth of her feeling remains obvious and urgent. "Oh I am more lost than ever without your father's society. I feel earth a wilderness."[45] Yet her conviction that they would someday meet again rescued her from despair and motivated her to continue in her activities to maintain her "usefulness."

Anniversaries, however, remained particularly difficult. Selina's deep awareness of the passage of time prompted her to commemorate special events often. She wrote to her children on their birthdays and always seemed alert to the approaching anniversary of an important event. Her searing memory of her husband's illness and death remained ever in her thoughts and troubled her often. She struggled to meet the challenge of sorrow by turning to the God who sustained her. "The return of the season that your dear father took his last illness (just this week) and the near approach of the anniversary of his death has a most peculiarly saddening effect," she wrote to William. "I feel as though all the affliction & solemn scene was before me. I realize it more than I could possibly thought I would."[46] On the fiftieth anniversary of her marriage, more than twelve years after Campbell's death, Selina turned to her writing to express her grief. She penned "An Address to the Departed Alexander Campbell," which she later included in *Home Life and Reminiscences of Alexander Campbell.*[47] The "imaginative discourse" encompassed several themes and attested to her continuing grief. In it she expressed her deep devotion to his memory and her admiration of his life and character. "It was not for the sake of victory that you labored," she wrote, "but for the establishment of *truth*." He also labored to free his fellow man from "the terrible entanglements which had been thrown around him in regard to religious knowledge," and Selina praised him for his devotion to the task. She also commended his labor, as evident from the "midnight oil" and constant travel. Other portions of the address recalled various aspects of their life together, including the sorrow of losing his five eldest daughters and her first born.[48] For a woman who felt the sorrows of life so deeply, it apparently afforded powerful relief to pour her feelings onto paper.

In the "wilderness" of separation from her husband, Selina often took comfort in reading his writings and heeding their call for return to a simple Christian faith. The words on each page probably brought to her mind the devotion of the man she so greatly admired, perhaps making him seem closer to her. But even they were a mixed blessing: "I am reading the memoirs with joy & with tears," Selina said. She reread her husband's writings for hours at a time. Through several years, she read not only the memoirs again and again but also the entire set of the *Millennial Harbinger* and almost all of her husband's published debates. All of these activities allowed her to work through her grief and at the same time attain her desire to fill her life with useful things.

At other times only her strong faith could comfort her in her husband's absence. Selina struggled constantly to respond in faith to her loneliness and without giving in to the frustration of grief at the loss of her husband. "Oh I feel the absence more than ever," Selina mourned one July evening, "& yet I realize how short the separation will be." Convinced she would see "Mr. Campbell" again when they met in heaven, she consoled herself in her loneliness on earth. Separation became more bearable with the promise of a blissful reunion, for Scripture promised that Christ would return to convey all who believed in him into the presence of God. Selina "meditated constantly" upon such thoughts. She also comforted herself by remembering how Mr. Campbell "kept all his promises to nourish & cherish me forsaking all others."[49] She often counted the blessings of her marriage to gain comfort in his absence. Though she enjoyed her new opportunity to pursue additional activities, she deeply regretted the price she paid in the loss of her life's partner.

Throughout her years as a widow, Selina enjoyed being at Bethany Mansion whenever she could, but she spent most of her time living with her children. She visited her daughters most often; her sons seemed to adopt too many troubling habits for her to enjoy spending time at their homes. The concerned grandmother especially mistrusted the child-rearing environment that prevailed at the home of Alexander, Jr. Apparently Alexander and Mary Anna had agreed to provide housing for Joe Pendleton, a family member of William Pendleton (Campbell's son-in-law and a professor at Bethany College), whom Selina characterized as an "evil outcast." The boy had been in some unspecified trouble before his aunt and uncle took him in. Selina was sure that "evil communications corrupt good manners," and she worried for her grandchildren because "the young mind is more ready to copy from example than from advice." Alexander's children were thus in great danger having their cousin under the same roof. She expressed her belief that other, more appropriate arrangements should be made. "He could get work elsewhere," she insisted, *"and get* it he should if I *had any influence."* Her letter to William on the subject declared that if she were at home, she would ask to keep her grandchildren with her to get them away from the bad influence. Thinking Mary Anna "too lenient" in her methods of discipline, she believed that only sorrow awaited her daughter-in-law if she stayed on her present course.[50]

The grandmother increasingly questioned whether or not Alexander was training his children for heaven. When invited, she hesitated to stay with him because "he is too much in the world & with worldly men & does not let his light shine as he ought." Alexander's mother refused to mix with the kind of company he kept and was "sorrowful at heart in thinking of these things," seeing "no relief."[51] Given her perception of the importance of good Christian parenting, her disappointment in her children's actions was telling. The deep commitment she felt to the importance of living a good Christian life of service and moral behavior undergirded her goals as a parent and grandparent. The situation was eventually resolved when Alexander, Jr., sent Joe Pendleton to live with his uncle, Mr. Burch, in Texas in 1871. He and William K. Pendleton agreed that it would be best to send him away.[52] Neither the two brothers-in-law nor Selina records the details of young Joseph's trouble, but the incident clearly indicates Selina's unshakable belief that one should associate oneself only with moral people, especially if one were a parent. She was invariably disappointed when her sons did not exhibit such a concern.

Selina's reaction to the plight of young Pendleton was directed not at the child himself but instead at the proper attitude for a Christian assisting those needing help. Alexander and Selina had themselves adopted an Indian boy they called Harvey. Harvey lived with the Campbells several years and kept in contact with Selina the rest of his life. From Selina's viewpoint, they struggled to manage Harvey's discipline, but she did not send him away to prevent him from contaminating her own children as she urged Alexander, Jr., to do. The situation with young Pendleton might have been different had Selina trusted her sons to protect their children from harmful influences. But their continual demonstration of poor judgment weakened her confidence in them and augmented her worries about her grandchildren. Thus, she felt they could not discharge their duty to little Joe Pendleton without jeopardizing their duty to raise good moral children.

Selina's disappointment with some of her children seemed not to affect her relationship with her grandchildren. Though Virgie was a favorite, Selina often demonstrated that she loved her other grandchildren just as much. She delighted in the birth of each of her grandchildren and always asked to be informed immediately when they were due. She often addressed notes to her grandchildren that she included in her letters to their parents. Several weeks after a visit from "Mr. Independent Patrick," the oldest child of William and Nannie, she wrote of missing his precious way of greeting her every day with "Good Morning Grand Ma." In a letter to the young boy, she told him how pleased she was with his visit and said that his affectionate behavior had won her heart. She also expressed her fondness for Patrick's sister Jeanette and her "lovely ways." Mentioned also was "the dear precious Argyle," the youngest brother.[53]

In 1875, Virginia Thompson experienced a severe financial crisis that troubled her mother acutely. Attorney William Thompson, Virginia's husband, had evidently developed a serious drinking habit that hampered his ability to provide for his family, and he built up debts he could not pay. Virginia faced a public auction to liquidate her possessions for his creditors. The gravity of Virginia's situation troubled her mother's heart, and she poured out her worries in a letter to her son William, a frequent confidante: "In a letter from my dear Virginia last night she sent me the notice from the [Louisville] *Courier Journal* of the sale of her house. She says it is now to be sold in a week or two with all her household things. She said if 'she could only save bedding by buying it in my name she would be thankful.'" Heeding the plea in her daughter's letter, Selina agreed to provide the money necessary to purchase the things Virginia wished to keep.[54]

Unfortunately, her offer of help strained her limited finances almost to the breaking point. Though her husband had died the wealthiest man in Brooke County, if not the whole state of West Virginia, by 1875

Selina had "only 4 dollars in the world . . . and that I am to pay for my papers with. . . . I gave my last 10 dollars to your dear sister when she was leaving." Though she still received an income from the interest on her husband's estate, she was forever donating most of it to people or to causes she supported. In order to recoup some of her expended resources, she wrote to William, who now had a law practice of his own, and gave him detailed instructions on collecting the debts owed to her. "If you examine *my account* I think you will [see] that there is some two or three hundred dollars of interest coming to me. The account you handed me, just as I was leaving is all right, except what you mentioned about not giving credit for Mr. Cavener's amount. . . . I would be glad to have the 15 dollars I said I would take from him for the 22 he is indebted. . . . Son Alexander said their[sic] was 44 coming to me from Mr. Fendly on the Lot and sent me the Deed to have signed." Though an able manager of all funds under her control, she was also quite generous and not as talented at raising money for herself as she was at managing her husband's estate. Realizing that her resources would not stretch to cover Virginia's needs, Selina asked William to "raise . . . a sum & send it or take it to Louisville the time of the sale to save the bedding and . . . a few articles of furniture." This was the minimum necessary, according to Selina, to prevent Virginia from being "turned on the pitiless world in the dead of winter."[55] At any moment the young woman could be ordered to remove from her house, and so quick action was required.

The exhausted mother also spoke of the great strain she was under and observed that it might have affected her perception of recent events. Though prone to worry over the condition of her children, Selina sought to avoid exaggerating the situation. "My head is so much affected for the want of sleep & the distress I am in about daughter Decima's illness," she told William, "that I feel like as if I was writing what is not true about the dreadful want of my beloved daughter Virginia."[56] The pathos of this admission also speaks to the emotional distress she felt concerning her insecure financial position and its dampening of her ability to care for her children. But she also acknowledged that she only wished the details of Virginia's situation were "fiction."

The reality was that Virginia had not married "in the fear of the Lord," and Selina feared that her current condition was part of a chastisement from God. At the same time she also admired her daughter's ability "to bear up" and believed her a "wonderful woman" with "her father's mind and strength." Selina too had hoped Mr. Thompson would live up to expectations and had not opposed the marriage that eventually brought Virginia so much pain. Thus she shared with her daughter the disappointment of Thompson's failures and expressed great pride when President Garfield appointed Virginia postmaster general of Louisville in the early 1880s.

Selina's financial troubles continued for the rest of her life. She took pride in her refusal to be indebted to anyone, but in the economic distress of 1876, she suffered from the inability of others to repay their debts to her. Thousands in principal still remained from the money left to her by her husband, but she used the interest to help Virginia move into a new house. She believed the money was needed more for her children's emergencies than for herself and that her advancing years meant she would not need money a great deal longer. "My wants for myself are not great nor will they in the course of nature be long now. But I feel for others. I feel for you *my son* that you are the least embaresed [sic] in your financial *affairs*. I feel for your dear sister [Virginia] in L——, who had a competency that her dear father left her but through want of thought she is brought to *penury.*"[57] As a mother she wanted to help her children in whatever way she could and was always saddened when she could not help them.

Though Selina Campbell as a widow faced challenges both financial and spiritual, she also expanded her many talents. Her reading habits especially invite close examination. In addition to reading the works of such men as Robert Owen (the Socialist who debated her husband in 1828 on the evidence of Christianity), she also read philosophers such as her favorite author John Newton, the author of the hymn "Amazing Grace," and James Wallis, the editor of the *British Millennial Harbinger,* the counterpart of her husband's journal. The list of newspapers and books she read is nearly endless. Selina herself claimed to be "a reader of almost every thing written, appertaining to the present Reformation, from the first number of *The Christian Baptist* down through the 41 volumes of the *Millennial Harbinger,* to the multiplied numbers that now issue from the press, by the prolific writers."[58] The breadth and depth of her reading together with her lively intellect enabled her to discuss a variety of issues both intelligently and profoundly.

Selina gradually earned the respect of many editors, who continued to publish her writings even as she received increasing attention from her readers. Her activities, especially her writing, gained favorable recognition from a number of journalists and public figures. One editor, writing for the *Memphis Appeal,* admired her as a woman who "employs all her spare moments in doing good, and setting an example of womanly endeavor in the cause of Christ."[59] The journalist for the *Appeal* also praised her efforts at preserving the articles and speeches of great men on important subjects. He mentioned her efforts to preserve her husband's series of writings entitled "Addresses to Young Men" as well as a speech she had recently read by Charles Spurgeon. Each of these compositions had been meticulously copied by Mrs. Campbell so that it would be preserved for the benefit of others. Many other speeches, articles, and essays were preserved in the same way. Some were sent to newspapers to be published, while others were carefully pasted into a scrapbook. All spoke to her awareness of a broad spectrum of issues in postbellum American society and religion. In particular, the editor of the *Appeal* noted that he found her "remarkable for her clearness of spiritual vision, for strength of conviction, and a devout interest in the affairs of her church."[60]

The comments made by the editor of the *Memphis Appeal* indicate the source of Selina's authority as an author. Given her relationship to such a prominent man, the question naturally arises: was she accorded respect because of her own talent or because of that of her husband? Did such a prominent woman receive so much public attention because she had married a prominent man or because she too achieved important things? The *Appeal* article suggests that the answer was a curious mixture of both. Early in the article, the editor describes in some detail his perception of the Campbell marriage, hinting that the wife's role was closely attached to—if not dependent on—the husband's: "It is pleasant to recall the fact that his [Campbell's] now aged widow was a helpmeet in sense, sustaining him in all his trials, comforting him and bringing as a reinforcement of his high purpose the encouragement of a true heart, and an intellect worthily mated with his own." But near the end of the article after discussing Selina's various activities during a recent visit to Memphis and her other interests, the writer concluded: "Mrs. Campbell occupies a peculiar position in life, one very far above that ordinarily filled by her sex, and is worthily regarded with affectionate reverence by those who are of her household of faith."[61] This peculiar position, the article suggested, did not occur in consideration of her husband's work. Rather Selina's activities won the esteem of her peers at least somewhat apart from her husband's influence. David Walk, the pastor at a church in Memphis and a visitor to Ingleside Plantation, bears out this idea in a brief article published in the *Christian Standard.* "What a blessed privilege I esteem it to be permitted to spend so much time with her," Walk wrote in 1868, "and to hear from her own lips the history of the Reformation in which she has borne so conspicuous a part!"[62] Such direct praise for her individual contributions to the cause she believed in so strongly testifies to her ability as a writer and thinker while also supporting the conclusion that at least some of the praise she received came because of her own contributions and not from her association with her husband.

Selina's writing also focused on issues close to her own heart. Many of these ideas appear in a "Letter to a Young Convert," which appeared in the *Millennial Harbinger* in 1858. In this letter, Selina broaches several matters about a young Christian of her acquaintance that truly concerned her. "I thought I saw in you a youthful gaiety and frivolity, that illy [sic] comported with the Gospel that you had professed. You are naturally kind, but impulsive; you are fond of pleasure, and will be apt to seek it (unless your heart is arrested) in a society, that will not contribute to your spirituality." Such concerns about the young flirting with the enticements of the world weighed heavily on Selina. When she observed how much those around her took pleasure in reading novels, attending local dances, and indulging in other amusements, she worried that their faith could suffer. When pursuing such activities a person was not seeking the things of God.[63]

Mrs. Campbell associated many frivolous activities with Satan, the adversary of all Christians. She had encountered his power as a young woman when her father, she believed, had fallen under his influence and contemplated suicide. The devil was the enemy of every person of faith attempting to live a pure, noble life—tempting them to stray from the path laid out for them by their Savior. Selina especially feared his influence on the vulnerable youth of her acquaintance. "You must arouse yourself, if you would not be *caught* in the snare of the adversary of souls forever!" she warned them. She also exhorted the youth to take action on the important issues of salvation. "You need to watch and pray earnestly, if you would obtain eternal life.—You cannot receive it by wishing for it—or by admiring piety in others. You will never attain to Heaven upon the righteousness of your father or mother." She encouraged young people to take control of their own spirituality and seek God with all their strength. To the young convert she included a strong reminder that his parent could not fix the way for him: "All the excellency of your now *sainted* and glorified mother, will not be to you a passport into the 'Celestial City.' You must labor, and toil, and overcome the world for yourself, if you would be counted worthy to receive a crown of glory." Again she returned to the importance of usefulness and hard work for success in the Christian life. Her plea was for action from the young in pursuit of a deep faith and knowledge of the Savior. The young man could not rely on the faith of those around him or on the strength of his upbringing; he must make his own choice. Just as she hosted many young people in her own home in order to provide a healthy environment in which they could grow and mature, so through her writing she encouraged other youths of her acquaintance to grow in their spiritual maturity. Her letter included some specific suggestions to help them fulfill her aspirations for them.[64]

Many of these suggestions also permeated Selina's other writings. One of the most important issues for her was the wise use of time. "On earth, time is not our own, it is the gift of God," she wrote to the young convert. "It becomes us, then, humbly and wisely to use it, both to our own benefit and for his glory." There were many reasons Selina offered to explain why using time wisely benefits a person. Her comments resonate with those of her Victorian peers who, as Daniel Howe has observed, viewed saving time as an important attribute of any activity.[65]

Selina felt most people, young or old, neglected to make the best use of the hours they had been given to "do good" and "improve themselves." They thereby isolated themselves from their Heavenly Father and ignored opportunities to help others, for they owed it to their Creator to use their time properly. "Ought we not as rational, immortal and accountable beings to value time, and our duties connected with our lives and our blessings, while sojourneying below?"[66] To evaluate the use of time Selina had some interesting suggestions. As she once wrote in a guestbook in 1855: "Tis wisely done to talk with hours, and ask them / What *report* they *bore* to *Heaven*."[67] This statement was quoted from an English author whose name Selina never mentioned but whose words she often heard recited by her husband. The hours that passed took on a life of their own complete with an intelligence capable of saying something to anyone living under the restrictions of time, and they impressed upon her the need to use her time to serve the God she loved.

The significance of the passage of time impressed upon Selina the need to make good use of it, but while other women organized societies to tackle the problems of postbellum society, for Selina there were other more important activities. Rather than join a temperance society or a mutual aid society, Selina sought action bent on improving the individual. To the young convert she revealed her suggestions for activities that make proper use of time: "Let many of your evening hours be set apart for reading valuable works that will strengthen your faith, and enlarge and ennoble your mind."[68]

Selina especially mistrusted the many activities that she associated with city life. These included such pastimes as dancing, theatergoing, and drinking alcohol, all of which she felt were at best distracting and at worst destructive of the soul. She observed that those who engaged in these activities seemed to avoid pursuing a deeper knowledge of their

Creator. "I am sorry to hear of the gayity [*sic*] & folly of city life," she wrote to William as he studied in the bustling city of Wheeling. "There is scarcely one who enters into the fashionable amusements that can draw a sober reflecting breath! They are enslaved by the whirl of fashion *dress* and amusements for these perishing bodies so that the high and ennobling nature of *man* is entirely forgotten!" Dancing and masquerading were "no . . . honorable amusement for a saint or sinner," Selina maintained. "The Shaking Quaker dances to shake the devil out. Vain man he shakes the devil in." She especially critiqued those "who look to Paris, the metropolis of atheism, sensuality and crime for any other fashion or custom than those which drown men in destruction and perdition."[69] These comments should not be taken to mean that Selina Campbell decried all social gatherings and amusements. Anniversary parties, singing socials in the Campbell parlor, and other similar events often filled the Campbell home with revelry of a sort that she regarded as appropriate. The difference between these activities and those Selina feared centered on the lack of occasion to converse with one another in public amusements and the distraction of the more frivolous activities like dancing and observing fashions.

To those caught up in the whirl of society, Selina offered some strong advice. Unless individual people rejected all these practices and worked for a reformation against them, Selina feared they "could not have any hope of salvation." She also observed that many of them complained of a dissatisfying life that left them longing for more. To those she imparted her belief that God wished the best for all those whom he had created, but neither salvation nor even true happiness could be found in frivolous amusements. She assured them that "the knowledge and company of the Saviour of the World is the only true source of human happiness!! He alone can teach us how to enjoy this life wisely and rationally and to look forward to enjoy an unending life in a world to come when *ages, of ages,* shall have rolled away!"[70] Thus, everyone should turn away from amusement and turn toward the Savior to find true happiness.

Scripture was the only "sure Guide Book" in directing a person toward activities of true worth. In Selina's opinion, no precedent in

Scripture could be found for "courtly balls and midnight masquerades"; they should consequently be rejected. She lamented the fact that "men . . . like the poor deluded Moth that flutters its wings around the lighted torch . . . would rather flutter a few moments and *dance* and die than to act soberly & thoughtfully and be happy now."[71] Whenever Selina found authors who she felt expressed particularly well the principles of sober living, she copied their comments and sent them to the various Disciple newspapers to help counteract antiscriptural activities. Often these remarks were published with her own brief commentary. The items she selected reflected her interests and further established her as a woman of character and position.

The newspapers published by various members of the Disciples of Christ in many ways represented on a larger scale the Victorian parlor described by Stevenson.[72] They represented an arena for discussion in which concerned individuals such as Selina Campbell could air their anxieties about certain aspects of church life or Victorian culture, bringing them to the attention of others. Letters to the editor often played a role as the response of readers to these concerns. Though the readers and essayists might never meet face to face, they were nevertheless able to discuss the intellectual and spiritual implications of many ideas through the written word. The lack of a formal denominational structure in the churches of the Disciples of Christ also served to enhance the importance of this forum.

The essays of Selina Campbell's favorite writer, John Newton (1725–1807), figured most prominently in the instructive excerpts she sent to the various newspapers. In 1853 she sent to Archibald W. Campbell, her brother-in-law and the editor of the *Millennial Harbinger,* an essay by Newton that discussed his definition of a Christian. Newton had converted to Christianity as a young man, turning away from his former life as the master of a slave ship. He lived the remainder of his life as a clergyman seeking to bring others to the same knowledge of God's love and grace that he described himself as experiencing. Selina immensely admired both his writings and his character. She especially enjoyed studying his definition of a Christian, which, according to the essay that she submitted to the *Harbinger,* emphasized the Christian cultivation of true humility, the enjoyment of the peace of God, and the entertainment of respect for "his fellow-creatures."[73]

The name "Mother Campbell," by which Selina was often known, indicates how her contemporaries saw her. The title resonates on several levels. First, it delineated her relationship to the students of Bethany College. Many of them spent a good deal of time at the Campbell home, interacting personally with the president of the college and his family. They called her mother in recognition of her deep interest in their experience as students. Even years later, alumni of the college referred to Mrs. Campbell with deep affection and respect.[74] Second, the title reflected her image as a woman of powerful intellect and with a capacity for generosity and scholarship. As her husband, "Father Campbell," had been a leader of many in the "Reformation of American religion" (his description of his work), so his wife was a recognized leader in the issues of family life and moral behavior.[75] Although she did not travel and speak publicly as her husband had done, she wrote over fifty published essays on a variety of topics, from the corrupting influence of public amusements to the proper realm of Christian behavior.

Her ability as a writer and an observer of current issues in the church also brought her to the attention of her peers as a recognized expert on many special issues. One of the most interesting was a request that Selina mentions having received from "Brother Reynolds." Reynolds apparently asked her to recommend women who might write for a Sunday school library he was compiling. Selina described the project as one directed toward creating a nonsectarian approach to teaching. She hoped to get back to Reynolds quickly, although her busy schedule threatened to interfere. On another occasion when she was asked to suggest some reading material for young sisters, she wrote a detailed essay for the *Christian Standard* on the subject. She intended to rectify a lack of appreciation for the more serious aspects of Christian life among the sisters that was, in her view, being fueled by "light literature" and "the pressure of domestic duties." To rectify this "neglect of reading solid works of instruction," Selina recommended works such as Brother B. A. Hinsdale's *Genuineness and Authenticity of the Gospels,* published in 1872. Other works that she suggested included Richardson's *Office of the Holy Spirit* and F. M. Green's *Christian Missions: Historical Sketches of Missionary Societies among the Disciples of Christ.* Selina considered these works to be of high spiritual value and capable of improving the mind of anyone who read them. In addition to works she felt beneficial for young women, she also suggested readings of value to preachers and teenagers. In so doing she showed judgment and a grasp extending beyond questions of gender to provide direction for all Disciples.[76]

In 1879 Selina began what might be called her magnum opus, *The Home Life and Reminiscences of Alexander Campbell.* The idea had been in her head for several years since the death of her husband. It gained particular currency after Selina read Robert Richardson's *Memoirs of Alexander Campbell.* She was said to have commented, "O the half has never been told, has never been told." Given her analytical mind, she probably craved the opportunity to put down on paper many of her observations about the man with whom she had shared her life. She firmly believed that the better people knew him, the more they would appreciate him.

Three years later *Home Life* appeared under favorable review by several editors. "It is a carefully prepared work, by one [in] every way competent to the task—the loving and devoted wife—who had been so long the partner of his labors, sorrows and joys," read one review.[77] *Home Life* clearly contained supplementary material to Robert Richardson's well-researched *Memoirs of Alexander Campbell* and often reflected more about Selina's character than it did that of her husband. Robertson had concentrated on the public persona of Alexander Campbell; Selina's focus on the private man offered new insights and preserved valuable historical information. The many anecdotes and essays appearing in *Home Life* testify to the nature of the couple's relationship and to the issues Selina regarded as important in her husband's life. She especially emphasized his leadership in developing a moral family life and his deep and abiding interest in the development of his children.

Selina lived for several years at Bethany Mansion, writing essays between visits to her children. By 1897, at ninety-five years of age, she was the oldest person in Brooke County. She could always be seen "dressed in a black satin dress . . . and a white mull cap [which] sat like a crown on her whitening hair." One of the most remarkable facts about Selina's long life was her mental alertness, which continued well into her nineties. All who visited her concurred that she was, as one journalist expressed it, "remarkably hale for one of her age." She continued to appear at public events, most often functions associated with Bethany College. Attending the commencement ceremony every year remained a high priority for her despite the considerable effort it required. In 1882, she was a participant in "a touching and thrilling scene" at the Commencement Day ceremony on July 4. Mary A. Campbell, her granddaughter, had just finished reciting a poem during the ceremony when her grandmother unexpectedly ascended to the stage and publicly embraced her. According to a journalist who witnessed the event, "the audience was transfixed." A thousand people remained silent for several moments in complete awe, and "Alexander Campbell, in his marble bust, was looking down upon the scene."[78] The incident illustrated some of the importance Selina attached not only to the college and its activities but also to the achievements of her beloved grandchildren.

Selina received a stream of callers at Bethany Mansion throughout the 1880s and 1890s. She also continued her constant visits to her children and enjoyed close relationships with her grandchildren. Even when her vision began to fail as she entered her nineties, she did not neglect her correspondence. Mother Campbell, like many octogenarians, focused often on her memories of people she had known in her youth and the friends of her husband who continued to drop in to pay their respects. Though Selina was forced to curtail her activities as she grew older, she accepted the deterioration of her body with equanimity and her usual measure of faith. Reading the Scriptures remained her most important pastime, especially as she contemplated the approach of death. "My dim vision admonishes me that I have passed much of my time here, and must shortly cross the silent River," she wrote to William in 1892. "Blessed be the Creator that I was born in a land, where the Book Divine, can be read and enjoyed. It is the only book, that can inform us of our origin & destiny." Selina was comforted by the things she read in Scripture, and her writings reveal no fear regarding the future. Indeed, she had been expecting death ever since her husband had passed away, and she was continually surprised at the number of years granted to her by her God. The phrase "before I die" often preceded any wish she expressed, indicating the tenuous way she viewed any plans she made.[79]

Death was another theme upon which Selina often reflected in her public and private writings. One of her favorite poets, Felicia Hemans (for whom Decima Hemans Campbell Barclay was named), wrote often on the subject. In contrast to many, this Christian sister neither feared death nor sought after it, but in a way she looked forward to unraveling the mysteries it would reveal. First of all, death meant instant reunion with the God Whom she served. Her writings on death engaged the subject on several different levels, including the writing of obituaries and discussion of the ultimate joy that death brings beyond immediate sorrow and of its function in the life of friends and family members.

Selina Campbell acutely recognized the sorrow that death brought to the lives of those who had lost a family member or close friend. But her reading of Scripture and her faith in the Author of her salvation convinced her that there was something beyond the sorrow, some hope available to the Christian and not to others. "What or who can take away the darkness the gloom of the grave?" she once asked. "No one, we all must respond, but the divine Saviour who endured so much to cure its horror & take away the sting of death." This was the deep source of the Christian's hope. The belief that Jesus Christ has risen from the dead after vicariously taking the punishment for all sins animated the Christian believer and offered salvation to all who believed. But Selina could hardly live in the world without seeing the harsh reality of death in the nineteenth-century United States. In 1868 she read of an epidemic in New York City that claimed a high number of victims. Selina was appalled at the death toll, and it turned her mind toward her faith that only the resurrection of Jesus Christ had broken the power of death over humankind "and brought life & immortality to light."[80]

In addition to writing about the spiritual aspects of death, Selina also wrote a number of obituaries published in the *Harbinger* and in other papers that focused on the significance of a person's life and death. Nearly every obituary, however, contained testimony of the last few moments of each person's life, not unusual in the culture of nineteenth-century America. These moments were considered by many editors, writers, and readers to be inspirational and very useful to all people who read them. They were often preserved by witnesses and written down for public distribution. One example of a death narrative is the diary of Mary Anna Purvis Campbell, which described the events of the last few weeks of Alexander Campbell's life. In his book, *The Quest for God: A Personal Pilgrimage,* historian Paul Johnson describes the Victorian attitude toward death. "In Victorian times," he write, "death was magnified, talked about, minutely examined and, almost, relished." This interest in death, which Johnson struggles to explain, can be seen in Selina's writings on the subject, for which Johnson does offer some valuable background. "Deathbed scenes were elaborately recorded or committed to memory," he explains. They "became part of family folklore, reverently told to children and grandchildren."[81] Selina Campbell shared this folklore not only with her family but also with the readers of the newspapers for whom she wrote articles on the subject.

One of the earliest pieces Selina wrote about death appeared in the *Ladies Christian Annual,* a popular periodical edited by James Challen of Cincinnati, Ohio. Challen had written the Campbells for information regarding the 1854 death of Thomas Campbell, Alexander's father, whose contributions to the Reformation had been admired by many. In her husband's absence, Selina penned a response to the editor, who was so moved by her letter that he included it in the next issue of his magazine. Selina's writing describes the progression of Thomas's illness, which began with the loss of his posture as he aged and then the severe inflammation of his face and mouth. She also detailed his attitude and activities during the final three weeks of his life. "He was patient and calm during all his illness. . . . His mind was as clear and as strong as when in health," she wrote. But the highlight of her essay was one particular incident that Selina identified as being of great value to those who witnessed it:

On the afternoon of his departure, about 4 o'clock, (and he died at 7 o' clock), his sons the Doctor and my husband, were not in. He suddenly grew worse, and we thought he would soon depart. His daughter, Mrs. McKeever [Alexander's sister Jane], and several others, were around his bed. I leaned over him and said, "Father, you're going to leave us. Do you know you're going to leave us, and that you will soon cross the Jordan?" To all of which he responded, by significant sounds—when I added, "You will soon see all THE DEAR LOVED ONES that have gone before." Then in the fullness of my heart I exclaimed, "O that an abundant entrance may be granted unto you into the everlasting kingdom of our Lord and Saviour Jesus Christ!" I had no sooner uttered it, than, to the astonishment of all around, he responded, in an audible voice, and in his emphatic manner, "AMEN!"—the last word I ever heard him utter. It shall be garnered in the recesses of my heart.[82]

Such recounting of the last words and final events of a person's life appeared often in Victorian culture, and many newspapers and magazines carried stories with such themes. Johnson affirms the custom in *The Quest for God*. "My mother related to me numerous accounts of the deaths of her relations . . . which were notable for their edifying circumstances, final sayings, last prayers and ejaculations." Many of the experiences he had as a child with members of previous generations reflect the scenes described by Selina Campbell in her writings.

Disciples put a special emphasis on death narratives and their spiritual significance. A person about to die was thought to be able to see into heaven. A great interest in the afterlife and reunion with the God who created human beings probably enhanced this reverence for the process of death. Moreover, the solemnity of the death scene and the suffering of the victim lent weight to any words they might convey. Johnson suggests that these scenes reflect the different nature of the experience of death in Victorian culture. He explains that, in those times, "death was a domestic, household, family affair, with the dying person upstairs in a well-attended bedroom with a fire in the grate, people downstairs walking softly and talking in whispers, straw in the street outside to muffle the noise of carriage-wheels."[83] Such a scene offers a dramatic contrast to the experience of death today, when most people die in hospitals, as Johnson points out, and when longer lifespans (the gift of modern medicine and technology), together with the physical distance separating members of most families, mean that people are far less willing to acknowledge the power of death.

Selina expressed many of her views about death in the obituaries she wrote between 1844 and 1882 that appeared in Disciple newspapers like the *Millennial Harbinger,* the *Christian Standard,* and the *Ladies Christian Annual.* All had to do with women except for that which she wrote about Thomas Campbell. Some of the women she described were close family members, but many of them were her friends or colleagues. Of Mrs. Martha Abbot James of Zanesville, Ohio, who died in 1859, Selina noted "her devotedness to her husband, and her consecratedness to the training of her children, in harmony with the teaching of the Bible," which rendered "her life as a bright *model* to others."[84] Almost all of the notices of death written by Selina reflect themes similar to those evident in the James obituary. She often praised the deceased's character and commitment to Christian faith and practice.

Another theme appeared in the obituary of Sister Ann Encell, the mother-in-law of Robert Richardson (Campbell's biographer), of whom Selina wrote, "It may be truly said of her, that she was a woman of peace and piety."[85] Selina's comments on the piety of her female subjects underscores her admiration for their Christian example and her belief in its usefulness in instructing others. But not surprisingly the most common trait that Selina praised in these notices was the devotion of the subject to her family. Selina's support of the role of women in the family found expression in her evaluation of the lives of the women she knew; their mutual devotion to the same ideals reinforced Selina's beliefs and informed her evaluation of the contribution of their lives.

Selina's admiration of the Christian women's strength shines through all of her descriptions of their deaths. Though assured of a glorious existence after death, the pain of severe illness and the tragedy of permanent separation impressed upon Selina the difficulty of the process. This awareness is especially evident in her description of the last moments of the life of her niece Mary Jane Campbell, which appeared in the *Harbinger* in 1844. "She departed without a struggle, a groan, or a sigh," Selina wrote, "so gentle was her exit, that it may be truly said she fell *asleep!* Never did I witness a more calm, a more delightful, and, I may say, a more desirable departure in my life."[86] The death of the seventeen-year-old Mary Jane saddened all members of the Campbell family, who drew comfort from each other by recalling her sunny disposition and her resignation to her fate. Before Mary Jane died, Selina also recalled how the girl comforted her uncle Alexander as he cried over her sickbed, saying, "Why weep?—Don't weep—I am going to a better country."[87] The sufferer looked forward to meeting the Apostles and the other saints who had gone before. Her last few hours were as peaceful as they were melancholy for those around her. Selina's lengthy article in the *Harbinger* evoked the family's feelings and the pathos of the moment.

The wife of Alexander Campbell found perhaps her greatest success as an advocate of women's issues in advancing the cause of foreign missions after the Civil War. Efforts to promote the Gospel overseas had drawn the attention of women from nearly every denomination in the years immediately before and after the war. By 1875 every major denomination boasted an organized women's missions society.[88] In that year the first women's missions organization for the Disciples of Christ, the Christian Women's Board of Missions (CWBM), was founded in Indianapolis. Though Selina did not play a direct role in the development of the CWBM, she took a large part in laying the foundation for the organization's support. Her fund-raising activities on behalf of Disciples missions began several years before the CWBM came into being and probably helped shaped the environment from which the association sprang.

In her 1974 book *The Shape of Adam's Rib,* Lorraine Lollis suggested three themes in the missions activities of all Disciples women, each demonstrating the importance of their scriptural roots. First, there was the belief in the "Great Commission" from the Gospel of Matthew, in which Christ instructed Christians to "go therefore and make disciples of all the nations." Then there was the emphasis on the unity of all Christians based on the Disciples' radical notion of *sola scriptura,* or the premise that the return to Scripture (and the corresponding rejection of all man-made creeds) would bring all believers together. The final theme was a reinterpretation of First Corinthians 14:34, which enjoined women to "keep silent in the churches" based on a new appreciation of Galatians 3:28, which argued "in Christ there was neither male nor female." The new emphasis on the Galatians passage mirrored the shift in the role of women after the Civil War. Under the directive of this Scripture, many women Disciples found a mandate to organize themselves in support of the cause of missions. While some viewed women's preaching as a spurious innovation, all could agree that women were an essential part of the Great Commission.[89]

Before 1874, women had been largely excluded from participation in public organizations of Disciples like the ACMS. Selina Campbell offered her support, drawing on her personal connections with many of the leaders of the ACMS, but women like her were the exception rather than the rule. Later, women's role in the home provided the locus of their influence because of the fundamental concern with motherhood and household management. But the quickening pace of urbanization and immigration that resulted in the increasing religious diversity in American cities drove the Disciples to tap women, a heretofore underutilized workforce. Women of other churches had already formed societies geared toward raising money for missions as early as the 1860s.

As the rising opportunities for female education and the higher level of public participation during the Civil War contributed to the desire of many women to take a larger role in the church, in 1875 three prominent Disciples women, Caroline Neville Pearre, Maria Jameson, and M. M. G. Goodwin formed the CWBM. This organization of women set out to raise funds in support of foreign missions, since the crisis of postbellum change in the United States seemed to threaten the spread of the Gospel. Organizations like the CWBM gained a special currency as they tapped the resources of the hitherto silent women who raised millions of dollars to fund thousands of missionaries, both male and female, in such diverse locations as Jamaica and Jerusalem.[90]

The new organization provided women with the opportunity to manage their own business, own their own property, and raise and administer their own funds. The founding of the Christian Woman's

Board of Missions also represented the first Disciples organization concerned with both home and foreign work. Pearre, through a letter-writing campaign, amassed significant support for the CWBM. Isaac Errett, editor of the *Christian Standard,* aided her by publishing an article, "Help Those Women," calling for widespread support of their efforts. Selina Campbell also threw her support behind the organization. These measures ensured that the organization was off to a strong start.

Selina also rose to the public defense of the CWBM. Though she was not among the founders of the organization, she would serve for nine years as president of its second chapter, the West Virginia chapter. When some charged that the CWBM would lead to women preaching, Selina objected vociferously. Her justification of the CWBM's mission appeared in the *Christian Standard* in 1880: "It is predicted by some that our sisterhood's Missionary Society is but a 'stepping stone' to get into the pulpit. If I thought so I would immediately sever myself from it, and give my aid, however small, in some other way."[91] She spent the rest of her life offering the society whatever assistance she could and writing articles in its support to various newspapers. Probably the power of her name contributed to the organization's success. By 1899, as the CWBM approached its twenty-fifth anniversary, nearly $1 million had been raised by the growing thousands of women members. It was by far the most successful fund-raising organization of the entire Stone-Campbell movement.

Selina Campbell's access to the *Millennial Harbinger* was probably one of the reasons she was able to take so prominent a role in a variety of women's organizations. It was a forum to which, despite her initial reluctance, she would return time and again. In November 1858, she published "Another Appeal" to her sisters on behalf of the "library to the 'Adelphian Society,'" also known as the "Preacher's Society" of Bethany College. The library's collection had been destroyed in the same fire that destroyed the college's main building in 1857. "Our young brethren preparing themselves for the ministry, greatly need the aid, in their studies, of a good library," Selina reminded her readers. She heartily embraced the cause of the preacher's society library and worked diligently to raise funds for its support. "Now, my dear sister, may we not look to you, both old and young, for your will and cordial co-operation in so laudable a work?" the article asked. Selina also had words of encouragement for her "younger sisters," to whom she renewed her recommendation to deny "themselves some superfluity of dress" to "invest . . . in so good a work." To collect the money, Selina asked that one woman in each church take charge and then forward the funds to her. "I want a *large* library—I *want* a *noble work* to the honor of my sisters in the good cause," Selina declared. Her donation of fifty dollars led the list of contributors published in the *Harbinger* two months later, and several other women (and also some men) sent in generous amounts.[92]

With such activity Selina's years passed quickly, yet the widow of Alexander Campbell never ceased to expect an end to her own life at any moment. She often seemed to welcome death—not in any suicidal manner but as one might long for reunion with relatives long absent. The following incident, related by Barton Campbell Hagerman (the husband of her granddaughter Mary), illustrates her feelings:

> I remember one morning about four years ago, she came to the breakfast room, and after she was seated began to tell us of a dream she had during the night. She said an angel had appeared, and had beckoned to her and then had vanished from her sight, this he repeated three times, and she asked what we thought the dream could mean? I knelt at her side, took her hand and said, "Mother Campbell, perhaps it means that God is to spare you to us here at least three more years." At this she broke out with almost a sob. "I can not stay here that long, I want to go to heaven"! So she looked forward to death with longing rather than dread and was often heard to repeat to herself, "How sweet to die with Jesus nigh, / The rock of my salvation."

Selina habitually used verse to express her desire to leave this life for heaven. She entitled one of her poems "I Want to Go Home." Its sentimental language reflected her faith in the beautiful life that awaited her in the "abode of the blest." The poem was published in the article containing B.C. Hagerman's funeral sermon and leaves little doubt as to her state of mind regarding her own passing.[93]

Another important facet of Selina's retiring years was her growing relationship with Julia Barclay. The two had become acquainted because their husbands had worked together in promoting Reformation. Julia Sowers Barclay was Selina's closest friend, and an important source of her inspiration. Selina often relied upon her intimate friends for encouragement and shared with them a deep affection that was nurtured through long visits, a voluminous correspondence, and a shared commitment to the importance of living a faithful life. Alexander Campbell believed his wife and Mrs. Barclay to be "well matched" and always appreciated their relationship. "He thinks I am like you," Selina wrote, "and so between Dr. Barclay's views and Mr. C—— I think we must feel it confirmed that there is a similarity both in person and taste."[94] These common tastes seemed to draw the two women together, as their religious convictions and preference for reading and Bible study provided topics for discussion and growing intimacy. Yet their backgrounds do demonstrate some of their differences.

When Miss Julia Sowers, daughter of Captain John Colson Sowers of Staunton, Virginia, married Dr. James Barclay on June 10, 1830, she was seventeen to her husband's twenty-three. Thomas Barclay, her husband's grandfather, "had been the warm and devoted personal friend of both George Washington and Thomas Jefferson, and was sent by Washington as first consul to France, from the then infant republic," according to Decima Campbell Barclay in 1900. Later, while Jefferson served as minister to France, Barclay was sent as commissioner to the emperor of Morocco and in 1786 negotiated a treaty of peace between the two countries. In 1828 his grandson became the first owner of Monticello after the death of Jefferson. After her marriage, Julia Barclay took over as its first mistress. Her two sons were born while the family lived at Monticello, and "both were rocked in the Jefferson family cradle."[95]

The Barclays stayed on the estate for several years, but soon the labor required to manage the house, the gardens, and the large number of visitors who clamored to see the home of Thomas Jefferson prompted the young couple to sell it and pursue their developing interest in serving as missionaries overseas. Julia Barclay sold her jewels to finance the missions effort, but James Barclay's frail mother could not bear to part with her son. The family therefore chose to wait until she had died before beginning its journey. The family left for Jerusalem in early 1851 as the first overseas missionaries for the churches of the Stone-Campbell movement.[96]

Neither Selina nor Julia recorded how they initially met, but the Barclays probably attended one of the meetings at which Alexander Campbell preached and were persuaded by his teachings. Perhaps Selina accompanied her husband to the meeting and there met her friend for the first time. On the other hand, Julia attended a school in Wheeling just a few miles south of Bethany, which was almost certainly where she met her husband, James Turner Barclay, and she might have met Selina there as well. However they originally met, the deep friendship between the two women outlasted both of their marriages and sustained them as widows. Unfortunately none of Julia's letters to Selina have survived, but the material in Selina's letters to her lifelong friend suggest much about the nature of their relationship. "I must say in all *sincerity* that I have never met with any friend (and I have a good *many* that I love and admire both for their personal and christian virtues) that I so fully appreciate their natural and christian *enthusiasm* than I do Sister J. A. Barclay," Selina said of her friend.[97] She constantly begged her friend for a visit and called upon Julia many times wherever she was living.

Throughout their lives Selina Campbell shared with Julia, during their visits and through her letters, some of her deepest feelings and struggles. The two commiserated regarding their heavy domestic responsibilities. Selina confided to Julia her anxiety over the lack of emphasis on foreign missions among the Disciples and her efforts to help Sister Williams, a missionary serving in the Holy Land. At the same time she told Julia of her great relief when the life of her husband, Alexander, was spared during a train accident. She confided her great thankfulness that "his *guardian angel was near & preserved him through* the *wreck* of *smashed cars.*"[98]

Through her letters, Selina conveyed her appreciation of and reliance on her good friend. Her words to Julia illustrate the depth of her affection: "And you my beloved sister may I say, that I *realized in you more than I had anticipated.* . . . I never was a flatterer. I fear you might think so of me but I must say that I *love* you all *dearly.*" She depended on her friendship with Julia for support and encouragement in the challenges she commonly faced. She could express her feelings to Julia, knowing that they would be received by an open, loving heart. "I have no language to express the high value & estimate I set upon your sympathetic heart!" she once wrote. She also judged Julia's heart to be "free from the hypocrisy of this sinful world and imbued with kind gracious & noble christian principles." She especially admired her friend's faithful devotion to the cause of Christ. Likening Julia to "a priceless jewel," she assured her friend that she did not expect a compliment in return. Her comments were sincere and deeply felt, for Julia was dearer "to me than any *one* of a christian female on earth *besides,*" as Selina wrote in 1859.[99]

When Julia's husband died in 1874, both women lived with their wedded children, and the bonds of friendship strengthened. Since the intermarriage of their children had cemented their relationship several years previously, during the last decade of Selina's life, they spent a great amount of time together at Bethany Mansion and in Alabama. In the later years of their lives, the two widows offered each other companionship during the twilight of their lives. Only eight years apart in age, they often spent their time sewing for their grandchildren or conversing about fond memories. They loved to read Scripture together, but when they could no longer "see to read very well," they read "from memory's pages," wrote one local journalist. Others observing their loving companionship "spoke of them as the dear old grandmothers, and always thought of them as sitting here in the same room, cherishing together the precious dreams of reunions soon with loved ones in the realms above sharing together these sweet immortal hopes for nearly a quarter of a century."[100]

In 1897, rumors flew as the newspapers began publishing stories with headlines that warned "She May Die: The Possibly Fatal Illness of Mrs. Alexander Campbell." An attack of influenza had left her bedridden, and Selina's family gathered around. Though it was hoped she would recover and live to see an entire century, after a few weeks her mind began to wander. The end seemed near. A few days later she slipped away "as quietly as one would lie down to pleasant dreams," according to one journalist.[101]

Following her passing, newspapers throughout West Virginia and Kentucky carried obituaries of the "Mother in Israel." Her funeral drew hundreds to Bethany Mansion where eight of her grandchildren served as pall-bearers. "The services opened with singing, and the reading of passages of scripture, favorites of the deceased," read one account. These activities were followed by the funeral sermon, preached by B.C. Hagerman. Published in the *Christian Standard,* Hagerman's comments emphasized Selina's longing to be reunited to her husband, her "remarkable natural powers," and "the history of [her] fellowship of labor and of love" with her husband. Hagerman stressed her welcoming attitude toward her own demise, and though many tears were shed, the funeral was not a tragic event.[102]

Perhaps Decima and a few others at the funeral recalled the scene over thirty years earlier when Selina's husband had reaffirmed his deep affection and love for her. That occasion had coincidentally marked the start of a new life for her that had culminated in the development of a new career. In the years to follow she improved those strengths of her personality that had lain somewhat dormant while she cared for her cherished family. Near the end of her life she assured William that she was "happy to remember that I have valued the time allotted to me."[103] A life of usefulness had left her feeling fulfilled in her calling.

When her obligations to her family had lessened with the passing of her husband and the marriage of her children, she experienced the freedom to pursue her own interests in a much deeper way. It was a role requiring the same vigor that she had tapped when managing her domestic affairs; she now drew on this energy in preserving her husband's memory and his writings. Though domesticity still influenced her life as she cared for her grandchildren and entertained visitors at Bethany Mansion, it only served to reinforce the contentment she felt in her service to those who depended on her. Now, freed from the minutia that domesticity entailed, she pursued personal interests such as reading, writing, and traveling. At the end of her life, however, Selina Campbell truly felt that she had lived a "useful" life even in the "wilderness" of pain and loneliness that followed her husband's death and the last years of her journey outside heaven.

Epilogue

The attributes of Victorian culture identified by Daniel Howe in the introductory essay of *Victorian America* are evident in many of Selina Campbell's observations about various issues in her life. This not only created the milieu in which she ordered her life but also provided the ideological framework for her public expression of women's proper work. Her preoccupation with saving time accorded with the Victorian dedication to efficiency in the home and in the workplace. Victorian culture and Selina Campbell also stressed the existence of a moral certainty that twentieth-century observers often dismiss as self-righteousness.[1] Selina's sturdy belief in the superiority of Christian teachings plainly demonstrates that she shared in this late nineteenth-century moral certainty. But above all, Selina's familiarity with Scripture linked her most closely with great numbers of her Victorian counterparts. Her comments on the world around her place her in the mainstream of Victorian culture and give her thought greater relevance to the experience of American evangelical women. Many aspects of her environment exerted an effect on her, but at the same time her faith played a formative role in shaping her Victorian perceptions.

The intellectual center of the Campbell household was, as in many other Victorian families, the parlor.[2] At midcentury, many Victorians emphasized the serious intellectual exchange that was expected to occur when families and friends met together in their homes and discussed the books they had read and other topics of interest. Such an exchange presupposed a certain level of education for all the members of the family that enabled everyone to participate. Selina also stressed the importance of education for every person. Her parlor, like those of her fellow Victorians, regularly attracted a host of intellectually active visitors. Her husband's status as a national celebrity brought into her home many distinguished guests. Moreover, his role as founder and president of nearby Bethany College further promoted the family's interest in education, helping maintain the quality of parlor exchange. Topics of spiritual interest were the most common, and the parlor was the most frequently chosen site for the family devotions that were another conspicuous feature of the Campbell home. Though the devotions were normally led by Alexander Campbell, Selina often filled in whenever he was absent and no other male could take on the task.

Selina wrote to her children often about the importance of education and frequently reinforced her advice to them with references to the teachings of her husband. She was like many Victorians in that an education afforded the basis for many of the things she valued most in life. She viewed the acquisition of knowledge as closely linked with a person's development of the best qualities of character and with instruction in the importance of faith and virtuous behavior. Such development she encouraged in both her sons and her daughters, rearing them in an environment that included their father's Bethany College and their Aunt Jane McKeever's Pleasant Hill Seminary for women, only a few miles away.[3]

Selina particularly emphasized the role of education in the general improvement of each individual. "I hope that every day that you will value more highly your opportunities for improvement," read one of her letters to William. "What is a Man without Education? If he had Mountains of Gold & Silver without it, he would be neither happy nor respectable. Every thing that tends to improve the Mind & enlarge the heart contributes to the happiness of Man!" It was education that complemented moral behavior and reinforced its foundations. William's mother also placed a premium on the ultimate worth of the education he was currently pursuing: "We live not for time— this as you have often heard your father [say] 'is only our birth place.' We should therefore add daily to our stores of wisdom & knowledge in things pertaining to a better existence." This better existence did not refer to acquiring material possessions or securing a higher standard of living, things often linked to a good education. As a child Selina had learned that "pleasure does not consist in earthly riches; but in a *firm belief* in *his word* and a reliance on his providence from day to day." Thus she warned William to "feel for what you are toiling adding to your knowledge! It is not to *figure* in this world for a few short years nor is it to enable you to lay up treasure upon earth. These considerations are too groveling for a *noble spirit* to be pleased & satisfied with."[4] An education's ultimate value, then, was not the wealth it might bring but the improvement it wrought in a person's character.

The mother also wished her son to understand that while the privilege of education came from God, responsibility for pursuing it fell to William. "It is the poor lost sinful man that breaks over all that God has made, that restraints [*sic*] & neglects to perform the things assigned him by his Creator and thus destroys his usefulness & happiness. . . . You will think I have been preaching a Sermon but I only wish to give you something to think about."[5] She believed fervently that God meant for his followers to pursue knowledge in order to know Him better. This belief she passed on to her children in the form of an exhortation to be diligent in their studies and to comprehend their education as a privilege coming from the Lord himself.

Selina thus impressed upon her son the importance of persevering in his education. Confident that he would learn to appreciate the worth of his studies, she encouraged him to do his best and openly complimented him on his progress. "I am happy to know that you are improving," she wrote. "You spell much better, and write much better than you did. And I have no doubt that you have greatly improved otherwise." Should he labor long enough, she was confident he would see the good result of his efforts and be inspired to continue. She told him so in one of her regular letters. "I suppose it is not so hard now to fix your mind pon [*sic*] any study as it was when you first began. And as your mind enlarges and you see the beauty of a good education you will love to study *more & more!!*"[6]

Another dimension of the proper education existed beyond the usual instruction in composition, reading, mathematics, and natural science. Selina's letters to William reveal a deeper concern for the moral aspects of education apart from the intellectual. She and her husband believed that no education was complete without training in moral as well as intellectual principles. Without a "moral cultivation," she reminded William, "you have heard your father say all the learning in the world would be of no account." Indeed, a lack of moral training could be disastrous, for as Selina believed, "many are made worse by being what is called *educated* without having the *heart* & the affections rightly trained."[7] The true value of education lay not in merely gaining knowledge but in developing a character guided by moral principles. It was the moral training that would prepare the Christian for the kingdom of God.

In the context of these observations about education, Selina reminded her son of the importance of reading his Bible and observing the Lord's day. This was the foundation of any moral teaching. Through studying the Bible William would learn how to "govern" himself and "how [to] treat your fellow beings as you should." His mother especially underscored the importance of developing a close relationship (through prayer) with Jesus Christ, for it is Christ "in Heaven making intercession for us." By studying the Scriptures daily, one received another kind of "goodly instruction" that comes from "the precious word of life."[8] This kind of education was deemed the most important —reflecting Selina's emphasis on morality over intelligence.

The middle of the century brought national conflicts to the doorstep of the Campbells. Some time before the assault on Fort Sumter and the first battle at Manassas Junction, Selina and Alexander had noticed that the northern and southern sections of the country were increasingly in conflict. While touring Fort Leavenworth in Kansas in 1859, for example, Selina commented on the "soldiers . . . on parade, preparing themselves for the horrors of war!!" She expressed her longing for the day when "nations shall 'beat their swords into plough-shares, and their spears into pruning-hooks; and study war no more.' "[9] Less than two years later, as she was returning home from a trip to Washington,

D.C., she and her husband learned of the attack on Fort Sumter and the start of the Civil War.

Selina Campbell's views on the war between the North and the South were shaped primarily by her experience living in what would become the new state of West Virginia and by her faith in her God. As a resident of one of the counties in the far northern part of the western Virginia panhandle, she was far removed from the centers of slavery, the most obvious source of the sectional conflict. Although her husband owned a few slaves, he had also spoken against slavery at the Virginia Constitutional Convention in 1829–1830 and had freed each of his slaves at the earliest opportunity. Neither Selina nor Alexander felt tied by the institution of slavery to one side in the conflict; both of them, but especially Selina, worried more about the horror of war than about the correctness of either side's ideology.

To Selina the appalling consequences of the war were immediately apparent. She regretted the impact of armed conflict on "many whom we thought the personification of meekness & good will." She was saddened to see those around her "exhibit wrath and the spirit of *war*!" But what especially troubled her was the question of whether a Christian could rightly fight in a war at all. In general, the members of the Disciples of Christ, like their counterparts in many other churches, joined both sides of the conflict between North and South. Perhaps because they had no structure through which to accomplish a division, the Disciples did not formally split over the questions surrounding the war.[10] Nonetheless discussion of the issue was bitter and filled with tension. Many Disciples considered pacifism the only response sanctioned by Scripture, while others felt called by duty or patriotism to fight on the side of their region or on the side of those whose convictions they supported. Like many who lived in the border states, Selina never expressed open support for either side. Instead, she regarded the war as a judgment on both sections of the nation. She called the first battle at Manassas Junction "a dreadful bother." Her only hope lay "in a God-hearing prayer that he will protect and defend mine in these perilous regions." She was also greatly distressed by the pillaging that followed the arrival of the "Yankees" in the southern states, but in all she saw the judgment of God in "Tribulation after Tribulation" accompanying the war.[11] Selina continually observed through the lens of her faith the greatest armed conflict that she would witness in her lifetime. While many chose to fight from loyalty to home or to a cause, Selina's loyalty to the God of her faith and to His cause created a spirit of neutrality within her.

It was, however, in the delicate realm of gender relations that the wife of Alexander Campbell showed some of her most brilliant abilities and indicated women's potentially active role in Victorian society and in church life. Occasionally frustrated with those who arbitrarily restricted women's activities and God-given aptitude, she labored arduously throughout her life to promote the cause of women's activism without ever undermining the ideal of true womanhood. At times her support might focus on financial matters; in other instances she provided critical emotional support to women seeking important new opportunities. She urged women who felt they had nothing to contribute to consider new ways in which they might be able to serve the cause of "Truth." Always her promotion of the proper roles for women focused on their relationship to the kingdom of God on earth and the need to promote this kingdom to inaugurate the coming millennium. These were the foundations of Selina's concept of truth.

Two aspects of Selina Campbell's life illuminate the subject of gender in the Stone-Campbell movement especially well. First, Selina mirrored the ideology of women's roles in the Disciples of Christ. The importance of domesticity, the involvement of women in mission efforts and fund raising, and the support of a specific female piety all find expression in her daily activities and at the same time reflect the experience of those around her. But on another level Selina Campbell also served as a motivator and a catalyst for change when she initiated new roles for women or provided unique apologies for current practices. She did not merely accept meekly the role that culture assigned to her. She actively pursued a dynamic part for herself and for her "Christian sisters in common faith." Nor did she agree with those who sought a wholly new role for women, for her views had little in common with those of the women's movement. Rather, she reinterpreted traditional female roles to meet the challenges of a new era and to enlarge the arena in which women could act.

The most common forums for Selina's concept of gender included her relationship with her husband, her close friendships with other women, her writing career, and her use of female networks. Within these arenas she developed her notions of the proper role for women and in some instances initiated new opportunities for them.

Sarah Smart, a close friend, shared Selina's interest in the abilities of women and in the power of the written word. Mrs. Smart participated with her husband in performing editorial duties for the *Christian Monitor* for most of the 1880s. Formerly known as the *Ladies Christian Monitor,* the paper continued to publish many items of interest to women even after its name and its focus changed. In letters and personal visits, the two women exchanged thoughts on a number of issues, and the topic of their correspondence most often centered on the role of women and items of related interest that had been published in other papers.

In one of her letters to Sister Smart, Mrs. Campbell affirmed the value of her friend's words: "Your precious favor of the 1st inst. came duly to hand; it was read gratefully & lovingly I might say with tears. It is comforting to realize that we are remembered by christian sympathetic hearts!" Selina drew encouragement from her friendship with Mrs. Smart. In her correspondence with this friend, Selina expressed her "great interest in the growing work of my Sisterhood!"[12] When she agreed to act as subscription agent for the *Monitor* in her area, the responsibility for signing up new readers for the publication allowed her to act in support of the issues that Smart championed, especially those related to promoting the involvement of women in church life.

Selina's strengths as a writer and as a faithful Christian frequently elicited praise from her peers. Those who knew her well acknowledged their respect for her unique gifts. Mrs. David Burnet, whose husband was a prominent Detroit preacher and later president of the ACMS, described "Sister Campbell" as a "good, zealous woman," a "genuine woman zealous with wisdom."[13] Mrs. Burnet had worked closely with Mrs. Barclay and Mrs. Campbell to raise awareness and support for the missionary society. They commonly supported and encouraged each other through regular correspondence. The respect expressed by friends with whom she worked so diligently would probably have warmed Selina's heart had she known about it, for she valued their friendship highly.

The issues facing the sisters of the Stone-Campbell movement both in the church and in the home consumed much of Selina's attention throughout her life. The many articles signed "Mrs. Alexander Campbell" reveal her commitment to spreading information about the opportunities available to women. She and her husband shared a high view of the abilities of the "gentler sex" and worked both together and separately to marshal the resources of the women in support of the churches. Most important, Selina valued the connection she felt with her "Christian sisters in common faith."

Within the Disciples of Christ and the Campbell home, the parallel dichotomies between the "home and the public" and the "world and the church" are important aspects of the separate spheres ideology. To many evangelical Christians the home took on a specific significance first for its education of children in the gospel and later for its activism in supporting foreign and domestic missions. Selina Campbell's life illustrates the connection between religious beliefs and the development of the separate spheres ideology among evangelical women. While many social and religious groups adapted to the new economic and social realities, the Disciples' concern with the spiritual world gave new meaning to the separate spheres in many unique ways.

Like most nineteenth-century American women, Selina Campbell attributed the advancement of women in the United States and within the Disciples of Christ to the influence of Christianity on Victorian culture. She explained the link between women's elevated position in the United States and the spread of the Gospel in an 1879 article in the *Christian Monitor.* "Women should indeed be unfeignedly thankful and grateful and most zealously and devotedly attached to our Redeemer," Selina wrote, "when she thinks of the humiliation and degradation he has raised her from, under the benign influences of his teaching, and the parts he has assigned her, and permitted her to take, in his death and resurrection; and indeed throughout his whole ministry."[14] Other writers assigned more temporal benefits to women from the Christian faith: "The religions of Christ, in spite of all that is said to the contrary, restores to woman her natural position and rights as the companions of man. The spirit of love, gentleness and tenderness, which Christianity inspires—a spirit entirely unknown to the ancient religions—working this reform for woman. In Christ there is neither male nor female all are one."[15] Thus, many Disciples, and many other Americans as well, concluded that Christianity had played a large role in elevating women. Their faith in Christian teaching led them to see its reflection in their society. Some noted that in areas where Christianity has gone, woman's position had improved, and in areas without the Gospel her position remained suppressed. Whether or not such global influence can accurately be attributed to Christianity, many Disciples believed such evaluations. Alfred Gilbert, one Disciple author writing in 1880, further described the benefits of Christianity to American women by comparing them with women in other cultures:

All the difference between a Christian home and a Mohammedan harem or Hindoo zenana, you owe to Christ. The mother and father-love that welcomed your birth in the family instead of casting you into a river, or smother[ing] your infant cry by firmly closed mouth and nostril you owe to Christ. Your position to-day as the peer of your brother and the prospective equal of your husband instead of his plaything and slave, you owe to Christ. . . . It is the strong arm of Christ that has lifted woman up from the abyss of degradation into which the heathen world combined to sink her, and placed her on the high vantage-ground she occupies in our own favored land.[16]

Such opinions manifest the confidence that many had in the advancing role of women. It was a role based on their faith and interpreted through it.

The validity of the Disciples' beliefs about "heathen lands" aside, the primacy of faith in their lives determined many of their responses to new ideas. Their faith was rooted in their belief of the divine origin of the Scriptures. Selina shared wholeheartedly in these beliefs and was certainly influenced by the many articles that appeared in the papers she often read. Moreover, she and others often located the core of the differences between the Christian world and the heathen world in the power of the Bible:

> Whether we admit or deny the Divine origin of the sacred volume, yet history compels us to allow that it has existed among us for centuries, and that its thoughts have blended with our thoughts, and as a consequence greatly influenced our conduct. We are also forced to grant that there is not another book except the Bible which exalts woman to her proper position as the "helpmeet" of man. You cannot find this doctrine in the sacred books of the East or the West, or the North or the South. This is saying much in favor of Scriptures, because the opinions that they furnish concerning the equality and rights of women are natural, are humane and just, benevolent and beneficial.[17]

Thus Selina and her fellow Disciples revered Scripture as the source of the woman's role and of the definition of her responsibility—not her husband or men in general. This was the real basis of Selina's active role in her marriage and in her church. As another Disciple sister explained, "the Bible is the woman's Magna Charta. In this blessed book her destiny is predicted, her duties defined and her privileges made sure by the inalterable promises of God."[18] Given such benefits from Christianity and the Bible through Jesus Christ, women regarded their service to God, church, and community as an expression of gratitude. Calls to female action based on such appeals appeared often in the pages of Restoration Movement journals and in the writings of Selina Campbell.[19] The Christian Women's Board of Missions stood as an example of the ultimate results of such appeals.

The change in the scope and nature of women's activities is significant. Fred Arthur Bailey has discussed it in terms of an evolution from the "true woman," the pious, submissive housewife, to the "new woman," the urban, female social activist. While Bailey and like-minded scholars have described this change as a shift from a passive role to an active one, the experience of women like Selina Campbell suggests that it may more aptly be characterized as a shift from a private, home-centered role with its own active elements to a more visible public role intended to counteract destructive social tendencies. The distinction is important in that it frees the analysis of the separate spheres arrangement from its restrictive roots in feminist thought. Now the nature of woman's sphere need not be interpreted through notions about sexual equality and the women's movement of the late twentieth century. Instead, it can be evaluated in terms of women's culture, religious identity, and individual experience.

Calls to action on the part of Disciples women increasingly reflected a new, almost gender-neutral aspect at the end of the nineteenth century that largely replaced the emphasis on the coming millennium. Although careful to respect the primacy of the domestic role for women, Selina Campbell and other authors nevertheless emphasized both the male and the female role in spreading the Gospel, the useful Christian's greatest call. The new challenges of the church in the closing decades of the nineteenth century demanded full mobilization of all resources, thus the more public role for women who had previously not participated publicly. Belief in the rapidly approaching return of Christ and the beginning of his millennial reign inspired calls for action to save a spiritually dying world. Appeals appeared in the newspapers asking women to commit more of their time and money to the missions effort. "Can a woman claim an individuality in the one great work which Christ has confided to his church to complete?" asked one female Disciple. "In the kingdom of Christ is there any exception to the general law in regard to woman and her work in the church? The salvation of the church, and also the salvation of the world, depend upon a oneness of all believers. . . . Our Savior has taught us that it is the duty of every individual to make the best possible use of every talent that has been given. In bestowing upon woman a being, has not he also given her capability for usefulness?"[20] Thus the role for women shifted in the face of new challenges encountered by the church but remained rooted in earlier conceptions of gender equality.

In addition to the growing concern for missions, the more Arminian aspects of nineteenth-century Protestant theology contributed to a greater degree of activism among women that relaxed some of the constraints on their behavior. Selina was among the women who found new meaning for activism in the new environment. The church historian Leonard Sweet observed that ministers' wives often assumed responsibility for organizing parachurch organizations such as temperance societies, missions organizations, and the like that reflected the new evangelistic theology. Sweet studied the lives of prominent spouses who were involved with their husbands' work but supportive of their own work as well. He concluded that these women because of their prominence were able to provide leadership for other women in many areas of church life.[21] This statement accords with many of Selina's activities affecting the role of women. As the wife of Alexander Campbell, she was in a unique position to lead the way in establishing organizations that offered support to the church but existed outside it. Examples include her support of the CWBM and her leadership in local money-raising efforts.

Beyond the women of the Disciples of Christ, Selina represented the thoughts and ideas of women who accounted for a significant portion of Victorian American society. Like her namesake Lady Selina, Countess of Huntington, she shared with millions of American women, and especially Protestants, a commitment to the Christian faith and its requirements of moral living, diligent promotion of the Gospel, and an active role for women. As a minister's wife she was also a prominent leader for her sisters. They could follow her example in ordering their own lives around marriage, motherhood, and service. Other women followed her lead in supporting missionary societies and in promoting a husband's career as his "fellow soldier." Her unique relationship to one of the nation's most prominent evangelists brought her into contact with countless women who made her their example.

Selina's experience as a Disciple and as a woman placed her in a significant group of Americans. In addition to the one million Disciples of Christ in 1900, millions more Protestants held similar beliefs. These were the people for whom faith was a daily experience of divine reality, not merely a function of their economic status or familial culture. The strong belief that Christ would return to rule the earth in the approaching millennium strengthened them in their daily labor. Then, when the concern for missions shifted their focus outward, the importance of the woman's role did not diminish. Instead, women's labor, still required, took a new form. It was not a revolution in women's role but rather an extrapolation of existing ideology.

Many evangelical women lived their lives according to strongly held beliefs that guided their actions. A strong belief in the divinity of Jesus Christ reinforced their reliance on Scripture as a blueprint for living. For many, as for Selina Campbell, death, women's preaching, motherhood, and a host of other issues found their significance and their final interpretation in Scripture. Like Lady Selina, Countess of Huntington, many American women devoted their entire lives to the spread of the Gospel as well as the maintenance of their household. Modeling their lives after the Christ of Scripture, they saw no void in their existence that could be attributed to their gender. As mothers, as missionaries, as advocates, and as writers, they did not hesitate to use their talents in advancing "the kingdom of God on earth" and in seeking to usher in the millennium. They found through their faith a life of service and dedication for which they sought a reward in the next life, not in their experience on earth. The life of Selina Campbell, "a fellow soldier" in the cause of reforming American religion, reveals that women's role extended well beyond the long undervalued domestic sphere and into a realm of eternal value.

Notes

Introduction

1. Alexander Campbell, "The Right Honorable Selina, Countess of Huntingdon," *Millennial Harbinger* (July 1845): 283–288. (The spelling of Huntingdon is used interchangeably with Huntington, the spelling of Selina Campbell's middle name.)

2. Ibid.

3. Welter, "The Cult of True Womanhood."

4. Braude, "Women's History *Is* American Religious History"; see also Ginzberg, *Women and the Work of Benevolence.*

5. Fred Arthur Bailey makes this argument in his dissertation, "The Status of Women in the Disciples of Christ."

6. Kerber, "Separate Spheres, Female Worlds, Woman's Place," 12–13. See also Kraditor, ed., *Up from the Pedestal;* Lerner, "The Lady and the Mill Girl." See Groover, *The Well-Ordered Home.*

7. See, for example, Berg, *The Remembered Gate,* and Smith-Rosenberg, *Disorderly Conduct,* 14, 21.

8. Douglas, *The Feminization of American Culture,* and Welter, "The Feminization of American Religion," 138; Hatch, *The Democratization of American Christianity,* 3–16.

9. Groover, *The Well-Ordered Home,* 198.

10. Cott, *The Bonds of Womanhood,* 64.

11. Alexander Campbell, Louisville, Ky., to Selina Campbell, Bethany, [W.] Va., March 12, 1839, Campbell Papers.

12. Cott, *The Bonds of Womanhood,* 197.

13. One magazine Selina read regularly that was examined by Welter was the *Ladies Companion.*

14. Campbell, *Home Life and Reminiscences of Alexander Campbell,* 354.

15. Alexander Campbell, "News from the Churches," *Millennial Harbinger* (November 1840): 521 (first quotation); Selina Campbell, Bethany Mansion, to Mrs. S. E. Smart, Saint Louis, Mo., December 23, 1880 (second quotation), Selina Huntington Campbell Papers, Disciples of Christ Historical Society.

16. See *Home Life,* 354, and Selina Campbell to Mrs. S. E. Smart, Saint Louis, Mo., December 23, 1880.

17. See Ryan, *Cradle of the Middle Class,* and Hewitt, *Women's Activism and Social Change.*

18. Daniel Walker Howe argues that Victorians were generally familiar with biblical rhetoric, in "Victorian Culture in America," in *Victorian America;* Selina Campbell, Ingleside Plantation, Ala., to William P. Campbell, Louisville, Ky., December 19, 1867, Campbell Family Papers; Hughes, *Reviving the Ancient Faith,* 32.

19. Selina Campbell, Wheeler Station, Ala., to William P. Campbell, Bethany, W.Va., December 3, 1884, Campbell Family Papers.

20. McAllister and Tucker, *Journey in Faith,* 154–55.

21. In recent years scholars of the Disciples of Christ have come to use this term to mean all groups owing their origins to the teachings of Barton W. Stone and Alexander Campbell. Today the three major bodies with origins in the Stone-Campbell movement are the Christian Church (Disciples of Christ), the Christian Churches/Churches of Christ, and the Churches of Christ.

22. For a discussion of the intellectual roots of the Stone-Campbell movement, see Tristano, *The Origins of the Restoration Movement.* For general histories of the Stone-Campbell movement, see: Earl Irvin West's four-volume series *Search for the Ancient Order,* vol. 1, *1849–1865* (Nashville: Gospel Advocate, 1964); vol. 2, *1866–1906* (Indianapolis: Religious Book Service, 1950); vol. 3, *1900–1918* (Indianapolis: Religious Book Service, 1979); and vol. 4, *1919–1950* (Germantown, Tenn.: Religious Book Service, 1987). See also Leroy Garrett's *The Stone-Campbell Movement: An Anecdotal History of Three Churches* (Joplin, Mo.: College Press, 1981); James DeForest Murch, *Christians Only: A History of the Restoration Movement* (Cincinnati: Standard Publishing, 1962).

23. Hughes, *Reviving the Ancient Faith,* 9.

24. Hatch, *The Democratization of American Christianity,* 74–75.

25. Such letters were probably not preserved, because Campbell received them as he traveled across the country, and he did not bring them home with him.

26. Fox-Genovese, "Two Steps Forward, One Step Back."

27. This did not, however, prevent several women connected with the Disciples movement from associating with movements such as the temperance movement. Two notable exceptions are Zeralda Wallace, stepmother to Lew Wallace, the novelist and Civil War general, and Carrie Nation. Both women figured prominently in women's reform efforts and yet maintained ties with the Disciples movement.

28. It was published by Isaac Errett in Cincinnati, Ohio, from 1866 onward and was one of the most widely read papers of the Disciples of Christ/Stone-Campbell movement.

29. *American Christian Review,* edited by Benjamin Franklin from 1856 to 1878 in Cincinnati, Ohio; *Christian Record,* edited by James Mathes from 1882 to 1892 in Bloomington, Indiana; *Christian-Evangelist,* St. Louis, Missouri.

30. Campbell, "The Right Honorable Selina, Countess of Huntington," 284.

31. Ibid.

32. William T. Moore, "Woman's Sphere and Responsibilities (an address delivered before the Morton Institute of Woodford, Female College)," *Millennial Harbinger* (October 1860): 591.

33. "How May Women Labor in the Gospel?" *Christian Standard* (March 30, 1872): 100; Mrs. H. W. Everest, "Let Us Do Good As We Have Opportunity," *Christian Standard* (July 27, 1878): 237.

34. Mrs. H. Jennie Kirkham, "What Can Women Do?" *Christian Standard* (April 11, 1878): 2.

The Bakewell Family

1. West, *Town Records,* 320–321; Lewis, *Topographical Dictionary of England,* vol. 3, p. 79.

2. In *The Bakewell Family,* Valerie Gould gives several possible origins for the Bakewell town name, including a family called De Basqueville that settled in the area soon after the Norman Invasion and the name Baquina, which referred to a local guide to tracks and mountain passes. Gould also notes that there is consensus only on the point that "Bakewell" has nothing to do with the occupation of baking, unlike the name "Baker."

3. Bakewell, *Bakewell History-Genealogy,* 45–47. Selina maintained contact with her English relatives throughout her life, and though she never returned to her homeland, she retained a fondness for her birthplace. Family records indicate that Samuel, Selina's father, was probably born near Kings-

ton, Staffordshire, but there is no definitive record. Samuel Roscoe Bakewell was the youngest of six sons of Thomas Bakewell, the grandson of the second John Bakewell of Castle Donington, a freeholder country gentleman, and Mary Chadwick Bakewell, a descendent of King Edward III and Phillippa. Samuel's elder brother Thomas, the second son, established the Springvale asylum, at Stone, Staffordshire, where he was the first to develop a system of nonrestraint in treating the mentally ill. Family genealogical records mention that Thomas Bakewell's portrait hangs in the city hall of Wakefield, Yorkshire, even today. He and his wife, Mary Keyes Bakewell, later immigrated to the United States and lived in Norfolk, Virginia, before she died in 1795 and he returned to England (see Bakewell, *Bakewell History-Genealogy,* 47). The year of Samuel's death is not mentioned in published histories of the Bakewell family, but it was most likely 1838. An obituary of Samuel Bakewell states that he died at "the residence of his brother, the late Dr. Thomas Bakewell." (See "Obituary," *Western Transcript* [Wellsburg, W.Va.], October 9, 1838, transcript in Theron Hervey Bakewell Papers.)

4. Ann Maria's parents, George and Ann Tudor Bean, had married in 1762, also at St. Chad's. The marriage records are found in serially published records from 1898 to 1935. Shropshire Parish Register Society, *Shropshire Parish Registers,* vol. 17.

5. As of 1847, one of the tombstones read: "Ann Bean, aged 62, Aug. 17, 1800." See Alexander Campbell to Clarinda Campbell, from Nottingham, June 15, 1847, reprinted in "Letters from Europe," *Millennial Harbinger* (August 1868): 475–476.

6. For information on the pottery industry in Staffordshire during this time, see Thomas, *The Rise of Staffordshire Potteries,* 168–186.

7. See Western Pennsylvania Genealogical Society, *A List of Immigrants who Applied for Immigration Papers in the District Courts,* vol. 1.

8. After the death of her mother at the establishment of the Campbell-Barclay Museum, Decima Campbell Barclay made a partial inventory of the items brought over that were still in the family's possession. A list of these documents is on file at the Disciples of Christ Historical Society.

9. Wellsburg was known as Charlestown until 1816, when its name was changed to avoid a duplication with another town in the eastern part of the state. The name "Charlestown" came from Charles Prather, the proprietor, but was later changed to "Wellsburg" for Alexander Wells, his only son-in-law.

10. Horatio N. Bakewell, Wellsburg, (W.) Va., to Samuel R. Bakewell, Tuscaloosa, Ala., March 29, 1822, Theron Hervey Bakewell Papers.

11. Ibid.

12. Selina Campbell, Wellsburg, (W.) Va., to Samuel Bakewell, Tuscaloosa, Ala., April 1, 1822, Theron Hervey Bakewell Papers.

13. The first was the congregation founded at Brush Run, several miles from Bethany. Several members of the Brush Run congregation lived in Wellsburg. They formed a new church that was also led by Campbell.

14. Wellsburg Church of Christ Minutes, 1823–1906, copy on file at Bethany College Archives. See also *The Second Church of the Disciples of Christ* (St. Louis: Christian Publishing, 1909).

15. Brooke County Deed Book No. 8, p. 114, copy on file at Brooke County Library, Wellsburg, W.Va. According to Selina (in her letter written to Theron on Christmas Day 1826), the land had been sold to Dawson by Mr. B. Wells (the "Wells" of Wellsburg) for $1,200.

16. Selina Bakewell, Wellsburg, (W.) Va., to Theron Bakewell, Washington, D.C., December 25, 1826, Theron Hervey Bakewell Papers.

17. I found the original article on microfilm in the West Virginia History Room, West Virginia University.

18. To Theron Hervey Bakewell, the sibling closest to Selina in age, historians owe a debt. By carefully preserving his correspondence, he gave us the most valuable glimpse of her family life. The over 500 items of Theron's papers richly describe his relationship with his sister and other family members and the family's experiences living on the western Virginia frontier. Theron Bakewell did not marry until late in life at the age of forty. His wife, Mary Bell Tomlinson Martin, was a widow with two children who lived in Morgantown, (West) Virginia. The couple eventually settled in Moundsville, (West) Virginia, and had several children, including one who was named Selina Huntington Bakewell after her beloved aunt. Theron and his sister remained close for most of their life even though they spent many years apart during their childhood. In fact, for several years after her marriage, Theron lived with his sister at Bethany Mansion. He eventually left to seek business opportunities in southwestern Virginia.

19. He died in his twenties unmarried; Selina Bakewell to Theron Bakewell, Washington, D.C., December 25, 1826, Theron Hervey Bakewell Papers.

20. Selina Campbell, Wellsburg, (W.) Va., to Theron Bakewell, Washington, D.C., February 28, 1827, Theron Hervey Bakewell Papers.

21. *Clarion and Tennessee State Gazette,* Nashville, July 15, 1817, pp. 3–5, copy supplied by the Museum of Early Southern Decorative Arts, Winston-Salem, North Carolina.

22. Theron returned home to Wellsburg and soon thereafter went to live at the Campbell Mansion with his then married sister, Selina.

23. Horatio N. Bakewell, Wellsburg, (W.) Va., to Samuel R. Bakewell, Tuscaloosa, Ala., March 29, 1822, Theron Hervey Bakewell Papers.

24. Horatio N. Bakewell, Wellsburg, (W.) Va., to Samuel R. Bakewell, Coffeville, Ala., August 14, 1823, Theron Hervey Bakewell Papers.

25. Ibid.

26. Selina Bakewell to Theron Bakewell, Washington, D.C., December 25, 1826.

27. Ibid.; Selina Bakewell, Wellsburg, (W.) Va., to Theron Bakewell, Washington, D.C., February 28, 1827, Theron Hervey Bakewell Papers.

28. Ibid.

29. *Home Life and Reminiscences of Alexander Campbell,* 327.

30. Alexander Campbell, after his marriage to Selina, stepped in to take over the responsibility of setting Edwin up in a career. He assisted Edwin in purchasing a ranch and several hundred sheep to start him out. Unfortunately, Selina's brother never repaid the loan from his brother-in-law, and the default strained the relationship between Alexander and his wife's family.

31. In the undated notes on her childhood written by Selina Campbell and held by the Bethany College Archives, she includes this interesting title for her future husband. It appears nowhere else. These notes may have been excerpts from her diary, which has not survived.

32. Selina Bakewell, Wellsburg, (W.) Va., to Samuel Bakewell, Tuscaloosa, Ala., April 1, 1822.

33. Richardson, *Memoirs of Alexander Campbell,* vol. 1, p. 357.

34. Ibid., 358.

35. *Home Life and Reminiscences of Alexander Campbell,* 20. The Brush Run church was the first and only Campbell church for several years before the formation of the Wellsburg church and was located twelve miles east of Brown's home.

36. Selina Bakewell to Theron Bakewell, Washington, D.C., October 2, 1825.

37. The *Christian Baptist* was the journal edited by Campbell from 1824 to 1830.

38. *Home Life and Reminiscences of Alexander Campbell,* 321–322.

39. Ibid., 354–355. Patterson later had a career as a distinguished Presbyterian preacher.

40. The origin of this assertion is unclear, but it is implied in Louis Cochrane's novel based on Alexander Campbell's life, *The Fool of God.*

41. *Memoirs of Alexander Campbell,* vol. 2, pp. 176, p. 177. Her husband later published this address (more than likely after significant editing) in the *Millennial Harbinger;* see *Memoirs of Alexander Campbell,* vol. 2, pp. 177–179.

The Making of a Partnership

1. Degler, *At Odds,* 8–9.

2. "Women Fit for Wives," by "A Country Parson," *Good Housekeeping,* November 28, 1885, p. 51, quoted in Degler, *At Odds,* 40.

3. Irving T. Green, "The Influence of the Campbell Home on the History of Disciples of Christ," *Christian-Evangelist,* (September 8, 1938): 984.

4. See Groover, *The Well-Ordered Home.*

5. *Memoirs of Alexander Campbell,* 295–296.

6. For a discussion of Campbell's role at the Virginia Constitutional Convention of 1829–1830, see Freehling, *Drift Toward Dissolution.*

7. Groover, *The Well-Ordered Home,* 54.

8. Cott, *The Bonds of Womanhood,* 197.

9. Alexander Campbell, Richmond, Va., to Selina Campbell, Bethany, (W.) Va., November 4, 1829, original at the Center for Restoration Studies, Abilene Christian University, Abilene, Texas.

10. Alexander Campbell, Morgantown, (W.) Va., to Selina Campbell, Bethany, (W.) Va., undated (probably August or September 1829), and Alexander Campbell, Richmond, Va., to Selina Campbell, Bethany, (W.) Va., October 12, 1829, Center for Restoration Studies, Abilene Christian University.

11. Alexander Campbell, Richmond, Va., to Selina Campbell, Bethany, (W.) Va., November 9, 1829, Center for Restoration Studies, Abilene Christian University.

12. Alexander Campbell, Richmond, Va., to Selina Campbell, Bethany, (W.) Va., December 10, 1829, Center for Restoration Studies, Abilene Christian University.

13. Ibid.

14. Alexander Campbell to Selina Campbell, November 9, 1829.

15. Alexander Campbell to Selina Campbell, December 23, 1829, Campbell Family Papers.

16. Alexander to Selina, October 12, 1829.

17. Ibid.

18. Alexander Campbell, Richmond, Va., to Selina Campbell, Bethany, (W.) Va., January 8, 1830, Center for Restoration Studies, Abilene Christian University.

19. *Home Life and Reminiscences of Alexander Campbell*, 468. See also *Campbell Mansion*, 14.

20. *Home Life and Reminiscences of Alexander Campbell*, 338–339.

21. Ibid., 51. See also *Campbell Mansion*, 16.

22. Fuller and Green, *God in the White House*, 141–142.

23. Irving T. Green, "The Influence of the Campbell Home on the History of Disciples of Christ," *Christian-Evangelist* (September 8, 1938): 984.

24. F. W. Emmons, Buffalo, N.Y., to Brother W. W. Ashley, August 10, 1830, Disciples of Christ Historical Society.

25. Selina Campbell, Bethany, (W.) Va., to Virginia Campbell, September 7, 1858, Bethany College Archives.

26. John Udell, Putah, Solano Country, Calif., to William K. Pendleton, Bethany, W.Va., in "Correspondence," *Millennial Harbinger* (March 1867): 152.

27. Selina Campbell, Bethany, (W.) Va., to Margaret B. Campbell, March 6, 1843, Bethany College Archives.

28. Selina Campbell, Bethany, (W.) Va., to Theron Bakewell, December 17, 1833, Theron Hervey Bakewell Papers.

29. For a comparison of southern men and northern women and remarks on the importance of kinship networks in the lives of southern women, see Friedman, *The Enclosed Garden.*

30. Selina Campbell, Bethany, (W.) Va., to Theron Bakewell, Elizabethtown, (W.) Va., June 16, 1842, Theron Hervey Bakewell Papers.

31. Ibid.

32. Selina Campbell, Bethany, (W.) Va., to Theron Bakewell, New Martinsville, (W.) Va., March 29, 1845, and February 9, 1846, Theron Hervey Bakewell Papers.

33. Selina Campbell, Bethany, (W.) Va., to Theron Bakewell, New Martinsville, (W.) Va., February 9, 1846, Theron Hervey Bakewell Papers.

34. Selina Campbell, Bethany, (W.) Va., to Theron Bakewell, New Martinsville, (W.) Va., January 30, 1846, Theron Hervey Bakewell Papers.

35. Ibid.

36. Selina Campbell, Bethany, (W.) Va., to Decima Campbell Barclay, Ingle-

side Plantation, Ala., November 28, 1876, Disciples of Christ Historical Society.

37. Ibid.

38. Selina Campbell, Bethany, (W.) Va., to Julia Barclay, January 30, 1856, Disciples of Christ Historical Society.

39. Selina Campbell, Bethany, (W.) Va., to Theron Bakewell, Fishing Creek, (W.) Va., May 25, 1841, Theron Hervey Bakewell Papers.

40. Ibid.

41. Richardson, *Memoirs of Alexander Campbell*, vol. 2, pp. 591–592, 595.

42. Selina Campbell, Baltimore, Md., to [William Campbell, Wheeling], (W.) Va., December 25, 1857, Bethany College Archives; Selina Campbell, Bethany, (W.) Va., to Julia Barclay, Philadelphia, Pa., January 18, 1858, Julia Barclay Papers; Selina Campbell, Washington, D.C., to Julia Barclay, Philadelphia, Pa., December 22, 1857, Julia Barclay Papers.

43. Richardson, *Memoirs of Alexander Campbell*, vol. 2, p. 633.

44. Ibid.; Selina Campbell, Bethany, (W.) Va., to Julia Barclay, Philadelphia, Pa.?, February 1, 1858, Julia Barclay Papers.

45. Selina Campbell, Bethany, (W.) Va., to Julia Barclay, Philadelphia, Pa.?, March 8, 1858, Julia Barclay Papers.

46. Ibid., echoing her husband's assessment.

47. Alexander Campbell, Jacksonville, Ill., to Selina Campbell, Bethany, (W.) Va., November 30, 1853, John Barclay Papers, Bethany College Archives.

48. See, for example, *Home Life and Reminiscences of Alexander Campbell*, 336.

49. Selina Campbell, Bethany, (W.) Va., to Virginia Campbell, Louisville, Ky.?, September 7, 1858, Campbell Family Papers.

50. Richardson, *Memoirs of Alexander Campbell*, vol. 1, p. 421. This tour included stops all over New England and down the coast to Philadelphia, Baltimore, and Washington, D.C.

51. Sweet, *The Minister's Wife*.

52. Alexander Campbell, Saratoga Springs, N.Y., to Selina Campbell, Bethany, (W.) Va., July 23, 1836, in ibid.; Richardson, *Memoirs of Alexander Campbell*, vol. 1, p. 417.

53. Richardson, *Memoirs of Alexander Campbell*, vol. 1, p. 417.

54. Alexander Campbell, Steamboat *Temper* on the Mississippi, to Selina Campbell, Bethany, (W.) Va., March 27, 1858, Campbell Family Papers.

55. Alexander Campbell, Evergreen Anderson District, S.C., to Selina Campbell, Bethany, (W.) Va., December 29, 1838, Campbell Family Papers.

56. Alexander Campbell, New Orleans, La., to Selina Campbell, Bethany, (W.) Va., January 23, 1839, in *Memoirs of Alexander Campbell,* 455.

57. Alexander Campbell, Lewistown, N.Y., to Selina, Eliza, Lavinia, and Clarinda Campbell, Bethany, (W.) Va., June 18, 1836, reprinted in Richardson, *Memoirs of Alexander Campbell,* 412–413.

58. Alexander Campbell, "Notes of a Tour to Illinois—No. 1," *Millennial Harbinger* (December 1853): 689.

59. Alexander Campbell to Selina Campbell, March 27, 1858.

60. Alexander Campbell, Baton Rouge, La., to Selina Campbell, Bethany, (W.) Va., original in Manuscript Collection, Public Library of Cincinnati, Ohio (copy in Bethany College Archives).

61. C.L.L., "A Letter of A. Campbell," *Millennial Harbinger* (January 1868): 30.

62. Selina Campbell, Huntsville, Ala., to William Campbell, Wheeling?, (W.) Va., April 4, 1859, Campbell Family Papers; Selina Campbell, Bethany, (W.) Va., to William Campbell, Wheeling, (W.) Va., February 18, 1859, Campbell Family Papers.

63. Selina Campbell, Bethany, (W.) Va., to Julia Barclay, Philadelphia, Pa., December 9, 1857, Julia Barclay Papers; Selina Campbell, Bethany, (W.) Va., to Julia Barclay, June 8, 1856, Julia Barclay Papers.

64. Ibid.

65. See Berg, *The Remembered Gate;* Cott, *The Bonds of Womanhood,* 74.

66. Smith-Rosenberg, "The Female World of Love and Ritual," in *Disorderly Conduct* (originally published in *Signs: A Journal of Women in Culture and Society* 1 [1975]).

67. Selina Campbell, Bethany, (W.) Va., to Julia Barclay, Philadelphia, Pa.?, April 24, 1856, Julia Barclay Papers.

68. Selina Campbell, Bethany, (W.) Va., to Julia Barclay, Philadelphia, Pa.?, July 21, 1857, Julia Barclay Papers.

69. Ibid.

70. *Home Life and Reminiscences of Alexander Campbell,* 455.

71. Ibid., 454–455.

72. Sweet, *The Minister's Wife,* esp. chap. 7.

73. Richardson, *Memoirs of Alexander Campbell,* vol. 1, 301–302.

74. See, for example, Alexander Campbell, "Mrs. Judson," *Millennial Harbinger* (September 1848): 524–528. In his review of Mrs. Judson's autobiography, Campbell mentions that the book was "put into my hand by Mrs. Campbell."

75. Alexander Campbell, "Woman's Rights," *Millennial Harbinger* (April 1854): 204–205; "Mrs. Sigourney on Woman's Rights," *Millennial Harbinger* (April 1854): 206–207. Alexander Campbell's article in the same issue entitled "Woman's Rights" introduces Mrs. Sigourney's comments.

76. Selina Campbell, Bethany, (W.) Va., to Mrs. Sarah E. Smart, Saint Louis, Mo., December 23, 1880, Julia Barclay Papers.

77. See also, in Chapter 4, the discussion of Selina Campbell's role in the Christian Women's Board of Missions.

78. Selina Campbell, "Woman's Work," *Christian Standard* (July 27, 1878): 238.

79. Bailey, "The Status of Women in the Disciples of Christ," 52–53.

80. A. Judson, "To the Female Members of Christian Churches in the United States of America," *Millennial Harbinger* (July 1832): 329, 331.

81. Selina Campbell, "Woman's Work."

82. Selina Campbell, "Women Preachers," *Christian Standard* (December 18, 1880): 402; Selina Campbell, "Woman's Work."

83. Ibid.

84. Selina Campbell, Bethany, (W.) Va., to Julia Barclay, Jerusalem, January 19, 1857, Julia Barclay Papers; Selina Campbell, "Women Preachers," 402.

85. See Joan R. Gundersen, "The Local Parish as a Female Institution: The Experience of All Saints Episcopal Church in Frontier Minnesota," *Church History* 55:3 (1986): 307–322; Sr. Elizabeth Kolmer, A.S.C., "Catholic Women Religious and Women's History: A Survey of the Literature," *American Quarterly* 30:5 (Winter 1978): 681–702; and Janet Harbison Penfield, "Women in the Presbyterian Church—An Historical Overview," *Journal of the Presbyterian Historical Society* 55:2 (1977): 107–123.

86. See Selina Campbell, Ingleside Plantation, Ala., to William P. Campbell, Bethany, W.Va., March 25, 1869, Campbell Family Papers; Selina Campbell, Bethany, (W.) Va., to Theron Bakewell, Fishing Creek, Tyler County, Va., May 25, 1841, Theron Hervey Bakewell Papers.

87. Selina Campbell, Bethany, (W.) Va., to Mary Bakewell, Elizabethtown, Marshall County, Va., October 8, 1841, Theron Hervey Bakewell Papers; Selina Campbell, Bethany, (W.) Va., to Mary Bakewell, New Martinsville, Tyler County, Va., August 23, 1846, Theron Hervey Bakewell Papers.

88. Selina Campbell, Bethany, (W.) Va., to Theron Bakewell, Elizabethtown, Marshall County, Va., March 1, 1848, Theron Hervey Bakewell Papers.

89. Ibid.; Selina Campbell, "Women Preachers," 402.

90. See Lasch, *The True and Only Heaven.*

91. Selina Campbell, "A Letter to Young Converts," *Millennial Harbinger* (December 1858): 708–712.

92. Selina Campbell, Bethany, (W.) Va., to Julia Barclay, Jerusalem, January 19, 1857, Julia Barclay Papers.

93. Selina Campbell, "An Appeal to the Sisterhood," *Millennial Harbinger* (February 1856): 119.

94. Ibid.

95. Selina Campbell, Bethany, (W.) Va., to Julia Barclay, Palmyra, Syria, April 1, 1856, Julia Barclay Papers.

96. Selina Campbell, "Sister Mary R. Williams, Missionary in Jaffa," *Millennial Harbinger* (April 1856): 936–937.

97. "Extracts of a Letter from Sister Williams," *Millennial Harbinger* (June 1857): 356; Selina Campbell, "Death of Sister Williams," *Millennial Harbinger* (March 1859): 172.

98. In 1906, when the formal split of the more conservative Churches of Christ from the main body of the Disciples was recognized, one of the most salient areas of conflict between the two groups was the suitability of the missionary society to the Restoration message.

99. Campbell often used the word "Church" to mean not a particular congregation or group of churches but rather the collective body and Christians throughout the World.

100. Selina Campbell, Bethany, (W.) Va., to Julia Barclay, Philadelphia?, February 6, 1857, Julia Barclay Papers.

101. Ibid.

102. Hughes, *Reviving the Ancient Faith,* 75–76.

103. Selina Campbell, Bethany, (W.) Va., to Julia Barclay, Jerusalem?, March 10, 1857, Julia Barclay Papers.

104. Ibid.

105. Ibid.

106. Hughes, *Reviving the Ancient Faith,* p. 85, quoting David Lipscomb, "Benjamin Franklin," *Gospel Advocate* 20 (December 5, 1878): 758.

107. Selina Campbell, Bethany, (W.) Va., to Julia Barclay, Washington, D.C.?, March 11, 1859, Julia Barclay Papers.

"An Abiding Interest and Love"

1. Selina Campbell, Bethany, W.Va., to William Campbell, Wheeling, W.Va., December 9, 1869, Campbell Family Papers. Much of the correspondence be-

tween Selina and her children survives in the archives of Bethany College. The many letters that make up the Campbell Family Papers yield a tremendous amount of information about the relationship between this mother and her children and about the nature of nineteenth-century motherhood itself.

2. D.C., "Woman's Work and Influence," *Christian-Evangelist* (September 20, 1888): 590.

3. Alexander Campbell, "Address to Christian Mothers," *Christian Baptist* (1824): 69.

4. H., "Woman and the Gospel," *Christian Standard* (June 6, 1868): 179; Bailey, "The Status of Women in the Disciples of Christ Movement," 123.

5. Alexander Campbell, "Address to Christian Mothers," 69; Ella F. Smith, "The Woman Helpers," *Christian Standard* (November 5, 1881): 353.

6. Alexander Campbell, New Orleans, La., to Selina Campbell, Bethany, (W.) Va., January 23, 1837, Campbell Family Papers. Alexander Campbell, Bethany, (W.) Va., to Decima and Judson Barclay, Island of Cyprus, May 6, 1864, in Richardson, *Memoirs of Alexander Campbell,* vol. 2, p. 650.

7. The book reads almost like a memoir in which her stated intent is to record all of her memories of her family for the benefit of her grandchildren and any others interested in the life of her husband.

8. Ibid., 21.

9. Richardson, *Memoirs of Alexander Campbell,* vol. 2, p. 462.

10. Ibid., 22.

11. Ibid., 23.

12. *Home Life and Reminiscences of Alexander Campbell,* 488.

13. Selina Campbell, Ingleside Plantation, Ala., to William P. Campbell, Bethany, (W.) Va., May 11, 1871, Campbell Family Papers.

14. Ibid., 24.

15. Selina Campbell, Bethany, W.Va., to William Campbell, Wellsburg, W.Va.?, July 28, 1879, Campbell Family Papers.

16. Selina Campbell, Ingleside Plantation, Ala., to William Campbell, Bethany, W.Va., January 29, 1876, Campbell Family Papers.

17. Proverbs 22:6, New International Version.

18. Alexander Campbell, Lake Erie, to Selina Campbell, Bethany, (W.) Va., June 11, 1836, in Richardson, *Memoirs of Alexander Campbell,* 412, from an 1853 letter to Selina Campbell reprinted in Richardson, *Memoirs of Alexander Campbell,* vol. 2, p. 608.

19. Selina Campbell, Bethany, W.Va., to William Campbell, Wheeling, W.Va., April 12, 1858, Campbell Family Papers.

20. Ibid.

21. Selina Campbell, Bethany, (W.) Va., to Theron Bakewell, Elizabethtown, (W.) Va., July 30, 1847, Theron Hervey Bakewell Papers.

22. Selina Campbell, "A Birthday Remembrance," manuscript in Campbell Family Papers. Melancthon in this context appears to be Philipp Melancthon (1497–1560), a German theologian, friend of Martin Luther, and author of one of the first extensive treatises on Protestant doctrine, *Loci communes rerum theologicarum* (1521).

23. Selina Campbell, Ingleside Plantation, Ala., to William P. Campbell, Bethany, W.Va., January 1, 1876, Campbell Family Papers.

24. Many items of correspondence were destroyed by family members who may have wanted to eliminate unflattering portrayals of themselves and their ancestors, and so it is impossible to draw final conclusions in this matter.

25. *Home Life and Reminiscences of Alexander Campbell,* 28.

26. Ibid., 29.

27. Ibid., 29–30.

28. Alexander Campbell to Brother Wallis, November 25, 1847, published in *Home Life and Reminiscences of Alexander Campbell,* 38.

29. Richardson, *Memoirs of Alexander Campbell,* 573–74.

30. Alexander Campbell, Bethany, (W.) Va., to R. L. Coleman, Cincinnati, Ohio?, January 12, 1848, in Richardson, *Memoirs of Alexander Campbell,* 574–75.

31. Davies, *The Story of an Earnest Life,* 281.

32. Margaret C. Ewing to Theron Bakewell, February 4, 1848.

33. *Home Life and Reminiscences of Alexander Campbell,* 28–29.

34. *Home Life and Reminiscences of Alexander Campbell,* 30. John Newton was a former slave trader who converted to Christianity and became a cleric. He is best known for writing the lyrics to the hymn "Amazing Grace." He was also Selina Campbell's favorite author.

35. Davies, *The Story of an Earnest Life,* 286.

36. Ibid., 291, 294.

37. Edwin Bakewell, Bloomington, Ill., to Theron Bakewell, Flower Mound, Va.?, April 4, 1848, Theron Hervey Bakewell Papers.

38. Selina Campbell, Bethany, (W.) Va., to Theron Bakewell, Elizabethtown, Marshall County, Va., March 1, 1848, Theron Hervey Bakewell Papers.

39. Selina Campbell, Bethany, (W.) Va., to Theron Bakewell, New Martinsville, (W.) Va., January 30, 1846, Theron Hervey Bakewell Papers.

40. *Home Life and Reminiscences of Alexander Campbell,* 30; Selina Camp-

bell, Bethany, (W.) Va., to William P. Campbell, Wheeling, (W.) Va., May 12, 1858, Campbell Family Papers.

41. Selina Campbell, Bethany, (W.) Va., to Theron Bakewell, New Martinsville, (W.) Va., January 30, 1846, Theron Hervey Bakewell Papers.

42. Bloch, "American Feminine Ideals in Transition," 100–101.

43. Ryan, *Cradle of the Middle Class.*

44. See Epstein, *The Politics of Domesticity.*

45. Bloch, "American Feminine Ideals in Transition," 18.

46. Current historiography on women during the Revolutionary War and the Early National period further illuminates the importance of these events. Mary Beth Norton (*Liberty's Daughters*) argues that a reassessment of women's status occurred at the turn of the century that was based on their role as mothers. Prominent revolutionaries such as Thomas Jefferson argued that the virtue necessary to sustain the republic must be preserved in order for it to survive. The domestic role perforce gained status as the center for the infusion of virtues necessary for the development and survival of a democracy. Distinctions between the public and private grew wider as new gender roles developed.

47. Alexander Campbell, "Schools and Education No. II," *Millennial Harbinger* (June 1839): 278.

48. Judge Hopkington, "Influence of Women," *Millennial Harbinger* (May 1844): 237.

49. Selina Campbell, Bethany, (W.) Va., to Margaret B. Campbell, Poplar Hill, near Frankfort, Ky., March 6, 1843, Campbell Family Papers.

50. Ibid.

51. Ibid.

52. *Southern Christian Weekly,* Mountain Home, Ala., 1872–79.

"Usefulness in a Wilderness"

1. *Home Life and Reminiscences of Alexander Campbell,* 349; Alexander Campbell, Louisville, Ky., to Selina Campbell, Bethany, (W.) Va., March 12, 1839, Campbell Family Papers.

2. Selina Campbell, Bethany, (W.) Va., to Julia Barclay, n.p., November 19, 1860, Julia Barclay Papers.

3. *Home Life and Reminiscences of Alexander Campbell,* 350.

4. *Home Life and Reminiscences of Alexander Campbell,* 350–351.

5. The ring had been purchased by Sister Pendleton, the third wife of W. K. Pendleton, as a keepsake that she donated to "enhance the pleasure of the com-

memorative occasion." See *Home Life and Reminiscences of Alexander Campbell,* 351.

6. "In Memory of Alexander Campbell," *Millennial Harbinger* 37 (December 1866): 536–537.

7. Selina Campbell, Bethany, (W.) Va., to J. W. Higbee, n.p., July 13, 1887, Selina Campbell Folder.

8. Selina Campbell, Bethany, (W.) Va., to Julia Barclay, n.p., October 12, 1863, Julia Barclay Papers.

9. "Diary of Mary Anna Purvis Campbell," as transcribed by George Miller, transcript and original in Bethany College Archives; W. K. Pendleton, "Death of Alexander Campbell," *Millennial Harbinger* (April 1866): 138.

10. Purvis diary, Campbell Family Papers.

11. See Sweet, *The Minister's Wife,* 7, and Berg, *The Remembered Gate.*

12. Washington, "In Memory of Alexander Campbell," *Millennial Harbinger* (December 1866): 520.

13. "Mrs. S. H. Campbell to Her Friends," *Millennial Harbinger* (July 1866): 332–333. People and groups mentioned in the letter include the Executive Board of the American Bible Union; the Board of the American Christian Missionary Society; the citizens of the town of Bethany and its vicinity; the "Christian Congregation" at Glasgow, Scotland; Maysville, Ky.; Paw Paw, Michigan; and about forty individuals all connected to the Disciples of Christ.

14. Sweet, *The Minister's Wife,* 89.

15. Selina Campbell, Ingleside Plantation, Ala., to William P. Campbell, Louisville, Ky., April 13, 1871, Campbell Family Papers.

16. Details relating to the terms of the will can be found in a lengthy newspaper article by M. Jacobs based on research in the Brooke County Records and published in the *Wellsburg Herald* beginning on January 21, 1898.

17. The original 1815 grant from John Brown came with 300 acres that he sold to Campbell for one dollar. In 1820, Brown deeded another 136 acres. By his death, however, Campbell, through his own management, had increased the holding to 1,949 acres. See Historic Bethany's "Campbell Mansion," 26.

18. James H. Pendleton, Bethany, W.Va., to T. M. Henley, n.p., April 1, 1866, Henley Papers.

19. Hughes explores this issue in *Reviving the Ancient Faith,* 43–44.

20. Selina Campbell, Bethany, W.Va., to Virginia Thompson, Louisville, Ky., January 25, 1867, Campbell Family Papers.

21. Selina Campbell, Bethany, W.Va., to Virginia Thompson, Louisville, Ky., January 25, 1867, Campbell Family Papers.

22. Jacobs, *Wellsburg Herald,* January 21, 1898, copy in Hagerman scrapbook, Campbell Family Papers.

23. Selina Campbell, Bethany, W.Va., to William Campbell, Louisville, Ky., February 15, 1867, Campbell Family Papers; Judson's brother Robert and Decima's cousin Emma had married in 1867; Selina Campbell, Ingleside Plantation, Ala., to William Campbell, Louisville, Ky., January 31, 1868, Campbell Family Papers.

24. Selina Campbell, Bethany, W.Va., to William Campbell, Louisville, Ky., June 19 and July 8, 1868, Campbell Family Papers.

25. *Home Life and Reminiscences of Alexander Campbell,* 52.

26. Selina Campbell, Ingleside Plantation, Ala., to William Campbell, Louisville, Ky., January 31, 1869, Campbell Family Papers.

27. Selina Campbell, Ingleside Plantation, Ala., to William Campbell, Louisville, Ky., June 12, 1871, Campbell Family Papers; Selina Campbell, Ingleside Plantation, Ala., to Nannie Cochrane Campbell, Louisville, Ky., September 20, 1876, Campbell Family Papers.

28. Selina Campbell, Ingleside Plantation, Ala., to William Campbell, Louisville, Ky., January 31, 1869, Campbell Family Papers; Selina Campbell, Bethany, W.Va., to William Campbell, Louisville, Ky., December 9, 1869, Campbell Family Papers.

29. Selina Campbell, Bethany, W.Va., to William Campbell, Louisville, Ky., November 11, 1869, Campbell Family Papers.

30. Selina Campbell, Ingleside Plantation, Ala., to William Campbell, Louisville, Ky., December 17, 1868, Campbell Family Papers.

31. Ibid.

32. Selina Campbell, Ingleside Plantation, Ala., to William P. Campbell, n.p., December 15, 1875, Campbell Family Papers.

33. Ibid.

34. Selina Campbell, Ingleside Plantation, Ala., to William P. Campbell, n.p., December 23, 1875, Campbell Family Papers; Selina Campbell, "Virginia C. Barclay," *Christian Standard* (September 30, 1882): 306.

35. There are several reasons why Richardson's work remains the most comprehensive treatment of Campbell's life even 130 years later. First, he had access to voluminous amounts of material that is no longer available. Second, his coverage of the life of Alexander Campbell is quite extensive and skillful. He probes many salient issues, including Campbell's place in the history of global religion, in a very informative manner. Not surprisingly, there is little real criticism of Campbell's thought and behavior, but in fairness, even

Campbell's critics found little to criticize about his manner. (See, for example, Jeremiah Jeter, *Campbellism Examined* [New York: Sheldon, Lamport, and Blakeman, 1855], in which this Baptist critic accuses Campbell of being sectarian and dogmatic but finds little fault with his character.) There have been a few works smaller in scope, including Perry Gresham's collection *The Sage of Bethany*. Apart from Edwin Groover's study and Richardson's biography, only two works mention Campbell's family life in any detail. One is the first biographical essay on Campbell after his death, Charles Seglar's introduction to Campbell's *Familiar Lectures on the Pentateuch*. His essay, however, contains little that was not included in Richardson's larger work, published later. Recently, the only other work to include significant information about Campbell's private life is Louis Cochran's "The Several Worlds of Alexander Campbell," 3–17.

36. Selina Campbell, Bethany, W.Va., to Robert Richardson, n.p., June 23, 1868, Disciples of Christ Historical Society; Selina Campbell, Bethany, W.Va., to William Campbell, Louisville, Ky., December 9, 1869, Campbell Family Papers.

37. Selina Campbell, Bethany, W.Va., to Sister Sarah Smart, Saint Louis, Mo., February 10, 1882, Disciples of Christ Historical Society.

38. The book was published in 1882. Selina wrote it between 1879 and 1881, just after she moved back into the mansion. It included, in addition to her comments about her husband, several letters and speeches, both hers and her husband's, that had not previously been published. The *Memphis Appeal* was a commercial newspaper in Tennessee with no direct connection to the religious world. *Home Life and Reminiscences of Alexander Campbell*, 417–418.

39. Ibid., 418.

40. Ibid., 371–372.

41. Today it sits prominently in the entrance to the Campbell Family Archives in the college library—a testament to the affection of his wife and the students and associates of the college he founded.

42. Selina Campbell, Ingleside Plantation, Ala., to Nannie Cochrane Campbell, Bethany, W.Va., September 8, 1876, Campbell Family Papers; Selina Campbell, Ingleside Plantation, Ala., to Nannie Cochrane Campbell, Bethany, W.Va., September 20, 1876, Campbell Family Papers.

43. Selina Campbell, Bethany, W.Va., to William Campbell, Louisville, Ky., October 21, 1869, Campbell Family Papers.

44. Selina Campbell, Bethany, W.Va., to William Campbell, Louisville, Ky., November 3, 1869, Campbell Family Papers.

45. Selina Campbell, Bethany, W.Va., to William Campbell, Louisville, Ky., July 15, 1868, pp. 1–4, Campbell Family Papers, and pp. 5–6 in the Julia Barclay Papers.

46. Selina Campbell, Bethany, W.Va., to William Campbell, Louisville, Ky., February 10, 1867, Campbell Family Papers.

47. Reprinted in *Home Life and Reminiscences of Alexander Campbell,* 367–370.

48. Ibid., 367–369.

49. Selina Campbell, Bethany, W.Va., to William Campbell, Louisville, Ky., July 15, 1868, pp. 1–4, Campbell Family Papers, and pp. 5–6 in the Julia Barclay Papers.

50. Selina Campbell, Bethany, W.Va., to William Campbell, Louisville, Ky.? December 19, 1867, Campbell Family Papers.

51. Selina Campbell, Bethany, W.Va., to William Campbell, Louisville, Ky., July 15, 1868, pp. 1–4, Campbell Family Papers, and pp. 5–6 in the Julia Barclay Papers.

52. Alexander Campbell, Jr., Wheeling, W.Va., to Selina Campbell, Bethany, W.Va., February 8, 1871, Campbell Family Papers.

53. Selina Campbell, Bethany, W.Va., to Patrick Campbell, Wellsburg, W.Va.?, ca. July 28, 1879, Campbell Family Papers; Selina Campbell, Ingleside Plantation, Ala., to Mrs. P. M. Cochrane, Louisville, Ky.?, November 4, 1875, Campbell Family Papers.

54. Selina Campbell, Ingleside Plantation, Ala., to William Campbell, Bethany, W.Va., December 23, 1875, Campbell Family Papers.

55. Ibid.

56. Ibid.

57. Selina Campbell, Ingleside Plantation, Ala., to William Campbell, Bethany, W.Va., February 2, 1876, Campbell Family Papers.

58. "Letter from Sister Campbell," *Old Path Guide* (March 1881): 211.

59. Article from the *Memphis Appeal* for May 27, 1874, republished in the *Christian Standard* (June 13, 1874): 187.

60. Ibid.

61. Ibid.

62. David Walk, "Items from Correspondents: Alabama," *Christian Standard* (September 23, 1871): 303.

63. Selina Campbell, "A Letter to Young Converts," *Millennial Harbinger* (December 1858): 708–712.

64. Ibid., p. 710.

65. Ibid., p. 711; Howe, *Victorian America,* 19.

66. Selina Campbell, Louisville, Ky., to William Campbell, Wellsburg, W.Va., January 19, 1886, Campbell Family Papers.

67. Copy of Guest Book at the home of William Boatwright, location unknown, dated November 20, 1885, in Campbell Family Papers.

68. Selina Campbell, "A Letter to Young Converts," 711.

69. Selina Campbell, Ingleside Plantation, Ala., to William Campbell, Bethany, W.Va.?, February 4, 1869, Campbell Family Papers; *Home Life and Reminiscences of Alexander Campbell,* 429.

70. *Home Life and Reminiscences of Alexander Campbell,* 430; Selina Campbell, Ingleside Plantation, Ala., to William Campbell, Bethany, W.Va.?, February 4, 1869, Campbell Family Papers.

71. *Home Life and Reminiscences of Alexander Campbell,* 429; Selina Campbell, Ingleside Plantation, Ala., to William Campbell, Bethany, W.Va.?, February 4, 1869, Campbell Family Papers.

72. See Stevenson, *The Victorian Homefront.*

73. Selina Campbell, "John Newton's Definition of a Christian," *Millennial Harbinger* 25 (June 1853): 344–349.

74. Article from the *Memphis Appeal,* May 27, 1874, republished as "Mrs. Alexander Campbell" in the *Christian Standard,* (June 13, 1874): 187.

75. Though Campbell often used the term "restoration" as an important concept in American religion, he rarely used it to define his entire theology and more commonly called his efforts "reformation" in the tradition of the Protestant Reformation begun by Martin Luther.

76. Letter from Selina Campbell printed in "Correspondence," *Christian Standard* (January 3, 1885): 3.

77. "Book Notices," *Christian Record* (July 1882): 219, and "Review," *Christian Standard* (May 27, 1882): 167.

78. Article in Hagerman Scrapbook, "The House of Alexander Campbell," probably from the *Wellsburg Herald,* ca. 1894, Campbell Family Papers; T. L. Fowler, "A Trip to Old Bethany," newspaper name and location unknown. The clipping appears in scrapbook of Mrs. B.C. Hagerman, Campbell Family Papers.

79. Selina Campbell, Bethany Mansion, to William Campbell, Wellsburg, W.Va., May 11, 1892, Campbell Family Papers; see, for example, her letter to Alice Campbell, June 3, 1890, Campbell Family Papers.

80. Selina Campbell, Bethany, W.Va., to William Campbell, Louisville, Ky.?, July 15, 1868, Campbell Family Papers; Selina Campbell, Bethany, W.Va., to William Campbell, Louisville, Ky.?, July 26, 1868, Campbell Family Papers.

81. Johnson, *The Quest for God,* 134.

82. Selina Campbell, "Thomas Campbell," *Ladies Christian Annual* 2 (March 1854): 298–299.

83. Johnson, *The Quest for God,* 134.

84. Selina Campbell, Obituary of Martha Abbot James, *Millennial Harbinger* (February 1859): 119–120.

85. Selina Campbell, Obituary of Ann Encell, *Millennial Harbinger* (June 1854): 359.

86. Selina Campbell, "Letter to Margaret B. Campbell," *Millennial Harbinger* (April 1844): 191–192.

87. Ibid., 192.

88. For general histories of the woman's missionary society movement, see R. Pierce Beaver, *American Protestant Women in World Mission: A History of the First Feminist Movement in North America* (Grand Rapids, Mich.: Eerdmans Publishing, 1968); Patricia R. Hill, *The World Their Household: The American Woman's Foreign Mission Movement and Cultural Transformation, 1870–1920* (Ann Arbor: University of Michigan Press, 1985); Dana L. Robert, *American Women in Mission: A Social History of Their Thought and Practice* (Macon, Ga.: Mercer University Press, 1996); Virginia Lieson Brereton and Christa Ressmeyer Klein, "American Women in Ministry: A History of Protestant Beginning Points," in Rosemary Reuther and Eleanor McLaughlin, eds., *Women of Spirit* (New York: Simon and Schuster, 1979); Shirley S. Garrett, "Sisters All: Feminism and the American Women's Missionary Movement," in Torben Christensen and William R. Hutchinson, eds., *Missionary Ideologies in the Imperialist Era, 1800–1920* (Aarhus, Denmark: Aros, 1982).

89. Matthew 28:19, New American Standard Version; Lollis, *The Shape of Adam's Rib,* 12; indeed, Bailey argues persuasively that this was one of the defining issues in the division of the Disciples of Christ into the Christian Church (Disciples of Christ) and the Churches of Christ.

90. Hull, "CWBM," 42.

91. Selina Campbell, "Women Preachers," 402.

92. Selina Campbell, "Another Appeal to the Beloved Sisterhood of the Churches of Disciples," *Millennial Harbinger* (November 1858): 652–653; "Contributions to the Adelphian Society Library, Bethany," *Millennial Harbinger* (January 1859): 56.

93. Barton Campbell Hagerman, "In Memoriam: Selina Huntington Campbell," *Christian Standard* (September 11, 1897): 1171.

94. Selina Campbell, Bethany, (W.) Va., to Julia Barclay, Palmyra, Syria, April 1, 1856, Julia Barclay Papers.

95. Barclay, "Jefferson's First Successor at Monticello," 10.

96. Ibid., 12.

97. Selina Campbell to Julia Barclay, April 1, 1856, Julia Barclay Papers.

98. Selina Campbell, Bethany, (W.) Va., to Julia Barclay, Palmyra, Syria?, August 13, 1856, Julia Barclay Papers.

99. Selina Campbell, Bethany, (W.) Va., to Julia Barclay, Palmyra, Syria, January 30, 1856, Julia Barclay Papers; Selina Campbell, Bethany, (W.) Va., to Julia Barclay, Palmyra, Syria?, December 22, 1857, Julia Barclay Papers; Selina Campbell, Bethany, (W.) Va., to Julia Barclay, Washington, D.C.?, March 11, 1859, Julia Barclay Papers.

100. "The House of Alexander Campbell," ca. 1884, Campbell Family Papers; Hagerman, "In Memoriam: Selina Huntington Campbell."

101. Newspaper article preserved in Hagerman scrapbook, Campbell Family Papers.

102. Ibid.

103. Selina Campbell, Bethany, W.Va., to William Campbell, Wellsburg, W.Va., May 11, 1892, Campbell Family Papers.

Epilogue

1. Howe, "Victorian Culture in America" in *Victorian America,* 3, 19.

2. See Stevenson, *The Victorian Homefront.*

3. When Pleasant Hill burned shortly after the end of the Civil War, the two schools united to make Bethany College coeducational. David Edwin Harrell points out that, though they were not the first, the Disciples were quick to adopt coed education. See Harrell, *Quest for a Christian America,* 206.

4. Selina Bakewell, Wellsburg, (W.) Va., to Samuel Bakewell, Tuscaloosa, Ala., April 1, 1822, Theron Hervey Bakewell Papers; Selina Campbell, Bethany, (W.) Va. to William P. Campbell, Wheeling, (W.) Va., November 12, 1858, Campbell Family Papers.

5. Selina Campbell, Bethany, (W.) Va., to William P. Campbell, Wheeling, (W.) Va., October 5, 1857, Campbell Family Papers.

6. Selina Campbell, Bethany, (W.) Va., to William P. Campbell, Wheeling, (W.) Va., October 5, 1857, Selina Campbell, Bethany, (W.) Va., to William P. Campbell, Wheeling, (W.) Va., January 24, 1858, Campbell Family Papers.

7. Ibid.

8. Selina Campbell, Bethany, (W.) Va., to William P. Campbell, Wheeling, (W.) Va., November 12, 1858, Campbell Family Papers.

9. Selina Campbell, "Letter from Mrs. Campbell," *Millennial Harbinger* (January 1860): 47, 48.

10. Though scholars are divided as to whether or not the Churches of Christ could split denominationally, northern Churches of Christ undeniably tended to remain in the Disciples movement, while southern churches tended to separate themselves into a new group (Churches of Christ). For a discussion of the issue, see Richard Hughes, *Reviving the Ancient Faith*, 128–132, and David Edwin Harrell, Jr., "The Sectional Origins of the Churches of Christ," *Journal of Southern History* 30 (August 1964): 261–277.

11. Selina Campbell, Bethany, W. Va., to Julia Barclay, n.p., September 11, 1861, Julia Barclay Papers; C. C. Goen makes this argument in *Broken Churches, Broken Nation*; Selina Campbell, Bethany, W.Va., to Brother James Black, Eramosa township, Ontario, Canada, December 31, 1862, transcription at the Disciples of Christ Historical Society (original owned by Mrs. Percy MacKinnon, Guelph, Ontario, Canada).

12. Selina Campbell, Bethany, (W.) Va., to Mrs. S. E. Smart, Saint Louis, Mo., December 23, 1880, Disciples of Christ Historical Society.

13. Sister Burnet, Detroit?, to Mrs. Julia Barclay, Jerusalem?, January 18, 1855, Julia Barclay Papers.

14. Selina Campbell, "Our Correspondence: Letter to Mrs. J. M. Mathes," 18 *Christian Monitor* (May 1879): 148. Mathes was the editor of the *Christian Monitor*, a paper geared toward the interests of women in the Stone-Campbell movement.

15. "Woman and the Gospel," *Christian Standard* (June 6, 1868): 179.

16. Alfred N. Gilbert, "What Can a Young Lady Do?" *Christian Standard* (September 11, 1880): 290.

17. Aaron Walker, "Woman as a Factor in Civilization," *Christian-Evangelist* (February 6, 1896): 87.

18. Mrs. H. Jennie Kirkham, "What Can Woman Do?" *Christian* (April 11, 1878): 2.

19. See, for example, "Woman and the Gospel," 179.

20. Mrs. J. M. Hughes, "Woman's Individuality in Church Work," *Christian-Evangelist* (November 29, 1888): 745.

21. See Sweet, *The Minister's Wife*.

Bibliography

Primary Sources

Manuscript Collections

Theron Hervey Bakewell Papers. Virginia Historical Society, Richmond, Virginia.

Julia Barclay Papers. Disciples of Christ Historical Society, Nashville, Tennessee.

Selina Campbell Folder. Disciples of Christ Historical Society, Nashville, Tennessee.

Campbell Family Papers. Bethany College Archives, Bethany, West Virginia.

Henley Papers. Virginia Historical Society, Richmond, Virginia.

Newspapers

American Christian Review. Indianapolis, Ind. 1869, 1870, 1884.

Christian. Quincy, Ill. 1878.

Christian Baptist. Bethany, Va. 1824.

Christian-Evangelist. St. Louis, Mo. 1888, 1896, 1938.

Christian Monitor. Indianapolis, Ind. 1879.

Christian Record. Bloomington, Ind. 1874, 1882–1884.

Christian Standard. Cincinnati, Ohio. 1868–1889.

Clarion and Tennessee State Gazette. Nashville, Tenn. 1817.

Ladies' Christian Annual. Philadelphia, Pa. 1855.

Millennial Harbinger. Bethany, W. Va. 1830–1870.

Missionary Tidings. Indianapolis, Ind. 1883.

Old Path Guide. Louisville, Ky. 1881.

Wellsburg Herald. Wellsburg, W. Va. 1898.

PUBLISHED MATERIALS

Barclay, Decima Campbell. "Jefferson's First Successor at Monticello." *Discipliana* 49 (Spring 1989): 6–12.

Campbell, Selina. *Home Life and Reminiscences of Alexander Campbell*. St. Louis: Christian Standard Publishing, 1882.

Davies, Eliza. *The Story of an Earnest Life: A Woman's Adventures in Australia, and in Two Voyages Around the World*. Cincinnati: Central Book Concern, 1881.

Richardson, Robert. *Memoirs of Alexander Campbell*. 2 vols. Philadelphia: J. B. Lippincott, 1868–70.

Seglar, Charles. "Introduction." In *Familiar Lectures on the Pentateuch*, by Alexander Campbell. Cincinnati: Bosworth, Chase and Hall, 1868.

Secondary Sources

ARTICLES

Bloch, Ruth H. "American Feminine Ideals in Transition: The Rise of the Moral Mother, 1785–1815." *Feminist Studies* 4:2 (June 1978): 1–126.

Braude, Ann. "Women's History *Is* American Religious History." In Thomas A. Tweed, ed., *Retelling U.S. Religious History*. Berkeley: University of California Press, 1997.

Cochran, Louis. "The Several Worlds of Alexander Campbell." In Cochran and Leroy Garrett, eds., *Alexander Campbell: The Man and His Mission*. Dallas: Wilkinson, 1965.

Fox-Genovese, Elizabeth. "Two Steps Forward, One Step Back: New Questions and Old Models in the Religious History of American Women." *Journal of the American Academy of Religion* 53 (1985): 465–471.

Hull, Debra. "CWBM: A Flame of the Lord's Kindling." *Discipliana* 48 (Fall 1988): 39–42.

Kerber, Linda. "Separate Spheres, Female Worlds, Woman's Place: The Rhetoric of Women's History." *Journal of American History* 75 (June 1988): 9–39.

Lerner, Gerda. "The Lady and the Mill Girl: Changes in the Status of Women in the Age of Jackson." *Midcontinent American Studies Journal* 10 (Spring 1969): 5–15.

Shropshire Parish Register Society. *Shropshire Parish Registers, Vol. 17: St. Chad's of Shrewsbury, Diocese of Lichfield, England*. Shrewsbury, December 1915.

Welter, Barbara. "The Cult of True Womanhood, 1820–1860." *American Quarterly* 18 (Spring 1966): 151–171.

———. "The Feminization of American Religion, 1800–1860." In William O'Neill, ed., *Insights and Parallels: Problems and Issues of American Social History.* Minneapolis: Burgess Publishing, 1973.

BOOKS

Bakewell, Stanley. *Bakewell History-Genealogy.* Bakewell: United Letter Service, 1983.

Berg, Barbara J. *The Remembered Gate: Origins of American Feminism, the Woman, and the City, 1800–1860.* New York: Oxford University Press, 1978.

Cochrane, Louis. *The Fool of God: A Novel Based upon the Life of Alexander Campbell.* New York: Duell, Sloan and Pierce, 1958.

Cott, Nancy. *The Bonds of Womanhood: Woman's Sphere in New England, 1780–1835.* New Haven: Yale University Press, 1977.

Degler, Carl. *At Odds: Women and the Family in America from the Revolution to the Present.* New York: Oxford University Press, 1980.

Douglas, Ann. *The Feminization of American Culture.* New York: Knopf, 1977.

Epstein, Barbara. *The Politics of Domesticity: Woman, Evangelism, and Temperance in Nineteenth-Century America.* Middletown, Conn.: Wesleyan University Press, 1981.

Freehling, Allison Goodyear. *Drift Toward Dissolution: The Virginia Slavery Debate, 1831–1832* Baton Rouge: Louisiana State University Press, 1982.

Friedman, Jean B. *The Enclosed Garden: Women and Community in the Evangelical South, 1830–1900.* Chapel Hill: University of North Carolina Press, 1985.

Fuller, Edmund, and David E. Green. *God in the White House: The Faiths of American Presidents.* New York: Crown Publishers, 1978.

Ginzberg, Lori. *Women and the Work of Benevolence: Morality, Politics, and Class in the Nineteenth-Century United States.* New Haven: Yale University Press, 1990.

Goen, C. C. *Broken Churches, Broken Nation: Denominational Schisms and the Coming of the Civil War.* Macon, Ga.: Mercer University Press, 1985.

Gould, Valerie. *The Bakewell Family.* Christchurch, New Zealand: Caxton Press, 1968.

Gresham, Perry, ed. *The Sage of Bethany: A Pioneer in Broadcloth.* St. Louis: Bethany Press, 1960.

Groover, Edwin. *The Well-Ordered Home: Alexander Campbell and the Family.* Joplin, Mo.: College Press, 1988.

Harrell, David Edwin. *Quest for a Christian America: The Disciples of Christ and American Society.* Nashville: Disciples of Christ Historical Society, 1966.

Hatch, Nathan. *The Democratization of American Christianity.* New Haven: Yale University Press, 1989.

Hewitt, Nancy. *Women's Activism and Social Change, New York, 1822–1872.* Ithaca: Cornell University Press, 1984.

Historic Bethany. *Campbell Mansion: A Guide to the Historic Home of Alexander Campbell.* Bethany, W.Va.: Historic Bethany and Bethany College, 1995.

Howe, Daniel Walker, ed. *Victorian America.* Philadelphia: University of Pennsylvania Press, 1976.

Hughes, Richard. *Reviving the Ancient Faith: The Story of Churches of Christ in America.* Grand Rapids, Mich.: Eerdmans Publishing, 1996.

Johnson, Paul. *The Quest for God: A Personal Pilgrimage.* New York: Harper Collins, 1996.

Kraditor, Aileen, ed. *Up from the Pedestal: Selected Writings in the History of American Feminism.* New York: Quadrangle, 1968.

Lasch, Christopher. *The True and Only Heaven: Progress and Its Critics.* New York: Norton, 1991.

Lewis, Samuel. *Topographical Dictionary of England.* Vol. 3. London: S. Lewis, 1844.

Lollis, Lorraine. *The Shape of Adam's Rib: A Lively History of Women's Work in the Christian Church.* St. Louis: Bethany Press, 1970.

McAllister, Lester G., and William E. Tucker. *Journey in Faith: A History of the Christian Church (Disciples of Christ).* St. Louis: Bethany Press, 1975.

Norton, Mary Beth. *Liberty's Daughters: The Revolutionary Experience of American Women, 1750–1800.* Glenview, Ill.: Scott, Foresman, 1988.

Ryan, Mary. *Cradle of the Middle Class: The Family in Oneida County, New York, 1790–1865.* New York: Cambridge University Press, 1981.

Smith-Rosenberg, Carroll. *Disorderly Conduct: Visions of Gender in Victorian America.* New York: Oxford University Press, 1985.

Stevenson, Louise L. *The Victorian Homefront: American Thought and Culture, 1860–1880.* New York: Twayne Publishers, 1991.

Sweet, Leonard. *The Minister's Wife: Her Role in Nineteenth-Century American Evangelism.* Philadelphia: Temple University Press, 1983.

Thomas, John. *The Rise of Staffordshire Potteries*. Bath, England: Adams & Dart, 1971.

Tristano, Richard M. *The Origins of the Restoration Movement: An Intellectual History*. Atlanta, Ga.: Glenmary Research Center, 1988.

West, John. *Town Records*. Chichester, Sussex: Phillimore, 1983.

Western Pennsylvania Genealogical Society. *A List of Immigrants who Applied for Immigration Papers in the District Courts of Allegheny County, Pennsylvania*. Vol. 1, 1798–1840. Pittsburgh: Western Pennsylvania Genealogical Society, 1978.

DISSERTATION

Bailey, Fred Arthur. "The Status of Women in the Disciples of Christ: 1865–1900," Ph.D. dissertation, University of Tennessee, Knoxville, Tennessee, 1979.

Index

About the Author

LORETTA LONG completed a B.A. in History at Pepperdine University in 1992, followed by an M.A. from Pepperdine in 1994 and a Ph.D. from Georgetown University in 1998. While at Georgetown, she focused on American and Asian History. In 1998, she joined the Department of History at Abilene Christian University, where she currently serves as Assistant Professor of History.

DATE DUE

amco, Inc 38-293